HOW TO ENJOY GOD and HOW TO PRACTICE the ENJOYMENT OF GOD

Witness Lee

Living Stream Ministry
Anaheim, CA • www.lsm.org

© 2006 Living Stream Ministry

All rights reserved. No part of this work may be reproduced or transmitted in any form or by any means—graphic, electronic, or mechanical, including photocopying, recording, or information storage and retrieval systems—without written permission from the publisher.

First Edition, March 2006.

ISBN 0-7363-3025-9

Published by

Living Stream Ministry
2431 W. La Palma Ave., Anaheim, CA 92801 U.S.A.
P. O. Box 2121, Anaheim, CA 92814 U.S.A.

Printed in the United States of America

06 07 08 09 10 11 12 / 9 8 7 6 5 4 3 2 1

CONTENTS

Title	Page
Preface	5
1 Enjoying God	7
2 God Desiring Man to Enjoy Him	19
3 God's Accomplishments for Man	33
4 The Way for Man to Enjoy God	43
5 How to Enjoy God in Prayer	57
6 How to Enjoy God in Reading the Word	67
7 Enjoying God by Eating and Drinking Him	81
8 Eating and Drinking—the Focus of God's Salvation	91
9 Enjoying God through Taking in the Spirit	103
10 How God Becomes Man's Enjoyment in the Spirit	113
11 How God Becomes Man's Enjoyment	123
12 Enjoying God by Praying at Set Times	135
13 Enjoying God as Food by Reading the Word	147
14 How to Enjoy God by Matching Reading with Prayer	159
15 Restricting the Mind and Exercising the Spirit in Reading the Bible	171
16 Learning to Be Simple to Pick Up the True Meaning of the Bible	179
17 Practicing Dropping Our Concepts to Pick Up the Central Thought of the Bible	187

18	Identifying the Central and Peripheral Matters in the Bible	197
19	Exercising to Pray in the Holy Spirit	211
20	Practicing to Pray according to the Sense of the Spirit	221
21	The Practice of Intercession, Beholding, Waiting, and Musing	231

PREFACE

This book is composed of messages given by Brother Witness Lee in 1958 in Taipei. The first section, chapters 1 through 14, covers the matter of how to enjoy God, and the second section, chapters 15 through 21, covers the matter of how to practice the enjoyment of God. These messages have been translated from Chinese.

Chapter One

ENJOYING GOD

Scripture Reading: Psa. 42:1-2; 34:8; 36:7-9; 84:1-2; 90:1; 91:1

In these messages I have a burden to speak concerning the way to enjoy God. This is a practical and intimate concern in the spiritual life of a Christian. We will spend some time to consider how a Christian can enjoy God.

GOD BEING ENJOYABLE

Some may consider the thought of enjoying God to be unusual, but the Bible clearly says that we can taste God. Psalm 34:8 says that we should taste and see that Jehovah is good. The Lord Jesus also said that He is our food; He is the bread of life. Because food is an enjoyment to us, His being food and bread must mean that He can be enjoyed by us.

A sweet thought recorded in the Word of God is that God is not only near us but that He has even given Himself to us to be our enjoyment. This shows the intimate relationship God has with us. When we enjoy our meals, the food we eat enters into us and becomes a part of us. Before we eat, the food is not a part of us, but after we take it in, it becomes our nutritional supply and strength. In addition, after passing through a process of metabolism, it becomes our inward element. The food we eat becomes a part of us, and we live by it. The relationship between food and our physical body is similar to the relationship between God and our entire being.

Psalm 23 is a favorite psalm among God's children; hence, it is difficult to find a Christian who does not know the words *the Lord is my Shepherd*. God, however, is not merely a Shepherd who leads us, protects us, and cares for us. God is more intimate than a shepherd. If He were merely a shepherd, He could care for us and shepherd us only in an outward way; He would be unable to enter into us to become a part of us. He could not become us. However, the Bible shows that God gives Himself to us for our enjoyment and works Himself into us. He can enter into us to be our life, our strength, our food, and our living water. He can meet the need of every part of our being. Those who have experienced God know that He is truly our enjoyment. We can enjoy God in His sovereign arrangements and provisions, and we can enjoy Him as the varied supply to our inward being.

Man is composed of a spirit within, a body without, and a soul between his spirit and body. When God is within us, He can supply the needs of our spirit, soul, and body. God can satisfy the needs of our spirit by supplying us from within our spirit. He can satisfy the needs of our soul, or our psyche, from within our soul. He can also satisfy the needs of our body by supplying us in our body. Although our God is invisible, untouchable, and intangible, those who have experienced God can testify that they enjoy Him in their spirit, their soul, and even their body. What a glorious blessing this is!

Since God is so intimately related to us, the Bible uses many ways to describe and illustrate our enjoyment of God. Let us briefly consider some of them.

God Being Our Life

God is our life. Immediately after creating man in Genesis, God placed man in front of the tree of life (2:8-9). At the end of Revelation the tree of life is still present (22:2). The tree of life signifies God Himself. God is the source of life. When God says that He wants man to come to the tree of life, He means that He wants man to touch Him. God wants to enter into man to be his life.

Life is something very close and crucial to man. It can even be said that life is man himself. Without life, it is impossible for man to be a man. The Bible shows that God desires to be man's life. Hence, we can say boldly that if a person does not have God within him as life, he has not come up to the standard of a human being. The life a person has determines the kind of person he is. Those with a lower life are lower, and those with a higher life are higher. The life we possess in our natural constitution, our natural life, is a lower life; it is impossible for us to be a higher person with only this life. In order to be a higher person, we must have a higher kind of life. God's life is the highest life. Hence, it is impossible for anyone to be a higher person if he does not receive God as the highest life.

A higher kind of man is noble, holy, loving, and patient, possessing no meanness or pettiness in his heart. Although there is a certain degree of magnanimity and tolerance in man's natural life, these virtues are limited. In order to be unlimitedly high, a person must receive the unlimited God as the highest life. When the infinite God enters into us and becomes the highest life within us, we become persons of an infinitely high standard. We can love what others cannot love, we can endure what others cannot endure, and we can forgive what others cannot forgive. We possess a nobleness and a holiness that no mere human being possesses.

Everyone who has the life of God can be unlimitedly high. A person who has God as his life should have a standard that is infinitely high. While others may say that a certain matter is overwhelming, those with God as their life can bear it joyfully. When others find a matter intolerable, those with God can gladly and willingly tolerate it. A person with God is a high person, an unlimited person. It is impossible to attain to this high living with only the natural life that man possesses. This living can be attained only when one takes God's highest life as his life. This highest life is the immeasurably high God Himself. He is life, and He is also the source of life. He not only dispenses His life into us but also enters into us to be our very life. He does not enter into us to be our life in small increments. On the contrary, He has fully entered into us. Day by day and moment by moment, He is in us as our life. Hence, we can enjoy Him every day. We can taste Him moment by moment.

We know the importance of air to human life. A man can be without food for seven or eight days, and he can be without water one or two days. However, if he is without air for five minutes, he will cease to exist. Air is vital to human life, and it is the most available item for man's enjoyment. We can breathe on the street and in houses. We can breathe in cars and in airplanes. We breathe when we are conscious of it, and we breathe when we are not conscious of it. We breathe while we are listening to a message and in our sleep. If we have a measure of spiritual experience, we will realize that God is just like air to us. God is Spirit, and the Spirit is like air. In the original language of the Bible, in both Hebrew in the Old Testament and Greek in the New Testament, *wind, breath,* and *spirit* are the same word. Spirit is breath, and breath is wind. God is Spirit, and God is also breath. The Bible describes the outpouring of the Holy Spirit on the day of Pentecost as a rushing violent wind, which was God Himself (Acts 2:2-4). The Lord Jesus also came to the disciples on the evening of His resurrection and breathed into them, saying, "Receive the Holy Spirit" (John 20:22). The Spirit is likened to breath. This Spirit is also the very God Himself. When God enters into us to be our enjoyment, He enters as the Spirit, and this Spirit is like wind and breath. Whether we open to Him or turn away from Him, He remains our enjoyment. Wherever we are and no matter the time, God as the Spirit is available to us for our enjoyment. We can touch and taste this Spirit. When the Spirit enters into us, He becomes the Spirit of life. This Spirit of life, this breath of life, strengthens our spirit and spreads from our spirit to our heart, which includes the soul, and from our soul to our body. In this way our whole being is saturated with the Spirit as breath; that is, we are full of the presence of the Spirit. This is the practical way to enjoy God.

God Being Our Husband

The Bible says that God is a Husband to us. As created and redeemed ones, we are a wife to God. There are many husbands and wives among us. The young people among us who are not yet married can see the relationship between a husband and wife from their parents. If we read through the entire Bible, we will see that the Bible begins and ends with life. The second thing spoken of after life is marriage; Adam married Eve. There is also a marriage at the end of the Bible. The Lamb of God marries a wife; that is, Christ marries His redeemed people. There are many places in the Bible that present God as our life. There are also many places that show God as our Husband, and we, the believers, as His wife (Isa. 54:5; 62:5; John 3:29; 2 Cor. 11:2). God's relationship with us is not only that of being life to man but also that of being a husband to a wife.

Let us consider this matter. A wife depends on her husband for everything. Her supply is from her husband. Her protection is in her husband. Her joy, comfort, and satisfaction are in her husband. We know what a husband is to a wife. There is no language to describe the intimacy, union, and oneness between the two.

When the Lord Jesus came to the earth, His forerunner, John the Baptist, declared, "Behold, the Lamb of God, who takes away the sin of the world!" (John 1:29). He also introduced Him as the Bridegroom, the One who is coming to take the bride (3:29). Christ is God incarnated in the flesh. He is the Lamb who bears the sin of the world. He is also the Bridegroom who is making us His bride and who is making the two one. According to the Bible, our being joined to the Lord is the same as a wife being joined to her husband. God is our Husband, and we are His wife. He is our satisfaction, and we are His satisfaction. A marriage relationship speaks of enjoyment.

God Being Our Food and Drink

The Bible uses food and drink to speak of the relationship between God and man. Man needs food and drink in order to exist. He needs to eat, and he needs to drink. Every day we depend on these two things. If we do not eat or drink, we will die. The Bible shows that God is our food, and He is our living water. He comes to us to be our bread.

In the Old Testament we see these types. When the children of Israel began their journey through the wilderness, they had no food or drink. Then God performed a miracle and supplied them with food and drink. Their food did not grow out of the ground but came down from heaven. Their drink did not come from wells, which they dug, but from a smitten rock. Those in the Old Testament did not know the significance of this. One day, however, the Lord Jesus came. He was God come in the flesh, God among men. His goal was to be received by man and to become man's enjoyment. He said that the manna in the Old Testament was only a type and that He was the bread that comes down from heaven (6:48-51). He is the true manna. He can satisfy man's hunger and fill man from within. The Lord also said that He would be lifted up and that His body would be broken and out of it would flow living water. The living water is the Holy Spirit. When the Holy Spirit enters man, He satisfies man's thirst and flows out of man as a river of living water to quench the thirst of others (7:37-38). These verses show that as God, Christ becomes man's enjoyment. He wants to enter into us to be our food and our living water. He wants us to eat Him and drink Him every day.

At the bread-breaking meeting everyone takes a piece of the bread on the table and eats it. Similarly, we take the cup and drink from it. We should have a strong realization of the significance of what we are doing. The Lord said, "Take, eat; this is My body" (Matt. 26:26). Then concerning the cup, He also said, "Drink of it, all of you, for this is My blood of the covenant, which is being poured out for many for forgiveness of sins" (vv. 27-28). He seemingly was saying, "You must take Me into you as your enjoyment. The real remembrance of Me is the enjoyment of Me. When you allow Me to be your food and your drink, you are remembering Me. I long to enter into you to be everything to you." The Lord wants to enter into us to be our life. He also wants to be our Husband, our food, and even our drink.

God Being Our Habitation

The Bible speaks of another kind of relationship between God and man. In this relationship God is our habitation. Every believer is a habitation of God, a temple of God, a house of God. God dwells within him. The Bible also says that God wants to be our habitation. This is wonderful. God dwells within us, and He allows us to dwell in Him. We are His habitation, and He is our habitation. Therefore, the Bible says that we abide in Him and He abides in us (John 15:4). When we abide in Him, we enjoy all that He is. When He abides in us, He enjoys all that we are.

We all know what a dwelling place is, and we all need a dwelling place. Without a dwelling place, we have no habitation, no place of rest, no place to set our feet, and no place to work. In order to rest, relax, and work, we need a dwelling place, a habitation. God is not only within us as our food and drink; He is even our habitation. We can dwell in Him, and He can dwell in us. We find eternal rest in Him.

God Being Our Light of Life

The Bible says that God enters into us to be our light of life (8:12). Light is needed for man to exist. Without light, we cannot live. In the daytime we have the light of the sun, and at night we have the light of the moon, the stars, and even lamps. We cannot exist without light. Light is a great necessity to us. Without light, man falls into darkness, which is an unbearable punishment. It would be a painful experience to be locked in darkness for twenty-four hours. Therefore, the Bible says that darkness is a kind of punishment. Man needs light in order to exist, live, and work.

The Bible says that God is our light. Those who follow Him shall by no means walk in darkness, but shall have the light of life. This means that without Him, apart from Him, or severed from Him, we are in darkness. He is so many things to us for our enjoyment. He is our life, our Husband, our food and drink, our habitation, and also our light. He is light, and He wants us to walk in the light.

God Being Our Strength

The Bible also says that God is our strength (Psa. 18:1). It is not sufficient for us to have only life. Although we need life to live, the life we have needs power. Because some people lack strength, they are weak and senile even though they have life. Hence, we need God to be our power, our strength.

God Being Our Love, Joy, and Comfort

In order for a man to live, he also needs love, joy, and comfort. The Bible clearly says that God is love (1 John 4:8). He is also our joy and our comfort (Neh. 8:10; Isa. 51:12). He is everything we need.

God Being Our Healing

If we need healing, God is the best healing for any sickness in our psychology, our soul, or our body. He is Jehovah Ropheka, which means "Jehovah your Healer" (Exo. 15:26). He is Jehovah, the God who heals. With Him we have healing.

God Being Our Guidance

In addition, we need guidance for our personal walk. We need to know when to move and when to stop, when to go forward or backward, and when to turn left or turn right. Thank God that He is our guidance. When we touch Him, we have guidance and direction, and we have a way to go on.

God Being Our All

When we read through the Bible and realize that it presents God as everything to us, we cannot help but praise Him. God wants to be our life, our Husband, our food, our drink, our habitation, our light, our strength, our love, our joy, our comfort, our healing, and our guidance. What He is matches what we need, and He provides Himself to us as that very item. Whatever we need, He is, and He provides us with Himself as that item.

GOD HUMBLING HIMSELF TO BE OUR ENJOYMENT

Regrettably, Christians today are full of common, religious concepts about God. They realize that there is a sovereign Lord in this universe who is great, holy, and bright. They also realize that as creatures they should worship such a sovereign Creator. This is not an erroneous concept, but it is altogether religious; it does not reflect the true revelation in the Bible. If we understand the Bible, our eyes will be opened to see that this great, holy, bright, and sovereign Lord has humbled Himself to meet with small, lowly, filthy, and sinful men such as we. Just as He was happy to speak with the immoral Samaritan woman by the well in Sychar (John 4:5), He is happy to contact us, the despicable sinners. He desires to dispense Himself into us. Even though He is our Redeemer on the cross and the Lord of all on the throne, He has condescended and lowered Himself to be as small and lowly as we are so that we can receive Him.

I sometimes have a wonderful thought as I meditate on the Lord, and I say, "Lord, You have become so small that You are even the same as I am. You have not made Yourself greater than I am; instead, You have become as small as I am. You lowered Yourself to be found in fashion as a man. If You were five feet taller than I am, I could not reach You. I know that You are as low as I am. This is the reason I can fellowship with You and be filled with sweetness and joy instead of fear." My fellowship with the Lord is sweeter and more intimate than the time I spend with my own mother. When I was young, my heart was filled with warmth and comfort every time I saw my mother. In the same way, there is absolutely no fear when I contact the Lord. I can say, "Lord, while I am touching You, I experience an intimacy and sweetness that far exceeds my feelings toward my mother." This is not because I have become as great as the Lord. No, it is because He has become low. I have not become tall; rather, He has become small. I am the same person. I have not changed. My sinful nature is still with me. I am wicked, depraved, in the old creation, and in the evil world. But I praise the Lord that I can fellowship with Him in my situation. I do not have the slightest feeling that He is in heaven and is greater than I am. Rather, I feel that He is small and lowly. He is the same as I am. I can fellowship with Him, touch Him, and enjoy Him.

The Bible reveals such a Lord to us. He is our enjoyment. We can enjoy Him as our life, our Husband, our food, our drink, our habitation, our dwelling place, our strength, our love, joy, comfort, healing, and everything we need.

When we worship Him, we should not consider Him as a great and sovereign Lord sitting far above all. We should not be afraid to approach Him. There is no need to pray to Him with trembling and trepidation. Approaching Him in this way proves that we have no revelation and that we have insufficient knowledge of Him; we are void of light and are filled with religious concepts. If we have revelation, we will see that while He is high and lofty, the Lord of glory and holiness, He also loves to dispense Himself into us. He wants us to draw near to Him. If He remained in heaven, we could neither be saved nor receive Him as life. If He remained on the throne, we could not touch Him or enjoy Him. But now He has stepped forward. He has lowered Himself, left the throne, and come to us. He is now where we are. He is as low as we are, and He is the same as we are. He has condescended and come to us in order to make Himself available to us for our enjoyment.

Every child of God needs to realize that the God whom we worship and serve is not the God of our religious concept. Even though our God is the Lord of all, He has lowered Himself, humbled Himself, to the extent that He has become the same as we are. He is the same as we are in everything except sin. He did this in order to make Himself available to us for our enjoyment and so that we can gain Him and experience Him. He wants us to receive Him into us as our everything.

HOW TO ENJOY GOD

Some may now be anxious to know how to enjoy God. Since God is life, food, drink, light, strength, and everything to us, how can we touch Him? Let us consider two points.

Turning to Our Inner Being

First, God is inside of us. If we want to enjoy Him, we should learn to turn to our inner being. We must turn in order to exercise our inner being. God is not outside of us. Even if we went to heaven today, we would not find Him there, because He is within us. He dwells in our spirit. We do not need to look for Him outside. He is very near to us; He is within us.

Being Calm

Second, we must learn to be calm before Him and pray to Him. In other words, we need to fellowship with Him. Although God is in us, we are often drawn to the outside world through busy distractions. To be busy is to have our heart drawn away by distractions. When our outer man is busy, our heart is dead to God. The Chinese character for *busy* is composed of the root words for *heart* and *dead*. When a person is busy, his heart is dead. Our heart may also be asleep even though it is not dead. The Chinese character for *forget* is also composed of the root words for *heart* and *dead,* but the character for heart is turned on its side. This shows that it is asleep. Forgetfulness means that the heart is asleep. This is not a joke. The heart should not be dead, and it should not be asleep. We do not want either situation. We should be normal and exercise our inward being in quietness in order to absorb God. The best prayer is one that absorbs God. Prayer has nothing to do with how many words we utter. It is a matter of finding a quiet time to turn our busy heart to the inner chamber in order to fellowship with God and to absorb His very being. We can then realize that He is our life, food, drink, light, strength, joy, and comfort. He is the answer to whatever we need. This is the meaning of being a Christian. We are not those in religion who worship a God who is high above and far away from us. A Christian does not worship in this way. Instead, he abides quietly in the inner chamber and touches God. He fellowships with God and absorbs Him in his spirit. In this way God abides in him and becomes his all.

CHAPTER TWO

GOD DESIRING MAN TO ENJOY HIM

Scripture Reading: 1 John 4:13, 16; John 15:5

GOD'S DESIRE BEING FOR MAN TO ENJOY HIM

In the Bible there is a very important principle related to the first mention of a matter that sets an eternal governing principle for that matter throughout the rest of the Bible. The way a matter is spoken of the first time determines the meaning of similar matters that are mentioned subsequently. In the first reference to God's relationship with man in the Bible, God presents Himself to man as food. This shows that God wants man to enjoy Him. After God created man, He placed him in front of the tree of life so that man would enjoy the fruit of that tree. The tree of life signifies God Himself. This shows that God wants to be man's enjoyment. God's first thought after creating man was for man to eat and drink, and the object of this eating and drinking was God Himself.

How can we prove this? When the Lord Jesus was on earth, He repeatedly revealed that He was food for man to eat and enjoy. Regrettably, when the Lord contacted man, no one had the concept that God could be man's enjoyment. Man's concept was that God should be worshipped and served. If we read the four Gospels carefully, we will see that the people who came to the Lord had many different opinions concerning Him. Some asked what they should do to inherit eternal life. Others asked which of the commandments was the greatest. Those who came to the Lord had different concepts, but no one had the correct view that man should come to God with the thought of enjoying Him.

One day the Lord performed a miracle. He fed five thousand

with five loaves and two fish, and there was much left over. When people saw this, they thought that He was the greatest prophet. They had hoped for such a prophet who would perform miracles among them and take care of all their needs. This concept was absolutely wrong; hence, the Lord spoke a word to change their concept. He pointed out that they were seeking for food that perishes, food that is of no eternal value. He did not come to give man corruptible food, but He came to give man incorruptible food from heaven. When they heard this, they did not understand what type of food the Lord wanted to give them. The Lord explained that He is the food; He wanted to give Himself to them as their food for their enjoyment. It was as if He were saying, "It is not enough to know Me as the Sovereign Lord who performs miracles. It is not enough to expect miracles and works of wonder from Me. I am much more than these things. I will not only perform outward things, but I will also be your food and enter into you to be your enjoyment. It is not enough to know Me as a great prophet or even as the Creator. You need to know Me as the Creator who has come to be your food. I have given My flesh to you for food and My blood to you for drink so that I can enter into you. He who eats My flesh and drinks My blood has eternal life, because this eternal life is just Me. If you eat Me and drink Me, I will enter into you, and spontaneously you will have eternal life." Those who heard this word thought that it was a hard word and could not receive it. Here was a wonderful person who told others that He was the bread who came down from heaven, that His flesh and blood could be their food and drink, and that He would enter into them so that they would receive eternal life. When they heard this word, they were baffled (John 6).

MAN'S CONCEPT MISJUDGING GOD'S DESIRE

Although we should understand the Lord's words when we read the Word, I would dare say that even today many Christians do not have the right concept concerning God. For example, we may have been saved for many years, but we might not have given much consideration to the matter of enjoying God. We might not have the concept that God has given Himself to us for our enjoyment. Perhaps, while we were contacting God and praying this morning, we still held the common religious concept that we should worship Him in a pious way. We may have considered what we should do today, and what we should not do today. Based on these dos and don'ts, we may have prayed, "God, be merciful to me so that I can please You by doing this and that." This kind of prayer is absolutely the result of religious concepts. God does not want us to pray this way. Whenever we draw near to God, He presents Himself to us as the fatness, the food for our satisfaction. He does not bargain with us whenever He fellowships and communes with us; rather, He presents Himself for our enjoyment. Fallen man, however, is incapable of recognizing this.

All of God's children should focus on this matter. According to the Bible, after creating Adam, God did not say, "You must worship Me in this way," or "You must serve Me in that way." On the contrary, after creating Adam, God placed him in front of the tree of life. God seemed to be saying, "Adam, come here. Just enjoy. I am the tree of life, and I am here for you to enjoy Me. I have no intention for you to do this or that for Me. I have no desire for you to serve or worship Me in this or that way. I only want to present Myself to you as food. My only desire is for you to enjoy Me."

In the four Gospels we see the same story. One day the tree of life came as the Word who became flesh, who tabernacled among us, full of grace and reality (John 1:14). Again He was placed in front of man as the tree of life so that man could "pick" the fruit from this tree. No one, however, knew that they could pick from this tree. In the four Gospels those who came to Him asked what they should do and which was the great commandment in the law (Matt. 19:16; 22:36). This was all they asked. But His answer was always the same: "I am the bread that came down from heaven. I do not intend that you do this or that for Me, or that you serve and worship Me in this or that way. I want you to receive Me, to enjoy Me. I am the tree of life. Life is in Me. I am life, and I have come that men may have life and have it more abundantly (John 10:10). I am like the tree of life that was in the garden of Eden. I have been placed before you as the tree of life so that you can stretch forth your hand in faith to receive me. I want to dispense Myself into you. I want to be your food to enter into you and be your very life. My thought is simply that you would enjoy Me."

Man's natural concept has dominated Christianity for two thousand years, and we are still not set free from its influence today. Even many servants of the Lord are unable to change their concept. We often think of how we should worship and serve God and of how we should do this or that for God, and it never occurs to us that the Lord Jesus does not care about this. The Lord simply wants man to enjoy Him. He was incarnated to put Himself in front of us as the tree of life. He said that He is life and that He came that we might have life. He did not come to ask us to do anything. He came with the intention that we would open to Him and receive Him. He wants us to receive Him every day and not just on the day of our salvation. Daily we should learn to abide in Him, and we should give Him room to abide in us. God has no intention for us to do anything for Him, and He has no desire for us to accomplish anything for Him. Rather, He desires to abide in us. The Lord desires all of us to open up to Him, to allow Him to abide in us, and to not turn Him away. If He can remain and abide in us, His riches and elements will become our enjoyment and blessing. When we enjoy Him and allow Him to become our blessed portion, all His riches become our supply and inwardly fill us. His riches even flow through us and bear rich fruit.

Fruit-bearing Being to Enjoy God

Although the branches of a fruit-bearing tree may bear much fruit, none of the fruit is the result of the work of the branches. The branches simply absorb the sap, the riches of the tree, and fruit grows. If we say to the branches, "You have worked too hard," they will respond, "This is not true; we are simply bearing fruit." Actually, they are enjoying. They do not contribute anything or perform any work. They simply absorb the riches of the tree. The more they absorb, the more fruit they bear. The more they experience this inward enjoyment, the more they bear outward fruit. Fruit does not come from the branches. Fruit comes from the tree, and the branches are merely channels through which the sap flows. This process of life passing through the branches is an enjoyment. This is the Christian life.

God has no intention for us to do anything for Him. He has no intention for us to worship Him or serve Him in a certain way. I hope we understand this word and not misunderstand it. God desires to be only one thing to us. He presents Himself to us and places Himself within us for the purpose of being our enjoyment. The more we enjoy Him, the more blessed we are. The more we enjoy Him, the more we know Him and are able to bear fruit. The more the branches abide in the tree, the more they allow the elements of the tree to abide in them. The sap and riches of the tree flow through the branches and from them bear much fruit. This is what God desires from us.

We must change our concept. We need to see a vision. I have met many children of God in different places, and the more I spoke with them, the more I shook my head. It is difficult to find a person who knows God. It is almost impossible to find a person who knows God's grace. When we meet a child of God, we may feel that he is a pious, God-fearing man who seeks God. However, it is not easy to find a man who knows that God desires man to enjoy Him.

Prayer Being to Enjoy God

A sister once complained to me that although she had been trying to exercise patience for many years, she still found it difficult. She said that she had been trying by praying. When I asked her how she prayed, she responded, "My patience is sufficient for only five trials. After that my patience runs out. Hence, I tell the Lord that I have no patience, and I ask Him to grant me patience. I can only ask the Lord to help me." This is the prayer of a novice. An experienced person would tell others not to pray such a prayer. The more we pray this way, the less patience we will have. When I asked if it was possible to forget about being patient when praying, she said, "But my problem is a lack of patience. I have to go to God to deal with my lack of patience. If I do not pray for patience, what should I pray for? Are you saying that if I lose my temper and am short of patience, it is wrong to pray? If I pray, should I not pray for patience?" I smiled and said, "Sister, it is right to pray, but some kinds of prayer are not really prayer. This can be compared to trying to eat with our nose rather than our mouth." This sister's problem was not a shortage of patience but a shortage of God. She did not need patience; she needed God. She needed to forget about patience and seize God instead. Some may consider *seize* to be a strong word. But she needed to spend time before the Lord and enjoy Him. She needed to absorb God. If God was added to her, she would have patience.

My word confused the sister, however, and she asked, "How can I enjoy God? How do I absorb Him?" This sister's confusion is typical of many Christians who are unclear about enjoying God. Even we are not clear; we are novices in knowing God, enjoying Him, touching Him, and fellowshipping with Him. While we want God, our way is often wrong and to no avail. We try to fellowship with God, but our way of fellowshipping is wrong. Many of our prayers are offered in a wrong way. We are wrong because we focus on things rather than on God; we lay hold of things rather than of God; we pray for things rather than for God. For this reason, we do not enjoy or absorb God.

Ministering the Word Being to Enjoy God

Let me use myself as an example. When I began serving the Lord, the most difficult thing for me to do was to minister the word. I had difficulty selecting a subject from the sixty-six books of the Bible. I did not know which subject to choose. Should I speak on Adam and Eve or on Peter and James? Should I speak on love and humility or on light and holiness? There were too many subjects, and this was a real problem to me. Even after I selected a subject, I worried about the content. How should I begin, and how should I end? How should each section be developed, and what examples should I use? I struggled with these points. When I could not come up with the right idea, I would pray. This seemed to be the Christian thing to do. However, as soon as I knelt down and asked the Lord about a subject, my mind started to spin.

Should the subject be heaven or hell, the cross or the manger, Jerusalem or Samaria? Such thoughts came all at once. Should I speak from Genesis, Exodus, Revelation, the Gospel of John, or Acts? My mind was full of subjects, but the Lord could not be found. I was often unclear even after half an hour. In the end, I would simply select a subject. But once I had the subject, I started worrying about the content and would pray again, saying, "Lord, what should the first sentence be? What should the last word be? How should I divide the message into various parts?" Since I was afraid of forgetting the points, I also prayed, "Lord, help me to remember all the points." While I was praying, I was occupied with these things; hence, I did not touch the Lord at all. When it was time to deliver the message, I was in fear and trembling. The result was often complete failure, and I would be totally devastated. Later I would wonder why the Lord did not answer my prayer. I suffered this agony for many years, but no one was there to help me find the right way.

After painfully searching for approximately ten years, I gradually found the key in the course of my Christian life. I found out that my experience of prayer was not prayer. Prayer is to absorb God and to enjoy Him. Let us again consider the matter of ministering the word. When praying concerning giving a message, there is no need to worry whether the message should be on Genesis, Revelation, the manger, or the cross. There is also no need to worry about what to say first and what to say second. There is no need to worry about any of these things. We need to go to the Lord to contact Him. We should forget about the message and the subject. We should simply contact and touch Him. As we contact Him, He will give us a sense that there may be problems, obstacles, and barriers between us and Him. We might be blaming others, holding grudges, or jealous of others. There may be other barriers between us and the Lord. We should deal with these barriers and remove them item by item through the blood. Then we can worship Him and, beholding His beauty in His presence, we can pray: "Lord, You are altogether lovely and sweet. You are my life and my strength. You are my word and my subject. You are everything to me." As we fellowship with Him this way, we not only stop praying for the message, but we also forget about the message. We are fully enjoying the Lord Himself. We are connected to Him in the same way that a light bulb is connected to the power source. As soon as we are connected, "electricity" flows into us. This is the way to pray for our speaking. There is no need to worry about the subject or the content. As soon as we are connected to the Lord, touch Him, and have His presence within, we can stand because the Lord is in us as our enjoyment and our everything. Ministering the word in this way can be compared to branches of a tree bearing fruit. Inwardly we are absorbing the Lord, and outwardly we are speaking the message. This is what it means to give a message.

The prayer of the sister who asked for patience was wrong because patience was the subject of her prayer. All genuine prayers have God as the subject. There is no need to be concerned with patience. We should simply spend time every day to contact God and to fellowship with Him. The more we enjoy Him, the more we will be filled with Him. When we are filled with Him in this way, we may not think of the word *patience* at any time but nevertheless experience patience in our living. Every situation will issue in joy because the God of joy fills our heart. We can endure everything joyfully, and nothing will trouble or irritate us. Inwardly we will be watered and filled with joy. We do not even think of patience. Although the word *patience* is not in our thoughts, and we do not speak of it, our daily life will be filled with patience. This patience comes from the God whom we enjoy. As we absorb Him and enjoy Him, He becomes our patience, our life, and our inward constituent. We will be inwardly watered, satisfied, and cheered. In whatever situation we encounter, there will be no need for us to exert any effort to be patient. On the contrary, patience will spontaneously be within us. This patience will not be the issue of our work; rather, it will be the living out of the God who lives within us. We might not say anything concerning patience, but everyone will say that we are full of patience. This is the wonder of the Christian life.

Preaching the Gospel Being to Enjoy God

Regrettably, most of our prayers are not prayers in which we absorb God; instead, they are religious prayers. We may pray, "O God, I am going to preach the gospel today. Be with me. Give me eloquence." While we pray, we are thinking of eloquence. "What should I say to the chemistry professor? What should be the topic of the conversation? Should I speak concerning atomic power or satellites?" Even though we may pray for half an hour, we are thinking only about eloquence and utterance. In fact, we have not really prayed. Such prayers are useless because they do not touch God, contact Him, or absorb Him.

If we want to preach the gospel, we should first spend half an hour or an hour contacting the Lord, beholding His glory, fellowshipping with Him, and praising Him. We should say, "Lord, You are too lovely. You are our Savior, and You are the Savior of all men. We come to enjoy You, to absorb You, and to live in the presence of Your countenance. We want to dwell in the house of the Lord." There is no need for us to think about preaching the gospel. There is no need to worry about our utterance or what we should say. We can forget about all of that. After absorbing the Lord and being filled with Him, we will not be the one speaking when we contact our professor. Rather, the Lord whom we have absorbed will be the One who is speaking through us. The words that we speak will be the very Lord whom we have absorbed, and it will be impossible for others not to be blessed.

Moses spent forty days and forty nights on the mountain before Jehovah, doing nothing other than absorbing Him. He did not feel anything when he came down from the mountain, but the children of Israel saw the shining of his face. Why was his face shining? God did not do anything for him. Moses merely spent forty days before the Lord, fellowshipping with Him and absorbing Him. He forgot about everything and was fully occupied with the Lord. For forty days and forty nights, Moses was fully absorbed with God and filled with Him. As a result, his face shone. When he presented himself before men, he did not need to say anything concerning God; they saw

God's glory in his face. This is the wonder of the Christian life. The more we ask for power, the more power eludes us. But if we forget about power and instead fellowship with God, absorb Him, and enjoy Him, we will have power without being conscious of it.

Receiving Leading Being to Enjoy God

I have often heard the brothers and sisters speak of receiving the Lord's leading. They do not understand how to receive the Lord's leading. Some have said, "Brother Lee, the more we seek the Lord's leading, the more confused we are, and the easier it is for us to make mistakes. Once we say that something is the Lord's leading, we discover that it is not. How can we know the Lord's leading?" Whenever I hear this, I ask, "Have you prayed in your seeking for His leading?" They usually respond that they have, and then I ask how they prayed. I typically find that they pray to receive leading instead of to enjoy the Lord. They pray, "Lord, should I go here, or should I go there?" While they pray, their mind is busy with these questions. They are not actually praying to the Lord; they are praying for things. After praying, they consider the options and then decide which option is according to the Lord's will and leading. This is the way many people pray. Hence, it is not surprising that they do not receive the Lord's leading. If we know what fellowship with the Lord is, we do not need to pray this way. We can forget about all these things and simply contact the Lord, absorb Him, and enjoy Him. This is the shortcut, the expeditious way. As we absorb Him and enjoy Him, we will have His presence, which is His leading. As long as we do not have His presence, we do not have His leading. His leading is His presence.

Let us consider the pillar of fire and the pillar of cloud. Their presence led the children of Israel. The pillar of fire and the pillar of cloud are simply God Himself. Do we have God's presence as we go to preach the gospel? Do we have His presence as we speak on a particular subject? If we are the only one active in preaching the gospel, and God neither moves nor gives us His presence, what we are doing is not under His leading. We do not have the pillar of fire and the pillar of cloud if we are the only one speaking, and God is not speaking. This is not His leading. He must speak in our speaking. Outwardly we may be speaking, but inwardly He must be speaking. Both He and we need to speak. This kind of speaking is full of the Lord's presence, and this kind of speaking constitutes His leading. This is not a matter of right or wrong, correct or incorrect, or good or evil. Everything depends on whether we have God's presence. With His presence, everything is right. Without His presence, everything is wrong.

THE SECRET OF THE CHRISTIAN LIFE BEING TO ENJOY GOD

God does not intend for us to do anything for Him. As God's children, we need to change our concept and see that God's only desire is to give Himself to us to be our enjoyment. The secret of the Christian life is not how much we work for Him, but how much we enjoy Him. It is not what we do for Him, but how we enjoy Him. We must learn this secret. There is no need for us to worry about doing this or that. We need to learn to simply turn our inner being to enjoy God. When we pray, there is no need for us to be concerned about our difficulties and burdens, such as a seriously ill child. We need to learn to come to God to enjoy and absorb Him, and forget about everything, even a child's illness. If we forget, the Lord will not forget, but if we remember, the Lord often seems to ignore the situation. Even when we say, "My brother Lazarus is sick," the Lord does not move faster for our sake. The more we want Him to come and take care of a matter, the more He does not come. He knows our "Lazarus" is sick, but He does not answer our prayer. Only when we stop does He come. The more we insist, the more He waits until "Lazarus" finally dies, is buried, and begins to stink. This is the Lord. He has no intention for us to do anything for Him. His only intention is that we learn to absorb and enjoy Him.

Martha was always busy for the Lord. She did not know how to stop and absorb the Lord. We must learn to stop ourselves. In particular, when we pray, we must learn to stop our involvement in so many affairs. We should not be busy with so many matters when we pray. Whether our prayer is for half an hour or only ten minutes, we should absorb and enjoy the Lord. We should feed on Him until we are full. Let the children be sick. Let the difficulties remain. Let the burdens take care of themselves. The Lord knows all about these things. We should enjoy Him and be fed by Him. We should simply enjoy and absorb the Lord again and again. If we do this, we will be filled with God, and our face will shine. We will be full of the Lord's presence. What a glory this will be!

Sadly, the opposite is true today. Many brothers and sisters are like the two disciples on the way to Emmaus. They are filled with sorrow. They preach the gospel with wrinkles on their foreheads. They visit people with sullen faces. They go with their sorrows, not with the Lord. As a result, the ones whom they visit have more sorrow. Some elders are sorrowful elders. When they consider hall twenty-eight, they shake their heads. When they look at hall two, they bemoan the situation. When praying in the morning, they say, "Lord, remember hall twenty-eight, and do not forget hall two." This is not praying to the Lord; this is praying about halls. The elders should forget about the halls. When they come to the Lord in the morning, they should behold His beauty, absorb Him, receive Him, and enjoy Him. As they are fed by Him and are filled with Him, their faces will shine. Then when they visit hall twenty-eight in the evening, all the brothers and sisters will say that "Moses" has come. They will marvel at the shining face and say, "The countenance of this elder has changed. His face is no longer sad but shining. When he stands up to speak, the Lord is expressed." This is the secret. This is what it means to be a Christian.

There is no need for us to pray for so many matters. We simply need to touch the Lord, to contact Him. Our relationship with the Lord is not based on matters. He has no intention for us to do anything for Him, nor does He have any intention of doing anything for us. Our relationship with the Lord is not based on doing things but on enjoying Him. He said, "Take, eat" (Matt. 26:26). This means that He wants us to remember Him, to take and drink Him. He has given Himself to us for our enjoyment. He has no desire to do anything for us. He simply desires to be our enjoyment. He does not want us to do anything for Him. He desires us to enjoy Him. That is all He desires, and this is all that matters. He has become our enjoyment. We simply need to enjoy Him, and His glory will be expressed through us. This is the Christian life. This is the meaning of being a Christian. Brothers and sisters, only in this way will we find light, power, victory, and holiness. This is how we will find the Lord of glory Himself.

CHAPTER THREE

GOD'S ACCOMPLISHMENTS FOR MAN

Scripture Reading: Psa. 27:4; 43:4; 1 John 2:27-28

GOD'S DESIRE BEING TO MINGLE HIMSELF WITH MAN FOR MAN'S ENJOYMENT

The Bible unveils that throughout the ages God has been doing one thing in man: He has been mingling Himself with man. The human concept is that God wants man to worship and serve Him. He is seen as the sovereign One far away in the heavens, and men on earth are expected to worship and serve Him. This is man's concept. The Bible, however, shows that God does not require such things from us. Rather, God wants to mingle Himself with us. He wants to work His entire being into us to the extent that He becomes our constitution. He wants to enter into us to be our content. He wants to be our life and our nature. He wants to be the love in our emotion, the thoughts in our mind, and the decisions and deliberations in our will. He even wants to be our ability and discernment. In brief, God wants to enter into us to be everything to us. We should simply be a vessel in the hands of God for His expression.

This divine intention is seen in the Lord Jesus. The Lord Jesus is unique among the human race. Outwardly, He was a man, a perfect man. In every aspect He was a complete man. But God was inside this man. Inwardly, He was filled with God, and God was expressed through Him. When He was on earth, those who followed Him often asked, "Who is this man?" He was hungry, and He was thirsty. He was tired and even exhausted. He was confined to a body the same as we. But if we look deeper, we will find that within this man there was unfathomable wisdom, unlimited power, immeasurable life, and eternal discernment. Hardly anyone could answer this question when He was on earth, but we know who He is today. He is God mingled with man. He is God entering into man, becoming man's life and nature and being expressed through man. The Lord Jesus manifests God's eternal intention for man.

Brothers and sisters, we must realize that unless God is mingled with us in our worship and service, they are not worth anything before God. The real worship rendered to God is one in which God is mingled with the worshipper. This also applies to service. Real service to God is one in which the serving one is mingled with God. When we are going to preach the gospel, we need to remember that the Lord, who is mingled with us, should be the one preaching the gospel. This is the only preaching that counts. When we are praying, the Lord must be the one who is praying through us, that is, praying by mingling Himself with us. Only such prayers are real prayers. If we are on earth, praying to a God who is far away in heaven, and we have nothing in common with Him, our prayers are not real but are merely a religious petition. In the genuine prayer that God desires, He enters into us, mingles with us, and prays through us. Every genuine prayer is a dual prayer; outwardly we are praying, but inwardly God is praying. Outwardly we petition, but inwardly He is petitioning. Outwardly we are speaking, but inwardly the Holy Spirit is speaking. Only this kind of dual prayer is genuine.

This applies to prayer as well as to preaching the gospel. If only I am speaking and the Lord is not, my preaching is worthless; it is merely human oration. The real preaching and release of the Lord's message is one in which the Lord in His humanity speaks through us. Outwardly we are speaking, but it is the Lord speaking from within. Outwardly it seems as if we are the source of the speaking, but the Lord is the source of the speaking. This speaking is a dual speaking, and only this kind of speaking has value.

This principle applies not only to our praying and preaching but also to the entire realm of our Christian life. When it is said that a man has a dual character, it often is spoken in a derogatory way; nevertheless, this is a very fitting description of the Christian life. The real Christian life should be a dual life. If we are living as an individual person, we are not living like a Christian; we are merely living like a human being. As genuine Christians, it seems as if we are the ones living, but inwardly God is living through us. Every Christian should be like Jesus of Nazareth; we should be God manifested in the flesh. Outwardly we are men, but inwardly we are God. The entire Christian life should be one in which God is mingled with man.

God's children need to see this basic issue: God does not desire worship or service from man; neither does He desire to do things for man or man to do things for Him. He only desires that every part of our being would be filled with His element by His mingling of Himself with us and becoming the constituent of our being. When we are filled with God's element, we will enjoy Him and know Him to the uttermost. Only when we allow Him to fill us and become every part of our being can we truly know Him as He desires to be known. This knowledge is not in doctrine, mental understanding, or intellectual apprehension. We can know Him deep in our being as the One whom we taste in our living and practical experience. This is to enjoy God.

THE FOUR STEPS OF GOD'S WORK
IN MAKING HIMSELF AVAILABLE FOR OUR ENJOYMENT

Let us now consider the way to enjoy God. How can God become every part of our being? How can we practically enjoy God in our daily living? We thank the Lord that He prepared the way for us long ago. In order for us to enjoy God and receive Him as the constituent of our inner being, He has taken four steps.

The First Step—Creating Man with a Spirit

In the first step God created man with a human spirit. Even though we have spoken of this matter often in the past, for the sake of the new ones we need to repeat this point.

God created everyone with a stomach so that we can enjoy our food. If we did not have a stomach, there would not be a place for us to receive the food we eat, and it would be impossible for us to enjoy our food. The function of our stomach is to enjoy the food we eat. Similarly, in order for us to receive and enjoy God, He created us with a spirit. The spirit within us is for receiving God and enjoying Him.

A poor man may think that he needs only clothes, food, a dwelling place, and transportation. As long as he can eat, is clothed, lives comfortably, and is mobile, he is satisfied. After being satisfied with these things, however, he will discover that there is another need within him. He may realize that he needs entertainment in his psychological being and then engage in different kinds of amusement, such as music, literature, or other diversions. After he has possessed these things and has tasted of their enjoyment, he will become keenly aware of yet another need deep in his being. This need is not physical or psychological; it originates from his spirit.

When a man is very rich, he thinks about worshipping God, and when a man is in pain or dire conditions, he also thinks about worshipping God, because when he is rich or in pain, he discovers that he has a need in his spirit. When man enjoys life because of his riches, tasting every blessing and every good thing that life can afford, he discovers that he still has a need in his spirit. When he is neither poor nor rich and neither in pain nor in joy, he feels no need to worship God. When he is not concerned with himself, he is not concerned with God. However, when he suffers greatly, experiences extreme poverty, or is sick to the point of dying, he begins to think about God. On the contrary, a person who is extremely rich and happy and who experiences all the blessings there are under heaven may ask himself, "What is the point of all these indulgences? These things do not satisfy me." He then begins to seek after God and to look for ways to worship Him. This principle holds true among all the races of human society, whether they are civilized or barbaric, refined or vulgar.

One will never see a dog, cat, or monkey worshipping God when it is desperate. Even when animals are at the height of their excitement or suffering, they will not turn to God or worship God. They have no need to worship God, because they do not have a spirit. Man is different. There is a spirit within man, and this spirit has a need. A nonchalant man does not feel the need in his spirit. But when he is brought to extreme circumstances, either extreme elation or extreme desperation, the need in his spirit is made manifest. He feels a deep need within him, a need that no person, thing, or matter on earth can satisfy. Nothing physical can satisfy this need. It is at such times that man thinks of worshipping God. There is a spirit within man, and God created man with this spirit in order that he could receive and enjoy Him.

The difference between man and all other creatures is that he has a spirit within him. It is no wonder the sages of old said that man is the spirit of all things. Only man has a spirit. Hence, of all the things in creation, only man possesses a spirit. Man is certainly the highest of all creation. Apart from God's life, man's life is the highest life, because there is a spirit within him. Man's spirit is an organ, prepared by God for him to receive and enjoy God.

The daily salvation of a Christian is a matter of his spirit. Whether he is rich or poor, suffering or joyful, every Christian can testify of the same experience. When he opens to God and fellowships with Him, he finds joy and satisfaction in his spirit, but when he does not open to God or fellowship with Him in his spirit, he feels that something is missing or lacking, and he is unhappy. We feel this way because we have not absorbed God. If we would spend some time every day to pray before the Lord, that is, to stop our mind, exercise our spirit, and fellowship with Him by contacting Him, absorbing Him, and opening ourselves to be filled with Him, we will experience unspeakable satisfaction, freshness, and relief.

If we remain in a room with closed windows for a long time, we will feel that the room is stuffy and soon want to go outside and breathe fresh air for five minutes. After breathing deeply we will feel relieved, refreshed, uplifted, and satisfied. As children of God who fellowship with Him, we can each testify of such experiences. When we would spend a little time to be with God every day, when we stop our thoughts and exercise our spirit to fellowship with Him, absorb Him, and be filled with Him, we sense indescribable sweetness, freshness, freedom, and satisfaction. This feeling proves that we have eaten and have drunk a satisfying portion of God.

We all should have had this experience. It is doubtful whether we are genuine Christians if we have never tasted the sweetness of God. Perhaps we are nominal Christians who have merely touched something of Christianity. We must see that God can be tasted; He is edible and drinkable. We can absorb God and enjoy Him. Sometimes as we are absorbing God in the morning, we need to say, "I will be very busy today, so I want to spend a little more time to absorb You and keep You within me throughout the day." We can have such an experience in our spirit. God has created us with a spirit, and this spirit is the deepest part of our being. It is the organ for us to receive God and the means for us to enjoy Him. This is the first step that God has taken for us.

The Second Step—Incarnation

In the second step God Himself became a man at the appointed time. This is the story of incarnation. When the Lord Jesus came to the earth, God was fully mingled with man. In six thousand years of human history there has been one unique man. He was truly a man, and every part within Him was God. The Lord Jesus was a man, yet He was God. The difference between the Lord Jesus and us is that every part within us is man, but every part within Him was God. The Savior we believe in and have received is not merely God, and He is not simply man. He is God mingled with man. Within every part of the man from Nazareth, our Savior, was God. Everything of God was mingled with this man in a full and undiminished way.

Our Savior is a wonderful person, and God demonstrated His eternal purpose in Him. God's eternal purpose is to mingle Himself with man to be man's element and his enjoyment. In order to accomplish this, when He saves man, He mingles Himself with man. Our Savior is the very One in whom God is mingled with man.

This may sound strange in the ears of a new believer, but gradually he will understand. In order for God to become our enjoyment, He not only created us with a spirit to receive

Him, but at the appointed time He also came into man to be fully mingled with man, thus becoming man's Savior. When we receive Him as our Savior, a mingling work is carried out in us.

The Third Step—Crucifixion

In the third step our Savior, who was both God and man, died on the cross. He accomplished two main things on the cross. First, the Lord shed His blood to deal with everything that prevents God from mingling Himself with us. In other words, His blood dealt with every barrier between God and us; He dealt with everything that frustrates us from contacting God or from touching Him, and everything that disqualifies us from standing boldly before Him.

If we want to contact the Lord and fellowship with Him, we must see the significance of the blood. God is altogether righteous, and we are altogether unrighteous. We need the blood so that we can fellowship with the righteous God. Whenever filthy and dirty men, such as we, want to fellowship with God, who is absolutely holy, the blood is needed. Without the blood shed on the cross, we would not dare come to God or even speak of contacting Him. It would be impossible for us to come near Him. We would die in His light; we would fall before His holiness. But now the blood shed on the cross has cleansed us. All our unrighteousnesses, filth, sins, trespasses, mistakes, and offenses against God as well as all that is incompatible between us and God have been removed by the cleansing of the blood. The blood has solved all of our problems. Now we can come boldly to God through the blood. We can joyfully contact God under the blood. We can even remain in His presence and live in His countenance. As sinners who are unrighteous, unholy, and filthy, we can now contact the holy God and live in Him, and He can live in us and fellowship with us. All of this is possible through the cleansing of the blood shed on the cross.

The Epistle of 1 John, a book on fellowship between man and God, begins by saying that God's life has entered into man and enables man to fellowship with God. God is light and He is righteous, but man is evil and in darkness. How can we fellowship with God? According to 1 John 1:7, we can fellowship through the blood of Jesus Christ. The blood of God's Son cleanses us from every sin. Through the blood we can fellowship with God, but apart from the blood there is no possibility of fellowship. In order for there to be fellowship between God and us, there is not only the need of life but also the need of the blood. The first aspect of the cross provides the blood, which removes all the barriers between us and God.

The second aspect of the cross is that it terminates the old creation. Through the death of the cross, our flesh, our self, and our old nature have been terminated. On the surface, it seems as if the only barrier to our fellowship with God is sin. As such, we are thankful to the Lord that His blood cleanses us from every sin and enables us to fellowship with Him. However, there is still a hidden problem in our being, which is the problem of the flesh, the self, the natural man, and the old creation. These frustrate our being mingled with God.

For example, a brother who is cleansed by the blood can boldly come to God and fellowship with Him. However, when he comes before God, he may be full of the self, full of his own views, his own thoughts, and his own desires. Everything about him is full of the self. This makes it difficult for him to fellowship with God. Although his sins are washed by the blood, his self remains intact. The death of the cross needs to be applied in this situation. The cross not only gives us the blood, but it also puts us to death. The blood of the cross takes away our sins, but the crucifixion of the cross deals with the self. It deals with our old man. This is the third step.

The Fourth Step—
Becoming the Spirit in Resurrection

In the fourth step, after our Lord was crucified on the cross, He resurrected from the dead and became the Spirit. Very few people understand fully the meaning of the Lord becoming the Spirit. We need to see that in resurrection He became the Spirit. In so doing He brought the perfect man into God. We have said that in incarnation the Lord Jesus brought God into man. Now in resurrection He brought man into God. If there were only incarnation, the mingling of God and man would be only half accomplished. God entered into man, but man had not yet entered into God. However, after the Lord Jesus' resurrection, the mingling of God and man was complete; God had entered into man, and man had entered into God. In incarnation the Lord Jesus brought God into man. In resurrection He brought man into God. Today in this universe the man Jesus is sitting on the throne. He is God who has become a man, and He is also man who has entered into God. This wonderful Savior is God mingled with man and man mingled with God. As this One, He is the Spirit. This word may be somewhat difficult for new believers. I hope that they will try their best to understand it. Gradually, they will apprehend this in their practical experience.

Our Savior today is the Spirit. He is beyond time and space. He is everywhere. No matter where we are, as long as we open our heart and our spirit, and we touch Him, His Spirit will come into us, and we will have "spirit-to-spirit" fellowship. His Spirit will touch our spirit, and our spirit will receive His Spirit. The Spirit does not only include divinity; there is also incarnation, the effectiveness of the blood shed on the cross to deal with man's sins, the killing of the cross that solves the problem of the flesh and the self, and resurrection that brings man into God. This Spirit includes so much. When we believe into Him and open our spirit to contact Him, He enters into us. When He enters into us, we enjoy and absorb God.

We have taken a brief look at these four steps. God created us with a spirit for the purpose of receiving Him. He also came in the flesh to be mingled with us. Furthermore, He was crucified on the cross. On the cross He shed His blood to remove the barrier of sin between Him and us, and He dealt with the self and the old creation. Finally, He resurrected and brought humanity into divinity, thus fully mingling God with man. God has taken these four steps to become our enjoyment.

Chapter Four

THE WAY FOR MAN TO ENJOY GOD

Scripture Reading: 1 Tim. 3:16; Heb. 10:19-20; Rom. 8:26-27; Jude 20

GOD'S FOUR STEPS BEING THE BASIS FOR OUR ENJOYING HIM

In the previous chapter we considered the four steps God took to become our enjoyment. In the first step He created us with a spirit. Our spirit is the organ for us to receive God. In the second step God became flesh in the fullness of time; He was mingled with humanity. This man was the Lord Jesus. In the third step the Lord Jesus was crucified on the cross at the appointed time. On the cross He shed His blood to remove everything that was incompatible with God. At the same time He crucified and dealt with the old creation and the self. In the fourth step He rose from the dead and became the Spirit. His death and resurrection brought man into God. Humanity is now fully in the Spirit. The items in the Spirit are very rich. They include God's entrance into man, the death of the cross, resurrection, and man's entrance into God. These riches are now in the Spirit.

Here is a simple example. When sugar, grape juice, and other ingredients are added to a glass of water, it is still a glass of water in a general sense. But if we analyze it, we will see that it contains other ingredients. Sugar has been added to the water. Grape juice has been added. If the glass is placed on a burner and heat is applied to it, the element of heat has been added to it. Other ingredients may also be added. It is no longer just a glass of water; it now contains water with many rich ingredients. Whoever drinks from this glass will receive all the rich ingredients.

In the same way, when the Spirit descended on the day of Pentecost, He was not just "water"; rather, He was a "drink" that included many rich elements. The elements of incarnation, crucifixion, the shedding of His blood, His termination of the old creation, His resurrection from the dead, and His bringing of humanity into divinity were all included in the Spirit that descended on Pentecost. Whenever a person receives the Spirit, all the rich elements in the Spirit enter into him. Whether or not he is aware of it, all of these elements are in him. This is like drinking a glass of water with many ingredients. Whether or not we realize it, all of the ingredients in the water enter into us. Today when a person receives the Spirit, the functions of all the elements contained in the Spirit, such as God's mingling with man, man's mingling with God, the cleansing of sins, and the termination of the self are activated. As we practice living in this Spirit, we will gradually experience all these elements that God has accomplished for us. The steps or ways for us to enjoy God are based on the four steps He has accomplished. Hence, there are now four steps for us to enjoy God.

The First Step—Exercising Our Spirit

The first step for us to enjoy God is to exercise our God-created spirit. Whenever we want to contact God and enjoy Him, we must first learn to exercise our spirit. What does it mean to exercise our spirit? When I hit Brother Hwang, I exercise my fist. When I speak, I exercise my voice. When I look at others, I exercise my eyes. When others listen to me, they exercise their ears. In order for us to contact God and enjoy Him, we must exercise our spirit.

In order to exercise our spirit when we come to God, we should pray according to the feeling deep within our being. We should forget about our thoughts and not be concerned with what we should say. We should simply turn and pray according to the inner feeling. The feeling deep within us is the feeling of the spirit. When we pray according to this feeling, we are exercising our spirit in prayer.

Regrettably, many brothers and sisters do not pray this way. We may pray for many matters according to our mind but never touch God. Hence, even though we pray, we are dry within. I believe that many of us have experienced this. Especially a new believer prays with his mind. He may consider how he should pray. He may consider whether he should pray for his father, his mother, himself, his finances, or his studies. When a wife prepares to pray, she may consider, "Should I pray for my husband and for his business, or should I pray that my children do not get into a car accident?" This is not the exercise of the spirit; instead, it is the exercise of the mind. It is right for us to exercise our mind when we are at school, but it is altogether wrong to exercise our mind in this way when we pray. The more we consider, the more God disappears. The more we exercise our mind, the farther God "runs from us." In reality God does not disappear and does not run away. We are simply using the wrong organ. We cannot use our eyes to hear or our ears to identify colors. If someone speaks of a dark red cup, the dark red will "disappear" if we try to see the cup with our ears. Or if some brothers try to hear a loud voice with their eyes, the voice will "disappear." Actually, the voice is still there, but the wrong organ is being used to substantiate it. In the same way, we cannot pray to God with our mind. God is not in our mind; He is in our spirit.

Let me say a further word to help us understand. In English we have the word *substance,* which means "matter" or "reality." From this noun we have the verb *substantiate,* which means "to make real" or "to materialize something." Sound is an example of a substance. It is something real, something substantial. However, if we do not have ears or if we are deaf, we will not realize that there is such a substance as sound; in other words, we will be unable to substantiate sound. The same is true with color. Although it is something real and substantial, if we do not have eyes or if we are blind, we will be unable to see this substance. In other words, we will be unable to substantiate color. We should remember that God is Spirit and therefore is "substance." Even though God is a "substance," and our spirit is a "substance," as long as we exercise our mind instead of exercising our spirit, we will be unable to substantiate God. If we exercise our spirit, however, we will immediately realize that God exists. We will substantiate God.

When we come to God, we should forget our considerations and pray with our spirit. Provided we use our spirit, we will immediately touch God, sense His presence, and receive Him. Once a believer learns this lesson, instead of exercising his mind, he will learn to pray from his spirit. The moment he kneels down, he will exercise his spirit instead of wandering in his mind with different thoughts. When he is convicted in his spirit of being full of the self, loving himself rather than God, he will cry out to God, saying, "I am full of the self. I only love myself. I do not love You at all." Such a simple prayer will immediately bring him in touch with God. Those who have some experience in this matter understand what I am saying. The more we pray from our spirit, the more we touch God, take Him in, and are filled with Him. After praying, we are persons filled with God. We are satisfied, refreshed, freed, comforted, cheered, and enlightened. This is a prayer of fellowship, a prayer that touches God, a prayer that involves the exercise of the spirit, and a prayer that counts.

Our mind, however, is often quite troublesome. While we are praying with an exercised spirit, a thought may suddenly come to us concerning our work or our family. Once we are interrupted by such thoughts, we turn from our spirit to our mind. These thoughts cut off our fellowship with God, and draw us out of the spirit. Then it is difficult to return to our spirit. This shows that contacting God through prayer is entirely a matter in the spirit. Whenever we are in the mind instead of the spirit, our fellowship with God is terminated immediately. We cannot fellowship with God in our mind. God meets with us in our spirit, and we meet with Him in our spirit. The Lord Jesus said that God is Spirit and that we must worship Him in spirit (John 4:24). To worship God is to fellowship with Him and to contact Him. May we learn to follow the steps that God has taken in the work He has accomplished in order for us to contact Him. His first step was to create us with a spirit. Hence, in contacting Him, our first step must be to exercise our spirit.

Dear brothers and sisters, we must set aside our troublesome and hindering thoughts whenever we pray. When we draw near to God in prayer, we must learn to set aside our thoughts. We must learn to reject and deny our thoughts. When we come to God, we must learn to turn to our spirit and to pray from our spirit. This is what it means to contact God by exercising our spirit.

The Second Step—
Applying the Principle of Incarnation

The second step that God took is incarnation, in which God is mingled with man. This is the great mystery of godliness. The second step that we take to contact God must be related to the manifestation of God in the flesh. This word may not be easy to understand initially. In order to understand how God's manifestation is related to contacting Him, we must clearly see the principle that God's will and fundamental desire is for us to provide Him with opportunities to mingle Himself with us. According to the common religious concept, God is far away in the heavens, and man on earth needs to worship Him. But this is not God's desire. According to the Bible, God's desire is entirely different from this concept. His unique desire is to enter into man and to be mingled with man. He has no desire to remain far away on His throne in heaven and receive man's worship from earth. This is absolutely not His intention. His sole intention is to come down from heaven to earth, enter into man, dwell inside of man, and mingle Himself with man.

God's desire can be seen in the New Testament and in the Old Testament. Although God dwells in His sanctuary in the highest and no one can touch Him, He desires to dwell with the contrite (Isa. 57:15; 66:1-2). While God desires that we praise Him, He does not desire one-sided praise. He is pleased with praise that comes from His being mingled with us. God wants us to worship Him, but He is not happy when we are the source alone. God desires worship in which He is mingled with us, and He worships through and with us.

The Christian life must be a life of two natures. Worship and service that has only one nature, the human nature, will not please God. Our worship must be mingled with God, and our service must also be mingled with God. Even our prayer must be mingled with God. If we are the only ones praying, and God is not mingled in our prayer, praying together with us, our prayer has only one nature. Such prayer will never be acceptable to God. Every prayer that is acceptable to God involves two natures. Outwardly, we are the ones praying, but inwardly God is praying through us. This prayer is the mingling of divinity with humanity.

Every prayer of worth that touches God, that touches the throne, is a prayer in which God is mingled with man. Outwardly we are praying, but inwardly He is praying. Andrew Murray once said that every prayer of true worth is a prayer in which the Christ within us prays to the Christ on the throne. This is a mystery. The God within us prays to the God on the throne. In such prayer God prays through us in our prayer. This prayer touches His throne and causes Him to respond. God never hears prayers that involve only one nature. All prayers that do not have the element of God's mingling are prayers that miss His heart's desire.

I believe many saints have experienced this. Sometimes when we go to God, we are the ones praying. Such prayers are absolutely our own prayers, originating from our own thoughts. In the example of a sister who thinks about her husband and children when she prays, the prayer was with the mind. In her prayer her spirit is not motivated, and the Holy Spirit is not invoked. Similarly, some people often pray according to their own choices and preferences. If they want to go and study in America, they pray, "Lord, be gracious to me and bless this endeavor." They never ask God His desire. This prayer is absolutely from the self. The Holy Spirit cannot move within such persons. The more they pray, the drier they will become, the farther they will be from God, and the harder it will be for them to sense God's presence.

This is not proper prayer. In proper prayer, either before or during our prayer, the Holy Spirit will initiate something within our spirit. He will operate first within our spirit. For example, many saints prayed for this meeting during the day. While they were busy with their work, the Holy Spirit was operating within them. Although they had many obligations in the world, there was a prompt in their spirit to pray for the meeting. When the Holy Spirit prompts us in our spirit, we must stop what we are doing and come to the Lord to pray, not according to our feeling or our thoughts but according to the moving within our spirit. Our outward prayer is the result of the inward moving of the Holy Spirit in us. I cannot enter into Brother Hwang and push him from within, but I can stand behind him and push him. When I push him once, he moves forward one step. As long as I push him, he will move forward. Although it appears as if he is walking by himself, I am actually pushing him forward. This is the way we should pray. We pray by the Holy Spirit pushing us from within. When the Holy Spirit pushes, we pray, "Lord, remember tonight's meeting." When the Holy Spirit pushes us again, we will pray further, "Lord, open our eyes to see that You are enjoyable." It seems as if we are the ones uttering these words, but actually the Holy Spirit is prompting us inwardly to utter these words.

This is the principle of incarnation. This is the Holy Spirit moving within us to the point that we pray outwardly. This is the great mystery of godliness. This is God manifested in the flesh. Whenever a brother or a sister truly prays this way, God is manifested in the flesh. God moves within them, and such moving is manifested in their speaking. I can testify that I once visited a brother who was praying in his room. Even though I did not see his face, I heard his prayer, and his prayer gave me the sensation that God was being manifested in the flesh. He was praying, yet I heard God's voice in his prayer. I heard God's sighing and God's yearning, and God's heart was fully revealed through such a prayer. This brother was God's mouthpiece and God's expression. God was manifested through his prayers.

This does not apply only to individual prayers. When the church comes together in the bread-breaking meeting, a fellowship meeting, or the prayer meeting, some brothers and sisters pray these kinds of prayers; their prayers are the result of the moving of the Holy Spirit. Their prayers do not involve merely one nature but two. Their prayers are prompted by the moving of the Holy Spirit within them. These saints are the mouthpiece of the Holy Spirit. When they pray, there is a sense that God is being manifested. Their prayers are an expression of God, a revelation of God, and a manifestation of God. These prayers are in the reality of the principle of incarnation, of God manifested in the flesh. A man in the flesh is praying, but he fully expresses God. God is manifested. God's desire, wish, and yearnings are expressed through man. It is difficult to say whether a man or God is praying. We can say that a man is praying, but we can also say that God is praying. In fact, God is praying in man and through man. Praying this kind of prayer is the way to touch God.

Whenever we draw near to God in prayer, we should first exercise our spirit. Second, we should learn not to pray by ourselves. Rather than praying simply by ourselves, we should let God move us in our prayer. When He wants to pray within us, we should pray with Him. I would like to offer a shameful testimony. Many times the Lord wants to pray, but I do not want to pray. It seems as if He is saying, "I want to pray now. Do you want to pray?" At times I reject Him, and He has to wait. At other times I immediately respond by praying, and the result is very sweet. At still other times I do not want to pray but quickly regret this and say, "Lord, please forgive me. I am ready to pray now." At such a time it is not unusual for Him to indicate His displeasure, seeming to say, "You are ready; I am not ready." Do not think that I am exaggerating. Those who have had intimate fellowship with the Lord have experienced this. Sometimes we can take the initiative and say, "Lord, I am ready to pray. Can we please pray?" We can inquire of Him, and God likes us to inquire of Him. If we sense that He does not want to pray, it is mainly because our condition is not that proper. If our condition is proper, He will respond, "Yes, I want to pray with you. I have been waiting to pray with you. I have been hoping that you could be My prayer partner." If we touch this key, we will realize the value of prayer. We will no longer utter vain prayers, uttering a mouthful of words that do not touch His heart. Such prayers are neither the Lord joining our prayer, nor our joining His prayer. These prayers involve only one nature. They are not prayers in the principle of God manifested in the flesh.

In matters great or small, the entire Christian life is altogether a story of God mingling with man. If I am the only one speaking, and God is not speaking in me, even this message is empty. It will not minister a spiritual supply to the brothers and sisters. God must be pushing and motivating me while I speak. Every word I speak must be one that He has already spoken within me. His speaking within me should constrain me to speak. Such words involve two natures; they are words uttered as a result of God being mingled with man. You may forget the words that are spoken, but something within the words will touch your inner being, and you will have no choice but to turn to God and draw near to Him. It is not the words themselves that convict us, but it is the very element of God, the element of the Spirit, behind the words that touches our inner being. This principle must govern every aspect of our Christian life. Whenever we draw near to God, we must seize the principle of incarnation. We must allow God to mingle Himself with us before we can enjoy Him in a practical way.

The Third Step—Applying the Blood and the Death of the Cross

The third step in enjoying God is to trust in the blood and the death of the cross. The blood deals with our sins, and the death of the cross deals with our person. When we come to God, exercise our spirit, and learn to cooperate and be mingled with Him, we will discover that we have two problems. We have the problem of sins outwardly and the problem of our person inwardly. There is the outward transgression and the inward self, the outward mistakes and the inward old creation. Those who have touched God's presence realize these two levels of frustrations.

Our lack of feeling that we are sinful and lack of realization that we are a problem are strong proofs that we have not touched God sufficiently; we are not living according to His countenance. Whenever we touch God and live in His countenance, we will see that we are dirty and full of sins. We will also realize that our person, which is of the old creation, is a big frustration to God. At such times we will immediately apply the blood and say, "Lord, cleanse me with the blood. Cleanse me with the blood." The more we go to God and exercise our spirit to cooperate with Him, the more we will be mingled with God and sense the need for the blood.

Every part of our being, from the circumference to the center, is full of defilement. The lack of the sense that we are defiled and filthy proves that we are not living in God's countenance. If we are living in His countenance, we cannot utter one word of prayer without pleading for His blood. Before the prophet Isaiah touched God's countenance, he could boast in himself. But as soon as he saw God's glory and came before His face, he cried, "Woe is me, for I am finished! / For I am a man of unclean lips, / And in the midst of a people of unclean lips I dwell" (Isa. 6:5). He was not able to stand before the Lord of glory. He needed the cleansing of the blood. Whenever we touch our spirit, and whenever we touch God and sense His presence and mingling, we will realize that we are unclean. Even if we spend one hour praying for cleansing, we will still need the cleansing of the blood in the next hour. Only when we touch God can we discover, realize, and see our filthiness. A believer once said, "Even my tears of repentance require the cleansing of the blood." We need to repent even for our repentance for sins.

How unclean are our inward parts! Our motives and thoughts are impure, and they are mixed with acts of the self and of self-interest. Our thoughts, views, words, and attitudes cannot withstand God's searching under His light. Even if we proclaim to be the cleanest of believers, we will find that we are in fact the most defiled once God shines on our inward and outward conditions. It is under this light that we find the cleansing of the blood most necessary.

Without the blood, God will not accept us. Without the blood, even our conscience will not approve us (Heb. 10:19; Rom. 2:15). An enlightened and cleansed conscience will always condemn us as being filthy; it will rebuke us. We may think that we said something in love, but our motive was impure. We may think that we love the brothers, but pride and self-glorification are hidden within our love. Our condemning of others for not having as much love as we have shows that our love is mixed with the expression and manifestation of the self. When the Lord shines on us, we will realize that what we consider to be a most holy love is altogether filthy and needs the thorough cleansing of the blood. For a long period of time I would spend thirty out of forty minutes of my prayer time confessing my sins. Only a few minutes were left for intercession. I can testify that the more one touches God's presence and His countenance, and the more one mingles with God and cooperates with Him, the more he feels a need for the cleansing of the blood.

In the morning we should each touch the Lord's presence, turn to our spirit, and pray by being mingled with Him. If we would do this, we will no longer be as free and careless as we have been in the past. Once we touch God and cooperate with Him, light will shine in us, and we will see that we are defiled in this item and wrong in that item. If we are wrong in our attitude toward our husband and in our thoughts concerning our children, we will confess, "Lord, cleanse me with Your blood." Before we finish this confession, another thought may come concerning how we wronged our parents. While we confess this, a third thought may come to us related to pride in our demeanor when we spoke with a brother. We may respond, "Lord, forgive me. Cleanse me with Your precious blood." As soon as we make this confession, another thought may come revealing that our prayer at the Lord's table was full of self-boasting and glorification. Immediately we should pray, "Lord, forgive me. Cleanse me again." As soon as we utter these words, another thought may come that we were improper in our behavior toward our household help. After confessing this, still another thought may come. Such feelings of condemnation touch one point after another. As we realize that we are full of problems, there is almost no way to proceed with our intercession. The entire time of prayer may be taken up with confession and prayer for forgiveness and cleansing. If this is our condition, we are blessed. We have touched God. We have met the Lord.

Our prayer is most likely outside of God if, without any

consciousness of sins and mistakes, it is easy to pray for this or that matter as soon as we kneel down. We have not touched God. We should read Daniel 9 again and consider his prayer. In effect, in his entire prayer, he said, "Our fathers have sinned against You. We have sinned against You, and I have sinned against You. If You do not grant us mercy, we have no way to proceed." Daniel was a man under the light. He knew himself, realized his corruption, and confessed and grieved at length. He made confession over and over again and prayed for forgiveness. After confessing, he simply made a short intercession at the end: "God, remember Your holy habitation and Your holy city for Your own sake" (cf. v. 19). Over ninety percent of that long prayer was confession; only the last part was intercession, but this was enough to touch God's heart.

Suppose a brother comes to God and prays in spirit by cooperating with God. He touches God and senses His presence, and God's light shines on him, exposing all his failures and hidden thoughts. At such a time he is aware of his evil doings and sins, and he trusts in the blood. He sees that the blood of the cross is not only for saving him from hell but also for maintaining his fellowship with God. When he draws near to God in this way, he enjoys the efficacy of the blood. He can point to specific incidents and say, "Lord, I apply the blood to this matter and to that matter." The more he prays this way, the more his conscience is purged, his spirit is revived, his heart is set at rest, and his inner being is filled with God's presence. Perhaps his entire prayer is simply a long confession, and he does not ask for much in his prayer. But after praying, he is inwardly filled with God's presence and is overflowing with God Himself. He has enjoyed God and has tasted God.

We need not pray for so many miscellaneous items. The Lord's Word says that we should seek first His kingdom and His righteousness, and all these things will be added to us (Matt. 6:33). The heathen pray exclusively for these things because they do not know God. As those who know God, we should not pray this way. We should touch God's presence in our spirit and pray by cooperating with Him. When we discover any sin in us, we should confess, ask for the cleansing of the blood, and enjoy the redemption that comes through the cross.

When we touch God, we will see not only the outward sins but also the inward self. We will see that our entire being is full of the self. The self is even the center of all our relationships. It is the center of our relationship with our husband, our wife, our children, our parents, and the church. Consequently, God cannot mingle Himself deeply with us; we are full of the hidden self. In everything our consideration is the self. We are number one. We are number two. We are number three. We are number four. We are the first, we are the last, and we are everything in between. The Holy Spirit will show that we are not only full of sin but also full of the self and the old creation. Then the Holy Spirit will lead us to the death of the cross. When the Spirit points out our sins, we receive the cleansing of the blood. In the same principle, when the Spirit exposes the self, we have no choice but to accept the death of the cross. We will condemn ourselves, abhor ourselves, reject ourselves, deny ourselves, and apply the death of the cross through the Spirit who abides in us. We will enjoy the death of the cross. Then the crucifixion of the old creation will no longer be doctrine to us; it will be our practical experience. In our fellowship with God in His presence we will experience the death of Christ in a very real and practical way. Through the Spirit who abides in us, the self will be put to death. On the one hand, we will experience the cleansing of the blood; on the other hand, we will experience the death of the cross.

The Fourth Step—
Living in the Spirit of Resurrection

As we experience the first three steps, we spontaneously will experience the fourth step, which is to be in resurrection. As cleansed, redeemed, and crucified persons, we will immediately be brought into resurrection and ascension. We will be in the Holy Spirit and be free and transcendent. The Holy Spirit will fill us, pour Himself upon us, nourish us, and mingle Himself with us. We will have the Spirit's presence in everything. Our sins will be cleansed, the self will be crucified, and our entire being will be in the Spirit of resurrection. We will be brought into the realm of resurrection, the realm of heaven, that is, the realm of God. We will be persons in God, enjoying God, filled with Him, and knowing how to apply Him in everything. God will not only be mingled with us; we will also be brought into the very being of God.

In such a realm of resurrection and ascension we will be sanctified, shining, and victorious. In such a realm God becomes our presence and our guidance. When we stand up to speak, God is our speaking, our message, and our eloquence. When we preach the gospel, God is our gospel and our power. In such a realm God is our all in all. He becomes whatever we need. Not only are we in God; He is also in us. In addition to contacting Him with our spirit and cooperating with Him in prayer, we will be cleansed and crucified, becoming persons who experientially enjoy the Lord's redemption and the crucifixion of His cross. In this redemption we are put to death, and the Spirit of resurrection brings us into the realm of resurrection. Our entire being is in God. We are fully in God, that is, in the spirit, in heaven, in resurrection, in life, and in the new creation. We are persons in the new creation, in life, in resurrection, in heaven, in the spirit, and in God. Moreover, our inner being is God Himself, and our outward expression is His expression. Every part of our being will be God, and we will be persons who fully enjoy God.

However, this is not a once-for-all experience; neither can a person reach this peak with one attempt. We need continual experiences of this. At a certain time we may feel that we have reached the peak. However, we will later realize that it was not the peak and that there is still a need to go deeper and higher. Although we may experience much grace when we touch the Lord's presence again, we will also sense our sins again and need the cleansing of the blood again. Under this shining we will discover more of our hidden self and realize our need to embrace a deeper death. Going through those experiences repeatedly, we will enter into a deeper resurrection and touch, absorb, enjoy, and appropriate God in a deeper way. This is the way to grace and blessing. May the Lord have mercy on us all and bring us into this realm!

Chapter Five

HOW TO ENJOY GOD IN PRAYER

Scripture Reading: Psa. 42:1-2; 27:4; 62:1; 104:34; 145:5; 29:2; 150:1; Gen. 18:22, 33

In this chapter and the next we will consider how we can enjoy God through prayer and reading the Word. Prayer and reading the Word are the most crucial means to receive and enjoy God.

Although prayer and reading the Word are quite common among us, there are many details to consider. Many people pray, but they do not know the meaning of prayer. Similarly, many people read the Bible, but they do not know the significance of reading the Word. The more common a practice is, the more science there is to it. We should never think that as soon as one becomes a Christian, he automatically knows how to pray and read the Word. It is not that simple. If a Christian truly touches the key to prayer and reading the Word, he is on his way to enjoying God daily. Let us now consider how to enjoy God through prayer.

PRAYER BEING TO BREATHE IN GOD

Prayer is not mainly a matter of coming to God to ask for something. The meaning of prayer is not to ask God to do something for us. The primary significance of prayer is to breathe in God, to absorb God. When we pray, we should not have a motive or intention of asking God to do something for us; rather, our intention should be to breathe in God and absorb Him. Regrettably, many Christians misunderstand the meaning of prayer. They think that we need to pray to God to ask for help because there are things that we cannot do.

Let me say strongly, this is not prayer. Real prayer has nothing to do with asking God for help.

Simply put, prayer is our spiritual breathing. We all know what it is to breathe. When we breathe out, we exhale the carbon dioxide that is within us. When we breathe in, we inhale the oxygen that is outside of us. This is what happens when we breathe in and breathe out. In prayer we do the same thing—we breathe out what is within us, and we breathe in what is in God. Everything that we have in our natural being can be compared to carbon dioxide, and everything that God is can be compared to oxygen. When we pray, we breathe out everything undesirable, and we breathe in everything of God.

Recently we found a good hymn on prayer (*Hymns,* #255). This hymn says that when we come to God, we breathe out ourselves and everything we have, and we breathe in God and everything He has. By this breathing in and out, we are delivered from ourselves and are put into God. This kind of breathing discharges what is within us and brings in everything of God. When we breathe out, our sins are exhaled, and when we breathe in, God's holiness is inhaled. By breathing out, we rid ourselves of weakness. By breathing in, we take in God's power. We may be full of sorrow and grief, but as soon as we come to God and breathe out, the sorrow and grief are gone. After breathing out, we must breathe in. When we breathe in, God's joy and comfort enter into us. This is the meaning of prayer. Prayer is to breathe in God, just as we breathe in air. Whenever we pray, we breathe in God. Prayer is our spiritual breathing before God and in God. Even though we often do not know what to say when we wait on God, there is a sighing within us. This sighing can be compared to breathing. Our experience shows that when we sigh a little, the weight on our shoulder disappears. We are fully released and rested, and we overflow with a sense of sweetness. We may often find ourselves sinking into darkness and confusion within, not knowing which path we should take, what we should do, or even how we should pray. But while we wait on the Lord, we utter a sigh from deep in our being. It is interesting that after sighing for a while, the darkness and confusion vanish, and we become clear and uncluttered, knowing the way to proceed. This wonderful experience is the meaning of prayer. Real prayer is nothing but waiting on God and breathing in God. When we breathe, we exhale everything that we are and inhale everything that God is.

Let us now consider ten points to illustrate how we breathe in God through prayer.

Appearing before God

In order to breathe in God through prayer, we must appear before God. The psalmist says that he thirsts for God. His soul pants for God as the hart pants for the streams of water. He says, "When will I come and appear / Before God?" (Psa. 42:2). Do we appear before God when we pray? Do we thirst to touch Him in our spirit? Whenever we breathe in God, we must first exercise to appear before Him. We should never think that God is only in heaven; He is abiding in our spirit. When we pray, we close our eyes not only to concentrate but also to stop our outward being. Our outward being often wanders with our eyes. By closing our eyes when we pray, we close the gate of our eyes, shut the door to the outside world, and turn the direction of our being to our spirit. After we stop our entire being and close the door to the outside world, we will be able to turn to the deepest part of our being and exercise our spirit. When we turn to exercise our spirit, we immediately touch God and appear before Him in our spirit.

Being Silent

After touching God in our spirit, we must learn the lesson of not opening our mouth quickly. We do not need to shout and cry when we touch God. We should be silent and calm. The more silent and calm we are, the better.

Many of us cannot pray once we are told to be silent. As soon as we are quiet, our minds wander, and we become confused. We need to shout and cry in order to concentrate. This proves that we have not learned the proper lesson in prayer.

We must learn a serious lesson in prayer. We must turn our entire being away from the outside world. We must stop our entire being and turn to our spirit so that we can appear before God. The psalmist says that he desires to dwell in the house of Jehovah to behold His beauty (27:4). The house of Jehovah is our spirit. We must turn our entire being to our spirit and remain there silently. This is a matter of practice.

In order to have prayers that breathe in God, we first need to turn to our spirit to touch God. After we touch God, we need to be silent before Him. This is true even in human communication. A person is probably not that close to us if we can only speak loudly to him once we meet. The more intimate we are with a person, the more silent we can be when we are with him. Simply by looking at each other, our sentiments are conveyed without speaking. The same can be said concerning one who is experienced in touching God. When he touches God, he is silent. Even if he is moved to tears, these tears are inward rather than outward. If he has anything to say, he speaks quietly; he does not need to shout or cry. Everyone who learns to breathe in God learns this lesson. As we touch God in our spirit, the best thing to do is to be silent before Him.

Beholding His Beauty

Although these points do not have a legal or fixed order, we should learn to behold the beauty of the Lord in silence (v. 4). Many Christians have never heard of this practice. Beholding the beauty of the Lord is to look at the Lord in our spirit and to gaze at Him. When we come before God in prayer, we must learn to stop our speaking, to cut off our words, and to simply turn to our spirit to appear before Him, touch Him, behold Him in silence, and gaze upon Him. We need to look at Him again and again, beholding, appreciating, and even treasuring Him. This is very sweet and necessary. We should never consider prayer to be merely asking God to do something for us. No, the object and subject of prayer are not things. Both the object and subject of prayer are God Himself. First we should touch Him. Then we should be silent before Him. After this we should behold Him by looking and gazing at Him. This is to absorb God and enjoy Him.

Inquiring

When we open our mouth, we do not need to ask or beg, but we can inquire. Many brothers and sisters have never inquired of the Lord. They only ask and beg. They say, "God, my son is sick. I have this need and that lack." Their asking turns into begging: "Heal my son. Take care of me. Give me what I need." What is this? This is begging. These are not good prayers. The best prayer is inquiring prayer. As we touch God, wait in silence, behold His loveliness, and converse with Him, we can ask Him, "Would You like me to mention a certain matter now?" This is the sweetest kind of prayer.

When Abraham stood before Jehovah (Gen. 18), he did not open his mouth quickly. He waited before God, inquired of Him, and looked at Him. There are times when we do things according to the index of a person's eyes; we speak according to the expression on their face. This is how we should pray. The psalmist expressed his desire: "To dwell in the house of Jehovah / All the days of my life, / To behold the beauty of Jehovah, / And to inquire in His temple" (v. 4). We must turn to our spirit, behold Him, and then inquire of Him.

I am afraid that many brothers and sisters have never prayed this way. It may be difficult for a sister who is praying for her husband's health to discuss the matter with God. It is difficult to find a person who would say, "God, can I pray for this matter? Can I bring up this subject now? What should I ask?" This is not how we usually pray. If a husband is sick, when his wife kneels down, she says, "God, my husband is sick. Please heal him quickly and promptly so that he will recover his health and even be healthier." How does this sister know that God wants to heal her husband promptly or to make him healthier than he was before? What if God wants him to be sick or wants to take him away? How does she know what God wants to do? She should discuss this matter with God. If she does not discuss this matter but simply implores God when she prays, in reality, she is the Lord in this matter; everything revolves around her. Brothers and sisters, have we learned the lesson of inquiring of God? Those who have never learned this lesson are wild and reckless in their prayers.

Our God is neither wild nor reckless. He will not deal with wild and obstinate people. Whether God is revealed as Jehovah in the Old Testament or as Jesus in the New Testament,

He is shown to be a very civil and fine person; He is not wild. John 11:1-44 is a good illustration. Martha and Mary asked the Lord to come immediately and heal their sick brother. This was wild and obstinate. The Lord, however, indicated that He was not ready. The two sisters thought that it was time, but the Lord was not yet ready. He remained where He was for two more days, and then He came. When Martha saw Him, she complained, saying, "Lord, if You had been here, my brother would not have died" (v. 21). Mary repeated the same thing. Although they were women, they were wild and reckless. However, the Lord was gentle and fine; He did not react in haste. Rather, He said that He was the resurrection and the life, and although her brother was dead, he would rise again. Martha had already responded, saying, "I know that he will rise again in the resurrection in the last day" (v. 24). This was a wild jump. She jumped from the present time all the way to the end of the age. After she said this, she went and called her sister secretly to meet the Lord, saying, "The Teacher is here and is calling you" (v. 28). This word came from Martha. Later the Lord asked where Lazarus had been put and requested that they take away the stone. Martha again spoke recklessly, saying that it was useless to open the tomb because it smelled. The Lord, however, told them to do as He said and then cried out in a loud voice, saying, "Lazarus, come out!" (v. 43). Lazarus responded and came out. The Lord said, "Loose him and let him go" (v. 44). This shows how the Lord answers prayer, and how differently people pray to Him. Many pray in a wild way, but the Lord answers in a fine way. He responds to man's prayer in a gentle and proper way.

It is difficult to find a person who does not pray to God in a wild way. We are not used to beholding His loveliness in silence; we are not used to living according to the index of His eyes. This is a pity. We must learn to be an inquiring person in our prayer. We should ask the Lord, "Can I bring up this subject at this time?" We should look at His eyes. If He is not happy, we should not continue. If He has an expression of approval, we can proceed by asking how we should pray. This is what it means to inquire. Some may say, "This is too slow. Things will be delayed, and people will die." We need to remember that time is in God's hand. He is beyond time. The Lord can save a brother if he is sick, He can resurrect him even if he has died, and He can make him fresh even if he smells. We must believe that our Lord never delays any work. The best prayer is inquiring prayer, but inquiring can only happen when a person is calm. If we have never touched God and have never been calm before Him or never beheld His loveliness, we do not know the meaning of inquiring.

Waiting

We should learn to wait on God. This is a trying lesson. Even in human relationships waiting is an important element. Suppose I want a brother to help me. If he is busy when I go to see him, I cannot make my request. I must wait until he is no longer busy before I can open my mouth. We should not think that we can skip this step when we pray. Many times when God asks us to do something for Him, He does not force us. He waits until we are ready. If God can wait on us, should we not wait on God?

The book of Psalms is filled with the matter of waiting on God. In the prayers of the psalmists the word *waiting* is uttered numerous times. We need to wait on Jehovah (37:9). Our soul should wait in silence for God alone (62:1). We cannot breathe in God without first waiting on Him. Waiting on God is to allow Him to determine the timing. We cannot dictate the time; He dictates the time. We need to wait. When we pray, we need to inquire of God, and we also need to wait on God.

Musing

We also need to learn to muse or meditate on everything about God. We must meditate on God's loveliness, His lovingkindness, His dignity, His glory, His attributes, and His acts. We must learn that when breathing in God through prayer, we should not only inquire of Him and wait on Him but also meditate on Him and ponder His acts.

We should not think that it is a waste of time to temporarily set aside other matters in our prayers while we meditate on God. God already knows our needs. What touches His heart the most and gives Him the sweetest thought is our musing on Him in His presence. This is the reason the psalmist says, "May my musing be sweet to Him" (104:34). We should remain in His presence and behold Him in silence. While we behold Him in this way, we inquire of Him, wait on Him, and muse on Him. We can muse on His dealings with us and on His dealings with the saints of old. We can also muse on the sweetness of His person. We can meditate on His desire, love, patience, character, glory, and sweetness. In this musing, we absorb God, and His elements fill us. We should gain this experience and learn this lesson.

Please trust in my word. We must leave our many affairs, our business, health, family, finance, and livelihood, in God's hand and remember His promise that our heavenly Father knows that we need all these things (Matt. 6:32). We must cast all our anxiety on Him (1 Pet. 5:7). There is no need to spend much time praying for these things. There is no need to pray for every point. We should believe that He bears the responsibility for all our needs. In our prayers we should forget about ourselves and spend more time to muse on Him, allowing Him and His acts to fill our spiritual eyes and inward senses. God treasures this type of musing; He appreciates this kind of meditation. When we enjoy Him in this musing, He dispenses Himself into us and takes care of all our other needs. We should be at peace and focus on His sweetness instead of focusing on our own affairs. We need to spend time to muse upon His sweetness.

Worshipping

As we touch Him, remain in Him, behold His loveliness, converse with Him, inquire of Him, wait on Him, and muse upon Him, we should worship Him. We should worship Him in our spirit and with our whole being. We should attune our entire being to His holy splendor and worship Him in holy splendor (Psa. 29:2). We should prostrate ourselves before Him and offer Him our worship.

Praising

We should also praise God. Praise always follows worship.

As we muse upon a certain matter, praises should flow forth from within us.

Interceding

We also should learn to participate in intercessory work. If time permits and we are able to spend more time before God, He will surely tell us things that concern Him. As soon as we know these things, we need to do the work of intercession. Abraham stood before God. As he remained in His presence, God seemingly said, "Shall I hide from Abraham what I am about to do? I have to let him know that I will destroy Sodom. But there is a child of mine in Sodom. On the one hand, I will destroy Sodom; on the other hand, I want to save Lot. This is My desire." Once Abraham heard this, he immediately began his intercessory work before God. In his prayer he said, "Suppose there are fifty righteous within the city; will You indeed destroy and not spare the place for the sake of the fifty righteous who are in it?...Shall the Judge of all the earth not do justly?" (Gen. 18:24-25). Abraham's intercession was absolutely in the form of inquiring; he did not ask or beg. Abraham kept inquiring all the way to the end. This is the best kind of intercession. As we remain in God, muse upon Him, worship Him, and praise Him, He reveals His desire to us, and we intercede by inquiring. This kind of prayer is sweet.

Allowing God to Finish His Speaking

We also need to allow God to finish what He is speaking. This was what Abraham did. He prayed, but God spoke. The Scripture says, "Jehovah went away as soon as He had finished speaking with Abraham" (v. 33). Many times in our prayers we go away as soon as we have finished speaking rather than letting God go away when He is finished speaking. In our prayers we have no thought of God's speaking. We simply speak what we want. After praying, we say, "In the name of Jesus, Amen." Then we leave. We do not care if God is leaving or staying. Let me say this jokingly: It is perhaps a good thing that God's presence is not with us during this type of prayer. If God were with us He would feel very lonely. It is very impolite to meet someone, not allow him to speak, and leave as soon as we are finished speaking. This, however, is the way many people pray to God.

Although Abraham inquired in his prayer, God was the One speaking. In his prayer Abraham did not finish speaking and then walk away. Rather, Jehovah finished speaking and then left. After Jehovah departed, Abraham left. Can we wait for God to finish speaking before we say, "In the name of Jesus, Amen"? Many times as soon as we finish our speaking, we say Amen. We may say Amen to such a prayer, but has God said Amen? We have finished, but God has not finished. This is a pitiful condition. We have never learned to absorb God, to receive God, and to breathe in God. We pray in a wild and reckless way. We have never been trained in the matter of prayer. We have never surrendered in this matter. We have never allowed God to speak. Consequently, we do not gain much God at the end of our prayers. We have not absorbed Him or received very much of Him.

In summary, when we come to God to breathe Him in, we must first turn to our spirit to touch Him. We should be calm, behold Him, inquire of Him, and learn to wait on Him. We should also muse upon Him, worship Him, praise Him, and learn to intercede before Him. Later we should allow Him to finish His speaking. Then we can let Him know that we are satisfied. This is the best kind of prayer. It is a prayer that receives and absorbs God. If we always pray in this way, we will surely receive and appropriate much more of God, and He will surely be our real enjoyment. This is what it means to enjoy God through our prayer. May the Lord graciously enable us to live in this reality!

CHAPTER SIX

HOW TO ENJOY GOD IN READING THE WORD

Scripture Reading: 2 Tim. 3:16; John 1:1, 4, 14; 6:63; Matt. 4:4; Heb. 4:12

In the previous chapter we saw how to enjoy God in prayer. In this chapter we will consider how to enjoy Him in reading the Word. In other words, we want to see how we should study the Bible. Since this is a broad subject, we will focus only on how to absorb God through reading the Word.

Whoever is experienced in fellowshipping with God knows that the way to receive and assimilate God is either in prayer or in reading the Word. Prayer and reading the Word are the two best ways for man to contact God. Although many people pray, they do not contact God, and although many people study the Word, they do not absorb God. There are different kinds of prayer, and there are different ways to read the Bible. In order to know how to assimilate God when reading the Bible, we need a basic understanding.

READING NOT FOR TEACHING BUT FOR ASSIMILATING GOD

In the last chapter we pointed out that prayer is not asking God to do many things, but it is breathing in God. Similarly, reading the Word is not digging out many teachings from the Bible but assimilating God. Although the Bible is full of teachings, and it is difficult to find another book that contains as many teachings as the Bible, when we seek God through the Word, we should realize that the Bible is not merely a book of teachings. When we study the Word, we should not look for teachings, just as when we pray, we should not ask for many things. The purpose of our prayer is to breathe in God. Similarly, the purpose of our reading the Bible is to assimilate God. The subject and the center of prayer is God Himself. The subject and the center of reading the Word should also be God Himself. Just as we breathe ourselves out and breathe in God through prayer, we deny ourselves and receive all that God is through reading the Word. The real reading of the Word has nothing to do with acquiring teaching in the mind. Rather, it is a fresh assimilation of God in the spirit.

God's children need this basic understanding. Whenever we come to the Bible, we should not have the concept that it is for the purpose of gaining some teachings. Instead, we should have the concept that we are here to touch God Himself. Instead of being taught by the Bible, we are here to assimilate God Himself through the Bible. Whenever we open the Bible, we should not desire teachings; our desire should be to gain God Himself. Considering the Bible as a book of teachings is not the proper Christian attitude in reading God's Word. The proper attitude for every child of God when coming to the Word is to consider it as another opportunity to contact God Himself. We should be deeply impressed by this, and we should have this basic change in concept. Let us now consider how to study the Word.

THE BIBLE BEING GOD'S BREATH

We should realize that the Bible is God's word, that is, His breath. In the universe words are a mysterious yet tremendous thing. The Bible says that God created all things by His word. By God's word we have the heavens and the earth. Not only are all things created by God's word, but the very existence of all things is also sustained by His word. Both the old creation and the new creation came into existence through His word. We are regenerated by His word, and every spiritual experience we have after our regeneration comes as a result of God's word. Our entire Christian existence is involved with God's word.

Unbelievers may consider us to be very odd people. Even though they may be attracted by movies, an avid moviegoer will still be bored if he visits the theater every day.

We Christians, however, meet every day, and the more we meet, the more we love to meet. Unbelievers wonder what we do in our meetings. In our meetings the only thing we do is speak and speak and speak. I spoke the night before last, I spoke last night, I am speaking this morning, and I will speak again next Lord's Day. We speak in the prayer meetings, and we speak in the fellowship meetings. We speak in the bread-breaking meetings, and we speak on Lord's Day morning. There is no place on earth that has as much speaking as in our meetings.

There is no end to our speaking. If we spoke every day for a thousand years, we would still be unable to exhaust our speaking. Speaking is a wonderful thing. Words can kill a person, and they can give life to a person. We can incite people to anger with a few words, and we can also make them happy with a few words. We can cause people to sit still with a few words, and we can cause them to stand up and leave with a few words. This shows the power of words.

God is the Word. In the beginning was the Word, and the Word was with God. He was not only with God; He was God Himself (John 1:1). The Bible is not a book of knowledge, science, or philosophy. The Bible is called the Word. The original meaning of the word *Bible* is "book," which is a collection of words. The Bible is a collection of words that were first spoken and then written. It is a collection of God's words, not man's words. In fact, these words are the embodiment of God Himself.

A man's words represent and express him. If I stood here without saying a word, everyone would see my outward form but not know what is inside of me. In order for others to know and clearly understand what is inside of me, there is a need for words. Once words come out, my desires and intentions are expressed. After speaking for an hour, others begin to know what is inside of me. In the same way the whole Bible is God's word, His breathing. Every word in the Bible, from the beginning to the end, is God's expression, His embodiment. In spirit these words become God Himself. Please do not misunderstand my words. This does not mean that the physical Bible is God Himself. That is mere superstition.

Reading the Word to Contact God Himself

When we contact the Word, we need to be clear that we are contacting God Himself. Whenever we open the Bible, our first thought should be to contact the living God. The living God has breathed out all that is within Himself as the Word. All the riches within Him are breathed out in the form of the word. Every word of the Bible, from the first to the last, is the breath of God. The Bible is not for us to study philosophy or literature. It is for us to contact what God has breathed out, what He has exhaled.

Brothers and sisters, this is not a light matter. Unless we have the concept that we are coming to God and contacting Him, our focus will be wrong. The first thought we should have, the first step we should take, when we open the Scriptures is to prepare ourselves to contact God. We are reading what God has breathed out. God has breathed His breath upon these words. We should not have the thought that we are reading teachings or literature. Rather, we are altogether contacting the manifested God, the God who has revealed Himself through His speaking. The God who dwells in unapproachable light, who cannot be touched or known, has revealed Himself through the Word. In fact He Himself is the Word, and He is embodied in the Word. Now He has put the Word, which is His breath, before us. When we study the Word, contact the Word, we are actually contacting God Himself.

Many people ask why they do not receive anything when they read the Word. I would like to ask, "When you read the Word, do you have the thought that you are coming to a book of letters, or do you have the thought that you are coming to the living word that has been breathed out from God?" This thought is very crucial. Many brothers and sisters do not have this thought when they come to the Word. They think that they are reading merely words printed on paper. At the most they think that they are studying teachings, commandments, or doctrines. It is no wonder they do not receive a living supply. We need a consciousness that the Bible is the Word of God; it is God's speaking. God has released Himself through His speaking. He is embodied in the Bible. Hence, when we come to the Bible, we should have the consciousness that we are contacting the revealed and released God. We are not touching merely letters; we are touching the living God. We are not touching merely teachings; we are touching a God who has breathed Himself out. In order to properly approach the Word, we must have this thought and prepare ourselves accordingly.

Exercising the Spirit Rather Than the Mind

With this initial understanding we can proceed further. We need to exercise our spirit rather than our mind whenever we study the Word. This is a trying lesson for many people. They may not agree and say, "Who can study without using his mind?" It seems as if this is an unreasonable demand. But I would ask, "Is there a difference between reading the Bible and reading a newspaper?" We will derive no value from exercising our spirit to read a newspaper. We should exercise our mind when we read a newspaper, asking ourselves about the content of an article or an editorial. We need to use our mind to analyze and understand international news, politics, and financial reports. But we must take a different approach when we read the Bible. When we come to the Word, our first thought should be that God can be released through these pages because these words are the very breath of God. God has spoken and revealed Himself through these words. We need to exercise our spirit, not our mind, when we read the Bible because God is Spirit (John 4:24). We must believe that the more we turn from our mind to our spirit, our reading of the Scriptures will be proper.

A brother once said that he received much light in his study of the Bible one morning. When I asked what light he had seen, he replied that he realized that Adam lacked one rib. I asked how he came to this conclusion, and he said that as he was reading Genesis 2, he pondered on how Eve could have been made from Adam's rib. He concluded that Adam must have lacked one rib. I pointed my finger at his head and said, "Brother, your mind has killed you! If you study the Bible in this way, you will never receive genuine light. You will forever be in darkness."

This is not the way to study the Bible. In reading the Word, we must turn from our mind in order to release our spirit. It is very difficult for one who has never received any education, who is illiterate, to read the Bible. However, those who are able to read the Bible need to turn from their mind and exercise their spirit in order to receive any benefit. There is much to learn in this matter.

Let us use an example to see the difference between reading the Bible with the mind or with the spirit. If a person exercises only his mind when reading Genesis 1 concerning God's creation of the heavens and the earth, he may wonder when the creation occurred. Was it six thousand years ago, or was it ten thousand years ago? There is no limit to the questions one can ask. If a person is a geologist or has books on geology, his mind will dominate. He may set the Bible aside and pull out a book on geology to investigate the subject. With ten minutes or even ten hours of this kind of reading, he will not touch God. On the contrary, he will lose God's presence when he reads in this way. His mind will be full of knowledge, but his spirit will be dry. When he comes out of his library, he will be irritable; any slight provocation will cause him to lose his temper. This shows that his reading did not bring God into him. Rather, it brought him into his flesh. This is not an exaggeration. God's children commonly face this difficulty when they come to the Word.

Even I studied the Bible in this way after I was saved. When I opened the New Testament to Matthew 1:1, which speaks of the son of Abraham, I asked, "Who was Abraham?" If I could not determine this, immediately I looked it up in reference books. I eventually determined that Abraham was the father of the Jews, the father of Isaac and the grandfather of Jacob. Then more questions came. Who was Isaac? Who was Jacob? I was so completely occupied with reference books that there was no time remaining to continue reading the Bible. The more I looked in reference books, the more confused I became, and the more I was distracted from the verse itself. My spirit was dry, my heart was ill-tempered, and I received no supply.

If this is the way we read, there is no value to it. Many new believers and even some long-time students of the Bible have only this kind of experience.

When brothers ask me to recommend reference books, I am reluctant because my recommendation could damage them. It is better to have fewer books at our disposal when we come to the Word. It is best if we have only one book—the Bible. We do not need to refer to any other material. If there is a need for a reference, that reference should be God. When we come to the Bible, our first thought should not be that we are coming to a book on knowledge or ethics; instead, we are coming to God who has revealed Himself through His speaking. When we come to the Word, we are contacting the living God. We do not need reference material, and we do not need to struggle with our mind. We only need to contact the living God by exercising our spirit.

If we read Genesis 1:1 with the exercise of our spirit, we will worship God, saying, "Praise You. You are the beginning. Without You there is no beginning. Everything begins with You." This will enable us to immediately touch God in our spirit, not in our mind. This is altogether a matter of our spirit touching the Spirit. We may read the verse again: "In the beginning God created the heavens and the earth." This may prompt us to worship God, saying, "You are the Creator. Everything is of You. You are the Initiator, the Inaugurator, of everything. Without You there is no beginning. Without You there is no heaven, and there is no earth. Without You there is no universe." This does not require the exercise of our mind. It is fully a matter of contacting the living God with our spirit. Studying the Bible in this way does not require ten minutes. Rather, our spirit can be filled in five minutes. As we leave for work in the morning, we still may be saying, "In the beginning God...In the beginning God...God created...God created...Praise You. You are the beginning of everything. You created everything." Just a few minutes and a few words enable us to touch God. Our inner being will touch God, and we will enjoy Him.

God's children need to see that whenever we come to His Word, we should be convicted in our heart that this Word is the speaking forth of the living God. We should not study it with our mind; instead, we should contact it with our spirit. There is no need to understand the Bible too much. Please give me the liberty to say that for many people, the more they understand the Bible, the worse their spiritual life becomes. This is not a matter of "understanding" the Bible but a matter of "contacting" the Bible. The Bible is indeed a wonderful book. The way to approach it is not to understand it but to contact it, touch it, and enjoy it.

Once a young brother asked me whether reading the Bible was useful since he did not understand much of what he read. He said, "I read the second half of the book of Exodus, and all I saw was the materials, the construction, and the dimensions of the tabernacle. The more I read, the more confused I am. What is the purpose of reading?" I answered, "Dear brother, let me suggest an experiment. Tomorrow morning when you wake up, change the way that you read, and see if there is a difference." The next day he came to me and said, "Brother Lee, there is a difference. This morning when I opened up the book of Exodus, I still did not understand much of what I read, but I had the intention of coming to God and putting myself under His shining." I said, "Brother, this is very precious. This is the right way." When we read the Word, we should place ourselves under the shining of God's light. We may read twenty-five chapters of Exodus, and our mind may lack understanding and be totally confused. However, after fifteen minutes of coming to the Word in this way, we feel as if we have passed under God's shining. We will be inwardly refreshed, cleansed, and enlightened. This is the most valuable kind of reading.

This does not mean that we do not need to understand or remember anything when we read the Word, but understanding and memorization are secondary. Our primary need is to pass through God's shining whenever we read the Word. The Bible is a book for us to contact rather than to understand. We contact sunshine every day even though we do not understand it. We do not understand water, but we contact it every day. To contact is one thing, and to understand is another. Similarly, to receive is one thing, and to comprehend is another. The Bible is not primarily for comprehension but for communication and reception. Whenever we read God's Word, if we acknowledge that it is His very speaking and contact it with our spirit, our inner being will touch God and receive Him.

Turning Mental Understanding into Meditation and Prayer

It is impossible for us not to receive any understanding when we contact the Bible. There will be some amount of comprehension no matter what chapter of the Bible we read. Once we receive some comprehension, we need to meditate on our understanding. At this point we need to exercise our mind. In the previous step we exercised our spirit, not our mind, to contact the Word. But in this step we need to involve our mind. However, this is meditation, not wild and unrestrained thinking. We should consider what we have touched and received and turn it into prayer. For example, there is no need for us to try to understand Genesis 1:1. Spontaneously there will be a realization within us that God is the beginning and that He is the Creator. At this juncture we can muse and consider and even turn our thoughts into prayer, saying, "God, may You be the beginning in all my ways. May my whole life and the beginning of everything that I do be filled with Your divine element." In this way we will be able to apply our realization of the Word to our daily living. When we do this, we are absorbing God.

We need to learn this lesson. Especially in the morning when we are reading the Word, we should not occupy our mind with reference books. This will not benefit us. Instead, we should practice this fellowship by exercising our spirit to contact the living word of God. When we contact Him, we should spontaneously turn our understanding into meditation and prayer and concentrate on absorbing God Himself.

Receiving More of God

We also need to realize that the issue of our musing and our prayer must be more of God in our inner being. Since the Bible is God's breath, His breathing out, and His spoken word, which is God Himself, whenever we receive Him, the result should be more of God in us. We should never congratulate ourselves for merely understanding some truths which we formerly did not understand. There is not much value in this. If the result of our coming to the Word is to receive knowledge, teaching, or truth, not the Lord Himself, our reading is a failure. When we read the Word, the ultimate result should not merely be the acquisition of more truth but the gaining of the Lord Himself. We are contacting the Lord, receiving the Lord, and praying to the Lord; therefore, in the end we should gain the Lord.

Let me elaborate on this point. If in praying for our business we take our business as the subject of our prayer, we have failed. The subject of every prayer should be the Lord Himself, not other things. All those who take other things as the subject of their prayer err in a fundamental way. This type of prayer never makes us clear; instead, it often makes us unclear. Even if we think that we are clear, we are actually quite confused. This type of prayer often results in a wrong impression of the Lord's leading. When we pray, we must first set aside our business and simply touch the Lord, breathe Him in, and contact Him. As we touch the Lord, we may feel peaceful and sense that the Lord's presence is with our business, enabling us to proceed with our business. Or we may lack peace and not sense His presence. In this case there is no need to pursue the matter further; we should simply drop it. This type of leading does not become clear to us as we pray about it. It becomes clear to us as we touch the Lord and gain Him in our prayer. The Lord becomes our very leading within us.

Most brothers and sisters have the same problem in reading the Bible. When they encounter problems that need to be solved, they go to the Lord to inquire concerning the matter. They also search the Scriptures to see what the Bible says concerning the matter. For example, when a brother is looking for a job, he may search the Scriptures for something related to jobs and careers. He may even use a concordance to find verses. He may eventually say that he is clear concerning the Christian perspective about a job. He may even say, "Lord, thank You for showing me Your will." However, this brother has received merely doctrine that can be retained in his mind. His mind may be somewhat corrected, taught, and educated, but this is the wrong way to read the Word.

When we have a problem with our job or when we are looking for solutions to other problems, we should not make these things an issue when we go to God. The Lord should be the subject of our prayer, and He should also be the subject of our reading. When we study the Word, we should say, "Lord, I want to contact You through Your Word. Your Word is Your very self." We should exercise our spirit to contact the Lord. Genesis 1 says nothing about jobs or careers. Verse 1 simply says, "In the beginning God created the heavens and the earth." However, if we touch God and contact Him through this word, it will turn us to meditate and pray so that we can absorb God and receive Him and His element within us. We will not need to say anything related to our business. However, after reading in this way, we will sense the Lord's presence within as we proceed with our business affairs. His presence will cause us to consider whether He has initiated our work and whether He is involved in it. In this light we may realize that we initiated our business, not the Lord. We may realize that we, rather than the Lord, are the founder of our business. He is not involved in it, but we are fully occupied with it. Then the Lord may give us a clear feeling that what has not been initiated by Him is not His will. In this way we will be clear about the Lord's will. This is not a matter of understanding the truth but of gaining the truth. As we contact the living Lord and as His element within us increases, He, the living God Himself, becomes our living guidance. He teaches us to understand God's will.

Being Enlivened and Shining in Spirit

Finally, if our reading of the Bible is proper, our inner being will be enlivened whenever we touch the Word. If our inner being is not enlivened, our reading is wrong. God's word is living (Heb. 4:12). His words are spirit and life (John 6:63). Whenever our spirit touches the living word of God, we will surely be enlivened, refreshed, enriched, enlightened, and empowered. In other words, when we read the Word in a proper way, our spirit will be filled after reading, our life will be strengthened, and we will be enlightened. This enlightenment is not related to the clarity of our mind. This is an entirely different thing. Some people become very clear in their mind after they read the Word, but their spirit remains dull. Others may not be that clear in their mind, but they are very clear in their spirit. They have discernment in their spirit. This is wonderful.

For example, the friends of a new believer may try to persuade him to go to a movie. He may decline because he is very clear in his spirit yet at the same time be unable to explain his reason for declining. He simply knows that he should not go. If we would learn to live in God's word and learn to contact Him through His Word, this will be our story. Although we may not understand many things and we may not know many doctrines, our spirit is clear. We are clear concerning what brings us into the Lord's presence and what causes us to lose His presence. We know when the Lord is walking with us and when He is far from us. We know when we are being mingled with Him and when we are separated from Him. Even though this type of knowing is not dependent upon our understanding, there is a clear shining in our spirit. This is the normal result of reading the Word.

When we read the Bible, we should realize that God is contained in His Word, and we should contact it in this way. We should exercise our spirit to touch the living Word. When we touch something in the Word, we should turn it into meditation and prayer. Consequently, we will gain more of the Lord, absorb more of Him, and our inner being will be enlivened, refreshed, strengthened, and enlightened. As a result, we will gain more God and enjoy more of Him. I hope that we will all learn to exercise ourselves in these two areas. We should exercise to have the kind of prayer we described in the previous chapter, and we should exercise to read the Word as described in this chapter. We should absorb God, gain Him, and enjoy Him through praying and reading. If we do this, we will express much glory, riches, and divine fullness. Furthermore, the church will rise to a higher plane. May we be faithful to continually learn to take this way and to live this life.

CHAPTER SEVEN

ENJOYING GOD BY EATING AND DRINKING HIM

Scripture Reading: Gen. 2:8-12; Psa. 34:8, 36:8-9; John 6:32-37; 7:37-39; Matt. 26:26-28; John 20:19-22; Rev. 2:7, 17; 22:1-2

GOD DESIRING MAN TO ENJOY HIM BY EATING AND DRINKING HIM

In this chapter we will continue the matter of enjoying God. I want to emphasize that God is man's enjoyment. Those who know the Bible and God's heart realize that what pleases God the most is for man to enjoy Him. This enjoyment is not an outward enjoyment. Rather, it is an inward enjoyment that can be compared to the enjoyment one experiences when he takes in food and water. God intends that man enjoy Him by eating and drinking Him.

We need to remember the principle related to the first mention of an item in the Bible. The first time an item is mentioned sets a principle for later references to similar cases. This is a set principle. After God created man, He presented Himself to man as food. This was His appearing to man. After creation, man's existence was not independent of eating and drinking. It is wonderful to consider that in God's creation He ordained that human beings must exist by means of eating and drinking. Without these two things, man cannot survive. Man needs to eat and drink in order to sustain the functions of walking, living, and working. In order to have the strength to do various things, man must eat and drink sufficiently. Without eating and drinking, he cannot do anything. In fact, if he does not eat and drink for a period of time, he will die. This is a God-ordained principle. Every physical thing in the universe is a sign of the invisible and spiritual things. When the Lord Jesus was on the earth, He considered everything He encountered around Him as a sign of spiritual things. In the same principle, God's ordination for man to eat and drink is a sign showing that He is man's food. Man must eat and drink of Him before he can live and work.

The Lord Jesus Being Man's Real Food

Everyone in the world thinks that the food he eats is real food and the water he drinks is real drink, but one day the Lord Jesus came and said that the real food was sent by God from heaven. This means that whatever grows from the earth is not real food. It is not real. Some new believers may not agree, saying, "The bread that we eat is real bread. How can you say that it is not real? The rice we eat every day is real food. How can you say that it is not real?" According to the Bible there is a different assessment of what is real and not real. In God's eyes, everything that belongs to this life, everything that is temporary and visible, is not real, because it does not last forever. We may say that a house we own belongs to us, but if it is burned down by fire, it is no longer ours. This indicates that the house is not real. Some sisters may wear an expensive watch. If the watch is stolen, it is no longer real to her. Anything that does not remain forever is not real. In the same principle, the food we eat cannot make us live forever; it cannot satisfy us forever. The water we drink cannot quench our thirst forever. Hence, they are not real. One day the Lord Jesus was by a well in Sychar and said to a woman that whoever drank of its water would thirst again but that the water that He would give was real, and those who drank of it would never thirst again (John 4:13-14). In another situation He told the Jews that He was the bread that came down from heaven and that those who came to Him would not hunger and that those who believed in Him would never thirst again (6:32-35). This is real food. The Lord's words indicate that God's ordination to eat and drink was merely a sign. Through eating and drinking, God intends to awaken man to his real need. When we are hungry or thirsty, we should remember that we have another need in our deepest part, and this need is our real need. Our experience proves this. After we are satisfied through eating and drinking, we still hunger and thirst in our deepest part. We are hungering and thirsting for the living God. God is our real food.

God Desiring Man Not to Work for Him but to Eat and Drink Him

After God created man, He did not say to man, "I am the Creator. Worship Me, serve Me, and work for Me." God did not do this. In His first contact with man He presented Himself to man as food in the form of the tree of life. He did not ask man to do anything. Rather, He made Himself available to man as food. He did not want man to toil for Him; He wanted man to enjoy Him. He presented Himself to man as food in the way of life. In other words, He became man's life in the form of food. This is a crucial matter.

If we were Adam and Eve before the Creator, we would probably respectfully confess: "Let us worship our Creator, serve Him, stand before Him, and wait for His command. Let us work for Him. Let us please Him." This is what we would do, but this is not in the Bible. Jehovah did not intend this for man. He had no intention that man would do anything for Him. When the Creator came to Adam and Eve, He did not come in His status as the Creator, sitting majestically on a throne and demanding worship and service. There is no trace of this. Rather, in effect, He was saying, "I have presented Myself to you as the tree of life, with the fruits of life hanging from its boughs. I have created you and ordained that you should live by eating and drinking. This means that you should eat and drink Me. I am the food you need. I am like the tree of life which is placed in front of you. My desire is that you would receive me. Although I am on the throne and you are on earth, My pleasure is to enter into you and be mingled with you. However, I cannot enter into you unless you receive Me. I will not force you to receive Me. You must choose Me and take Me into you." Brothers and sisters, this is not too much. This was God's intention at the beginning when He placed Adam and Eve in front of the tree of life.

Some have asked me, "Brother Lee, how do you know that the tree of life refers to God?" If the tree of life in Genesis 2 does not refer to God, what else can it refer to? Psalm 36 clearly says that with God is the fountain of life (v. 9). God is the source of life. Life is in God. The Bible clearly says that when the Lord Jesus came, life was in Him. He is the life, and He came that man may have life (John 1:4; 10:10). These words are clear. The tree of life that man was placed in front of in Genesis signifies God Himself. It also signifies that God is life to man.

As soon as man was created, God placed Himself in front of man in the form of food. He did not come as a God demanding worship and service. He came as food. In effect, He said to man, "Eat Me. Do not be concerned with loving your wife or obeying your husband. I know that if you do not eat Me, you will beat your wife and rebel against your husband. If both of you do not eat Me, surely you will argue with each other about everything. But I also know that if Adam eats Me, he will love his wife. And if Eve eats Me, she will obey her husband. If you eat and drink Me every day and are filled with Me, you will surely be a loving couple. The love with which one loves is simply Me. If you eat Me, you will have love. The obedience with which one obeys is also Me. If you eat Me, you will have obedience. When I enter a husband, there is love, and when I enter a wife, there is obedience. When electricity operates in a bulb, it is light; when it operates in an amplifier, it is sound; and when it operates in a fan, it is wind. As soon as a bulb receives electricity, it lights up. As soon as an amplifier receives electricity, it produces sound. As soon as a fan receives electricity, it moves and produces wind. I do not need to give you any laws. I do not need to require anything of you. I only need to minister Myself to you. However, I also must warn you. If you eat something other than Me, you will die, because only I am life. Apart from Me everything else is death."

It may seem as if this is a simple illustration, but we need to be deeply impressed with this picture. We may still have the concept that we should worship and serve God and that we need to work for Him. Before the Lord's grace came to us, we loved the world and sin. After being revived and loving Him, our thought is to worship, serve, work, and be zealous for Him. Formerly we loved the world, sin, and evil things.

Now we are zealous and want to serve God and do good things. However, both the evil things we did and the good things we want to do are related to the same tree, the tree of the knowledge of good and evil (Gen. 2:9). We still have not seen the tree of life. The tree of life is not related to doing evil or doing good. The tree of life does not need anything from us. It indicates that all things are ready for us to come and enjoy. The fatted calf has been killed, the blood has been shed, the flesh of the lamb is available, the unleavened bread is prepared, and all things are ready. Do not come to worship, serve, or work. Come and eat!

The first picture unveiled in the Bible has nothing to do with our work or effort but with our eating. A Chinese expression describes some people as "a pair of shoulders with a big mouth." This refers to people who eat all the time, and while this may not be a compliment as far as man is concerned, it is wonderful to God. He simply wants us to eat.

Some may ask, "If we do not need to worship or serve Him, what should we do? If all these things are related to the tree of the knowledge of good and evil and do not have anything to do with God, what should we do? If God wants us to eat Him, drink Him, and breathe Him, where is He? How can we do this?" I know this question is in us. But for the moment we should not worry about this. Forget about doing things. It is all right if we cannot serve and work for Him. Instead, we should say to Him, "Lord, I cannot do anything. I cannot worship and serve You. I know that it is wrong to try to do things for You, but what should I do?" If we can groan before the Lord this way, we will breathe in God. When we say, "Lord, I can't make it," we are breathing Him in. When we say, "I am wrong in this and I am wrong in that," we are taking in another breath. Even saying, "Lord, I am confused. I do not know what is proper anymore," this is another breath. We should thank and praise the Lord. This is to breathe out our sorrow and to breathe out our sin. We cannot breathe out without breathing in, and once we breathe in, God comes in, and His element increases within us.

Whenever we breathe deeply, we first must breathe out and then breathe in. The more we breathe out, the more we can breathe in. We do not need to pray that much, nor do we need to spend that much time to worship or serve God. We need to see this picture in the Bible—God first appeared to man in the form of food. He had absolutely no intention for man to worship Him. I can say this boldly even though some theologians may condemn me. They may say that it is heresy to say that God does not want man to worship Him. But I now have the boldness to speak of God's desire for man because I know that He presented Himself to man in the form of food.

God Desiring Man to Be Transformed and to Be Like Him by Eating and Drinking

We should consider the situation when Adam was placed in front of the tree of life. Beside him was a river flowing, and where the river flowed, there were gold, bdellium, and precious stone (vv. 11-12). This picture depicts the desire of God's heart. Adam, who was made of earth, was placed beside Eve, who was made from Adam's earthy rib. This was an earthy husband with an earthy wife, an earthy male beside an earthy female; both were earthy. Do we think that the God whose appearance is like the shining of gold and precious stones craves worship of earthy creatures? God is not a god of earth and dust. He has no intention for earthy men to worship and serve Him. In effect, God was indicating that there was no need to serve and worship Him, but rather to be fed and satisfied with Him. He is golden and like precious stone. He is different in nature from the earth, the clay, and the dust of our constitution. We need to eat and drink Him and allow His nature to enter into us in order for us to experience transformation. This will make us the same as He is—gold and precious stones.

God's word is even clearer in the New Testament. Second Corinthians 4:7 clearly says that we have this treasure in earthen vessels. God is a treasure, and we can be transformed when this treasure is hidden in us, the earthen vessels. At the end of Revelation there is a city with the tree of life and the river of water of life flowing in it. This city is not an earthen city but a golden city of precious stones and pearl. That is the ultimate manifestation of the glory of the believers. Hence, the first picture that God shows in the Bible is that He wants to be food to man. He wants to be eaten so that man can be transformed in his nature. This is God's intention.

Some may think that I am too excited, but I have a burden within me. God has no intention for us to worship or serve Him. He simply wants us to eat Him. Although we would rather worship and serve Him, this thought is absolutely contrary to His desire. Our thought and God's desire are incompatible. We must eat Him; we do not need to worship Him.

This picture needs to be seared into our being. God is for us to eat. I have heard many brothers and sisters praising God, saying, "I praise You that a man as vile and lowly as I am can worship You as the holy God." This type of praise comes from those who do not truly know God. If we knew God and knew how to enjoy Him, we would say, "I praise You that a man as lowly and vile as myself can eat and enjoy You even though You are great and holy." Every Lord's Day we praise the Lord in the bread-breaking meeting, saying, "Lord, we love You so much. You died on the cross for us. You have shed Your blood and borne our sins. You rose from the dead and ascended on high to be our interceding High Priest. We thank and praise You." Almost every Christian says this. After this type of thanksgiving, we may make a resolution, saying, "Lord, give me the strength not to shame your name but to walk and behave according to Your will so that I can preach the gospel with zeal, attend every meeting, and read the Bible and pray every day." The Lord's response to this is, "Foolish one, I do not want any of these things. My body was broken for you. Take and eat. My blood was shed for You. Take and drink. Remember Me in this way." Eating and drinking the Lord in remembrance of Him means to take the Lord by eating and drinking Him. When we break the bread, we need to realize that we are not worshipping or serving Him; rather, we are eating and drinking Him. The loaf of bread before us symbolizes the Lord's body, which was sacrificed for us. The cup before us symbolizes His blood, which was shed for us. Both of these are for eating and drinking. This is altogether a matter of eating and drinking.

We must understand this. God's relationship with man is not based on things but on His being food. In Genesis 1 we see the matter of eating and drinking. The tree of life is for us to eat, and the river of water of life is for us to drink. Through God becoming food, an earthen man can become golden. A man without God can become a man full of God, and the human element can be transformed by participating in God's element. God has absolutely no intention for man to do anything for Him. He just wants man to eat and drink Him. When we break the bread, we are eating and drinking God. When we contact Him in the morning, we are also eating and drinking Him. Even our meetings are a kind of eating and drinking of Him.

The Subject of the Bible Being Eating and Drinking God

The sixty-six books of the Bible focus on this one subject. This is the unique subject. If the Bible speaks of love, it is a love that is lived out through our eating of God. If the Bible speaks of patience, it is a patience that is lived out through our receiving of God. If the Bible speaks of holiness, it is a holiness that is manifested through our digestion of God. If the Bible speaks of zeal, it is a zeal that comes from the fire that burns within us through our breathing of the fiery God. The things of God that are recorded in the Bible are only God Himself.

This is the story of the Bible. Genesis begins with God becoming man's food. In the Psalms the psalmist says, "Taste and see that Jehovah is good" (34:8). Tasting involves eating and drinking. Psalm 36:8 says that we can be saturated with the fatness of His house. The fatness of His house is simply God Himself. Without God the house has nothing. God Himself is the fatness of the house. Hence, to enjoy the fatness of the house is to enjoy God Himself. This verse also says that we can drink of the river of His pleasures. This water is God Himself. The fatness and the water are for eating and drinking. This continues the thought in Genesis 2. Psalm 36:9 says that with God is the fountain of life and that in His light we see light. These descriptions and expressions are found in the Old Testament. However, these are not merely descriptions; they are the genuine experiences of the psalmists.

In the New Testament the Lord Jesus came. He said that He is the bread of life that comes down out of heaven. He came to give man life. In other words, He said that He is the tree of life in Genesis 2. He is able to dispense life into us in the form of food. He wants to be our food so that we may have life. Those who contact Him will not hunger, and those who believe into Him will not thirst. One day the Lord Jesus declared that if anyone thirsts, he should come to Him and drink, and that those who believe into Him will have rivers of living water flowing out of them. The Bible explicitly points out that this refers to the Spirit, whom those who believed into Him would receive (John 7:37-39). The Spirit is the realization of God. God became flesh, died, resurrected, and became the Spirit. The Spirit is the very God who was incarnated and raised from the dead. The Spirit is also the God who enters into man. The God who became flesh, died, resurrected, and entered into man is the Spirit. When such a Spirit enters man, He becomes rivers of living water in man to satisfy his thirst and to flow out of him. Here the Lord Jesus is again speaking of eating and drinking. This is the thought in Genesis 2. Before He died, He established the Lord's supper in which He took bread and blessed it and said to His disciples, "Take, eat; this is My body." And He took a cup and gave thanks, and He gave it to them, saying, "Drink of it, all of you" (Matt. 26:26-28). This is eating and drinking; it is the thought in Genesis 2. When He came to the disciples on the evening of His resurrection, He breathed into them and in a sense said, "Receive the holy breath" (John 20:22). By this breath the Holy Spirit entered the disciples. This is a kind of eating and drinking of the Lord Himself. In the book of Revelation God says that He would be the hidden manna to the overcoming saints who love Him. From the beginning to the end of the Bible, God's thought is to make Himself available as food and drink. He wants man to eat and drink Him. At the end of Revelation the entire divine record concludes. The Bible begins with the tree of life and a flowing river, and it concludes with the tree of life and the river of water of life. From the throne within the city, that is, from God Himself, the river of water of life flows. On both sides of the river is the tree of life, bearing fruits for man's enjoyment. The Bible begins with the tree of life and concludes with the tree of life. In the beginning God reveals Himself to man as food for eating and drinking, and in the end He presents this same picture.

The line that runs through the entire Bible, from beginning to end, is God becoming food to man. He wants man to eat Him, drink Him, and enjoy Him. He wants to be life to man. Once we know this, we can understand that the relationship between God and man is not a matter of worship or service or a matter of doing some work for Him. These are secondary and ancillary. The crux of the issue is that we must eat God, drink Him, absorb Him, and enjoy Him.

CHAPTER EIGHT

EATING AND DRINKING—
THE FOCUS OF GOD'S SALVATION

Scripture Reading: Exo. 12:3-4; 16:14-15; 17:5-6; 1 Cor. 5:7; 10:3-4; 1:2; 1 Pet. 2:2-3; John 6:54-57; Matt. 22:1-2; Luke 15:18, 21; Acts 2:4; Eph. 5:18

THE LORD'S DESIRE BEING FOR US TO LIVE HIM THROUGH EATING AND DRINKING HIM

In the previous chapter we emphasized that God wants man to enjoy Him through eating and drinking Him. Although some may think that this is a crude and unrefined way of speaking, the New Testament speaks of God offering Himself to us for our food and drink. Although the expression *eating and drinking* may seem common and even vulgar, God often uses common expressions to convey extremely mysterious things. In describing the relationship between God and man, it is insufficient to say that man should receive God. This can be understood as receiving something purely in an objective way. Even if we speak of receiving God into us, this may not convey the thought adequately, because receiving something into us does not necessarily mean digesting it into our being so that it becomes our very constitution. The most direct and clear way is simply to say that God wants man to eat and drink Him. This is because everything we eat and drink is assimilated into us and becomes a part of us. "Eating" God is the clearest description of this thought.

Regrettably, the concept of eating and drinking God does not exist in man. Our concept is to worship God, serve Him, be zealous for Him, and do something for Him. When we first hear the expressions *eating God* and *drinking God,* we may consider them as hard sayings that are difficult to understand. The Lord Jesus said that He is the bread of life that came down out of heaven, and that those who come to Him would no longer hunger, and those who believe into Him would no longer thirst (John 6:35). He said that His flesh is true food, and His blood is true drink (v. 55). This word confounded the Jews. How could they eat His flesh, and how could they drink His blood? This was a hard word. Who could hear it (v. 60)? But the Lord Jesus said that His flesh is true food, and His blood is true drink. He who eats His flesh and drinks His blood abides in Him, and He in him. As the living Father abides in Him, and He lives because of the Father, in the same way those who eat Him will live because of Him (v. 57). We live because of Him when we eat Him, because after eating Him, He enters into us and is digested by us. He becomes our nutrients, our element. This is not difficult to understand. We live today because of the food we eat. If we did not eat, we would cease to exist. This is the reason the Lord said that we should eat Him. If we eat Him, we will live because of Him.

Man's Concept Being to Work, Not to Eat and Drink

When man considers Christianity, his first thought is that he should do good or achieve some work. People often say that Christianity is a good religion and that it teaches people to do good. Then they claim that they are good and do not need Christianity. They say that only those who are evil and poor need Christianity. Some friends have said to me, "I know you are trying to convert me for a good reason. But I cannot give up my drinking or my gambling; therefore, it would not be good for me to join Christianity." These statements show that people's concepts are based on behavior.

What about the concepts of Christians who are saved by grace? Although our gospel proclaims that we are not saved by works but by grace and although we readily acknowledge and confess this with our mouth, when we become a Christian we immediately place ourselves under a kind of bondage. For example, we say, "In the past I often rebelled against my parents, but from now on I will no longer rebel against them. I often lost my temper and abused my wife, but from now on I will no longer do these things." Some sisters say, "I used to argue with my husband all the time. It was terrible, but from now on I will be a good wife. Tonight I am being baptized. As soon as I rise from the baptistery, I will be a new person and will act like a new person." However, no one can produce this kind of "newness." After only a few days, the old man will resurface. Because this is our situation, we never have the concept that God is for us to eat, drink, and enjoy. I have never seen a person on the day of his baptism prostrate himself before the Lord and say, "Lord, I thank and praise You. You do not want me to do anything or behave in any way. You simply want me to enjoy You, receive You, eat You, drink You, and take You into me." I am afraid no one who is baptized has ever uttered such a prayer. Rather, everyone has the concept that following his baptism he should make a resolution to refrain from certain things. As Christians, we focus on acts and behavior. Rarely do we think about eating and drinking God. We can say that Christianity knows nothing about eating and drinking. It only knows about work and behavior. Christianity is a work and a walk with an empty stomach. But this concept is far from the record of the Bible.

The Lord Being Our Savior by Entering into Us through Eating and Drinking

We always say that the Lord Jesus is our Savior. However, in what way is the Lord Jesus our Savior? Someone drew a picture with a man in a miry ditch and next to him was the Lord with an outstretched hand. This person considered that this is how Jesus saves us. That is, after a person is saved, he needs the Lord to hold him by his right hand in order to progress in his spiritual journey. But is this the way the Lord Jesus acts as our Savior? No! The Lord Jesus does not save us in an outward way or hold our hand in a physical way. Rather, He is the Lord whom we eat and drink. We eat Him and drink Him, and He saves us from within. As the edible and drinkable One, the Lord Jesus would say to the man in the miry ditch, "Poor man, are you hungry? Eat Me. Are you thirsty?

Drink Me." When this one takes the living Lord into him through eating and drinking, he will experience an inner operation, an inner strength, which will bring him out of the pit. After he is saved, the Lord does not need to hold him by the right hand. He is in him, supporting him and living and walking through him. There is no need to teach him to take the right way or to exhort him to be good. He only needs to take a drink of the Lord Jesus in the morning, and the Lord will live, move, and operate within him. Then it will be impossible for him not to take the right way.

This is our Savior. We often say that we trust in the Lord, but the New Testament never speaks of trusting in the Lord Jesus in an outward way. When the word *trust* is used in the Chinese Union Version, it is often an inaccurate rendering of the original language. For example, in Philippians 4:13 Paul says, "I am able to do all things in Him who empowers me." The Chinese Union Version translates this as, "I am able to do all things by trusting in the One who empowers me." We do not do things by trusting in Him. We are in Him. We can be in Him because He is in us. We have taken Him in through eating and drinking. He is mingled with us, and we are mingled with him. We are not merely trusting in Him, but we are joined to Him. He is mingled with us and has saturated our entire being. Hence, we are in Him. Because we are in Him, we can do all things. Actually, it is not we who are able to do all things, but it is He who is doing all things through mingling Himself with us. The Lord does not give us an outward, objective deliverance. He does not remain in Himself, and we remain in ourselves. He is not merely offering us a helping hand. He is not our Savior in an objective way. Our salvation is absolutely subjective. It is absolutely a matter of the Lord coming into us to become our food and our salvation.

Salvation Being a Matter of Eating and Drinking

In the Old Testament Types

This is clearly portrayed in the Old Testament types. In the picture of God delivering the children of Israel in the book of Exodus, He did not lift His mighty hand and pull His people out of Egypt one by one. Rather, in this picture of God's salvation, God commanded His people to prepare one lamb per household. In the evening they slaughtered the lamb, and ate its flesh. How did they eat it? They ate with their staff in their hand and their sandals on their feet. This typifies a journey. The strength for their journey came from the flesh of the lamb. There was not an outpouring of power from on high that delivered them out of Egypt. It was the flesh of the lamb they ate that became their inward supply and strength and sustained them when they were thrust out of Egypt. They were able to leave Egypt by the strength of the food they ate.

Because there was no food, they became weary again when they reached the wilderness. However, God did not say, "Do this or do that"; rather, He sent manna from heaven and daily fed them to the full so that they had the strength to continue. When they became thirsty, God did not tell them to do this or that; instead, He cleft a rock and out came water, which quenched their thirst. Prior to reaching Mount Sinai, God's deliverance of the children of Israel was altogether through eating and drinking. They ate the lamb, unleavened bread, and manna, and they drank water from the rock. This eating and drinking brought them onward in their journey. God did not command them to do anything other than eat and drink. It was their ignorance of God and of themselves that forced God to give them the law that spoke of His requirements upon them. The law was not God's original intention. His original intention was for them to enjoy Him by eating and drinking.

What were they eating and drinking? In the Old Testament the people were not clear, but in the New Testament we are very clear. The lamb they ate was Christ. First Corinthians 5:7 says, "Our Passover, Christ, also has been sacrificed." We are eating the same Lamb. Praise the Lord, He is not only the redeeming Lamb who takes away the sins of the world, but even more He is an edible Lamb who dispenses Himself into us. As a Lamb, He not only redeems us from our sins but also avails Himself to be our food and satisfaction.

We should read Exodus 12 again. The flesh of the lamb was eaten by the Israelites, and the blood was put on the doorposts and the lintel. The Israelites did not obtain their strength from the blood; the blood could only expiate their sins before God. It was the flesh of the lamb, which they consumed, that afforded them the strength for their journey. In the same principle, if the Son of God had shed His blood on the cross merely to redeem us from our sins, we would have received only the forgiveness of our trespasses before God. We must thank and praise Him that He also has given Himself to us. As we take Him in, He becomes our life. He is not only the Lamb who shed His blood but the Lamb who has become our food.

Why do we remember the Lord by breaking bread? Why do we eat the bread and drink the cup when we remember the Lord? The Lord seemed to say, "This bread is My body, broken for you; take and eat. This cup is my blood, shed for you; take and drink." When He died on the cross for us, He not only made propitiation for our sins before God but also became food for us to eat. A lamb or chicken cannot be our food unless it is first killed. In the same way, the Son of God was slain in order for us to eat Him. It is a pity that poor, degraded, and deformed Christianity does not know anything concerning this aspect of the Lord Jesus' death. Many Christians are only aware of a redeeming Christ who was crucified for them. They do not see that as a Lamb, who shed His blood for us, He is also our food who can be eaten by us.

Let us consider manna. Manna is a type of the Lord Jesus. When the Israelites were in the wilderness, God did not come down from heaven to hold Moses, Aaron, and Miriam by the hand to take them through the wilderness. Instead, God sent manna from heaven, and Moses, Aaron, and Miriam took it and were filled with it in order to continue with their journey. This is a type. What is manna? We know that manna is a type of Christ, but the people who ate it did not know this. They saw only a small, white thing that came down from heaven and looked like coriander seed and bdellium. They asked, "What is this?"—which is the meaning of the word *manna*. We are often like the Israelites, enjoying the Lord Jesus, eating and drinking Him, but we do not know that it is the Lord we are enjoying. We too ask, "What is this?" Perhaps we rise up in the morning to pray, and in our fellowship with Him we sense a power welling up from within that enables us to endure what we previously were unable to endure. In the past if our wife said something to us, we would lose our temper. But now we are happy and joyful no matter how much she complains. We may wonder, "What is happening? I used to lose my temper, but today I have not lost my temper once. What is this?" This is manna. This is Christ. Christ has another name that is given to Him by those who are not very familiar with Him: *What is this?* Because He is food that cannot be found anywhere in the world, we do not know Him, but we enjoy Him. We know the food that we regularly eat. However, here is a wonderful food that becomes our strength once it enters into us, yet we do not know what it is. Hence, we continually ask, "What is this?" Instead of asking what it is, we should joyfully declare, "This is Christ. This is our glorious Lord. He has become our food. He has become our satisfaction. Not only so, He has also become our living water that quenches our thirst whenever we drink Him. Christ is the spiritual rock that follows us."

In the Old Testament the lamb, unleavened bread, manna, and living water are all types. When the Lord Jesus came, the reality, the body of the shadows, came. The God who is the tree of life to man, who was unleavened bread, manna, and the living rock, became incarnated. He came among men for the purpose of presenting Himself to man to be his full contentment and satisfaction.

In the New Testament Parables

In the four Gospels men came to the Lord Jesus, but they did not know about eating or drinking Him. They only knew to work. Everyone, male or female, seemed to ask the same question: "Teacher, what should I do?" (Luke 10:25), or "Teacher, which is the great commandment in the law?" (Matt. 22:36). Those who came to the Lord Jesus were bound by the concept of working and doing. The Lord Jesus said that He is the bread of life and that He came that we may have life. He said that His flesh is true food, and His blood is true drink. He also said that if we believe into Him, He will enter into us, and we will be born again. When He spoke these words, the listeners were confused. Even the aged Nicodemus was confused. He asked how an old man could enter his mother's womb and be born again. He did not understand the Lord's word. No one could understand. As we have been speaking concerning enjoying God, many have also considered this as a hard word. They think that this is too deep. However, if like a scribe and a teacher, I said that we should not take alcohol, play mah-jongg, or lose our temper, but we should submit to our husbands and love our wives, everyone would easily understand this. But when I say that we should not do anything, not try anything, and not consider anything, it is difficult to accept these words because we are short of the concept of eating and drinking God.

The Lord repeatedly spoke of His being food for man because He faced this concept when He was on earth. The parables in Matthew 21 and 22 illustrate this concept. At the end of Matthew 21 the Lord Jesus spoke a parable concerning a vineyard. He said that God leased a vineyard to vinedressers in order for them to work on it. However, when God came to collect the harvest, there was no fruit. This parable was meant for the Jews, and in essence the Lord was saying, "You desire to do something, and you are trying to work. But your work has no result, no fruit. You cannot do anything." In chapter 22 the Lord spoke another parable. He compared God to a king preparing a wedding feast for his son. He had slain the oxen and the fatted cattle and made all things ready. He then invited many to come to the feast. No one who comes to a feast comes with the thought of working or doing something; instead, he goes with a mouth ready to eat. God seemed to say, "All things are ready. Come. I do not want you to come to work or to do anything. I want you to come to eat, to enjoy." In these two parables the Lord Jesus was saying, "Even though you desire to do something, God has absolutely no intention for you to do anything. He desires that you come and eat." The Lord was eventually slain like the oxen and given to man to eat. The cross can be compared to a big feasting table. The Lord was slain on this table and placed on it for men to eat. God has no desire for us to do anything. He has no desire for us to work. His desire is to give us His Son for our enjoyment. His Son is simply His embodiment. God wants to become food to us in the person of His Son.

This also applies to the parable of the prodigal son in Luke 15. In this parable there are two sons. The younger one went astray but later repented. He resolved in himself, seeming to say, "I am no longer worthy to be called my father's son. I will go and be his hired servant." The meaning of being a son is to enjoy; a son enjoys all that his father has, but a hired servant works and has no share in the enjoyment. The son resolved within himself to be a servant. But when he reached home, his father saw him from afar and ran toward him and kissed him. While the son proceeded with his clumsy speech, the father interrupted him and ordered the servants to put the best robe on him. The father also said, "Bring the fattened calf; slaughter it, and let us eat and be merry" (v. 23). This is a clear description of our salvation. When the younger son came home, the joy consisted of eating the fattened calf and being merry. We should notice that the Bible speaks of a fattened calf, not an ordinary calf. Who is the fattened calf? It is the Son of God, our Lord Jesus Christ. He is the calf God has prepared and given to repentant sinners for their eating and enjoyment.

The Lord presented a full picture of salvation in this short parable. The father first put the best robe on the son. However, the best robe alone does not offer much joy. The son came home with an empty stomach. If the father merely said, "Come, child, let us sit down and be merry," this rejoicing would lack something because the son's stomach would still be empty. But the father killed the fattened calf and fed him. For a period of time the son's longing was only for carob pods, but now suddenly he had the fattened calf. This was true merriment to him. His merriment was not merely in the best robe but in the eating and drinking.

While God's salvation has an aspect of putting on a garment, there is also an aspect of eating. When man was in the garden of Eden, only the matter of eating was important. There was not even a question of clothing, because man had not yet fallen. Eating is God's original intention. Clothing is a remedy for man's fall. If man had never fallen, there would never have been a question of shame, and there would never have been a need for clothing. Spiritually speaking, this means that there would have never been a need for justification. Man was undefiled and uncorrupted when he was created. In the eyes of God he was justified and good. Therefore, he did not need clothing; he needed only to eat. However, man became fallen; he was like a prodigal son. He completely lost his standing of beauty and acceptability before the father. He became a feeder of hogs, and his clothes became ragged, old, and dirty. Consequently, it would not be enough for this prodigal son to return to his father's house and partake of the fattened calf without first exchanging his ragged clothes for his father's robe. Hence, he must first put on the robe of righteousness to match the fine clothing of his father. When the son matches the father, the fattened calf can be brought in. Only then will he fully match his father.

The same can be said of a sinner. When he first turns to God, he is cleansed by the blood and given the Son as his righteous robe, having been forgiven, justified, accepted, and freed from condemnation. Then he is given the Son as food for his enjoyment. It is a pity that many of us have only put on the robe; we do not know that we should eat the fattened calf. We are all properly dressed outwardly, but we are still hungry. Hence, our Christian life is weak, lifeless, and malnourished. Today in Christianity most people see only the side of justification, not the side of enjoyment. They see only the putting on of the robe, not the eating of the fattened calf. Strictly speaking, the robe is a remedial measure; God's original intention is that we eat and drink Him. Because of our fall and defilement, we must first be cleansed and justified in order to eat and drink Him. These are remedial measures; they are the means to make us worthy to eat and enjoy Him. Putting on the robe does not make us merry; eating and drinking make us merry. When we have taken in the Son of God, when we have eaten the lamb and the fattened calf, there is genuine merriment within us. When we eat Him and drink Him, we practically enjoy the riches of salvation and are inwardly filled. Then it is so easy to live a life that is according to His will. These are the central matters of the Bible. They are the very heart and marrow of the Bible. We must realize that the focus of God's salvation is that He wants to be our food, drink, and enjoyment.

CHAPTER NINE

ENJOYING GOD THROUGH TAKING IN THE SPIRIT

Scripture Reading: Psa. 27:1; John 6:63; 7:37-39; 14:6; 15:4-5; 1 John 2:27-28; 3:24; 4:13; 5:20

BEING DRUNK WITH THE HOLY SPIRIT

I would like to emphasize the word *eats* in John 6:57 and *drink* in 7:37. After speaking concerning eating Him in 6:57, the Lord said that anyone who thirsts should come to Him to drink in 7:37. We should never consider that the thought of eating and drinking the Lord is something we invented. Our speaking is based entirely on the Lord Jesus' words.

Drinking the living water refers to drinking the Spirit. At the time the Lord Jesus spoke this word, the Spirit was not yet, because Jesus had not yet been glorified. Hence, on the evening of the Lord's resurrection He came and stood in the midst of the disciples and breathed into them, saying, "Receive the Holy Spirit" (20:22). From that day on the disciples drank of the Spirit. On the day of Pentecost the Holy Spirit descended and filled the disciples. This was a greater drinking of the Spirit. Once they were filled with the Spirit, they began to speak in different tongues. They were like drunken people speaking. Those who heard them could not comprehend them. They could not understand what was happening, and they remarked that the disciples were filled with new wine. They definitely were filled, not with new wine but with the Spirit. They were drunk with the Spirit, not drunk with wine. The Spirit is the realization of God. They were drunk with God, not with wine. They were "crazy" because of God, not "crazy" because of wine. I believe that the

Lord would allow me to say this. When a man is drunk, he becomes crazy and speaks deliriously. He speaks whatever he wants to speak; there is no fear or reservation in him. On the day of Pentecost the disciples were indeed drunk. They were drunk with God. They were filled with God. Therefore, they were "crazy" in their behavior.

We should not be surprised when we hear the word *crazy*. Strictly speaking, if we have never been crazy in our experience as a Christian, our faith in Him is not very strong. In 2 Corinthians 5:13 Paul says, "For whether we were beside ourselves, it was to God." Being beside oneself is being crazy. God can make a person beside himself. As Christians, have we ever been beside ourselves? The verse goes on to say, "Or whether we are sober-minded, it is for you." This means that the apostle was sober toward men but was crazy toward God. Some Christians are sober before men and sober before God; they have never been crazy, because they have never been drunk with God.

Another place in the Bible, Acts 26:24-25, also speaks of being beside oneself. These verses say, "As he was saying these things in his defense, Festus said with a loud voice, You are insane, Paul. Much learning is driving you insane. But Paul said, I am not insane, most excellent Festus, but I am uttering words of truth and soberness." In Paul's mind he was uttering words of truth and soberness, but to his interrogators he was insane. He was speaking in an insane way while he was defending himself, not in an ordinary way. Paul was "insane" because he was inwardly filled and drunk with God. He was filled with the Holy Spirit.

Many of us can testify that when we breathe in God through our prayer, we are filled with the Holy Spirit. The Spirit can be compared to new wine; the more we drink Him, the more we are inwardly filled with Him. When we are full of the Spirit, we cannot help but be beside ourselves, because it seems as if we have been swept off our feet. Our praise is no longer common praise, and our singing is no longer common singing. We are as those who are "insane" before God; we are drunk with God.

We not only need to eat God and drink God, but we also

need to be drunk with God. This is an intense drinking, not a small sipping. We need to drink to the extent that our whole being is filled with God. Then our preaching of the gospel will be powerful, and our witnessing for the Lord will be bold. The fact that some brothers and sisters are afraid of testifying for the Lord proves that they do not have enough God, not enough of the Spirit, within them. Everyone who is drunk with the Spirit is bold. Whatever God entrusts them with or commissions them to say is carried out without any fear. They are like Peter who declared before the rulers, "Whether it is right in the sight of God to listen to you rather than to God, you judge" (4:19). The apostles were indeed in a drunken and crazy state. They testified that the Jesus whom the Jews had crucified on the cross was raised up by the God of their fathers, for it was not possible for Him to be bound by death. They seemed to be saying, "We stand here today to testify of His resurrection. If He has not resurrected, we would not have such boldness. He is living, and He is living within us. As the Spirit, He has entered into us, has filled us, and has intoxicated us. Therefore, we are not afraid of anything."

We must see that God is not only edible and drinkable but also intoxicating. Not only can we eat God and drink God; we can be intoxicated by Him and be drunk with Him.

EVERYTHING CONCERNING GOD BEING IN THE SPIRIT

Those who came to the Lord Jesus when He was on earth thought that He was a teacher, a rabbi, and that He came to teach men how to behave. However, the Lord Jesus showed them again and again that He did not come to teach men. He was not a teacher or a rabbi. He is life; He is the bread of life. He came to be eaten by men as food, not to teach men. Hence, He often spoke of being eaten by men. Sometimes He used parables, and other times He spoke in plain words. The clearest passage is in John 6 where the Lord said to the crowd around Him that His flesh is true food and His blood is true drink, that those who eat His flesh and drink His blood have eternal life, and that those who eat Him will live by Him.

When the people heard this word, they did not understand it. They thought, "How can this man be eaten? How can we eat

His flesh and drink His blood?" The Lord went on to explain that it is the Spirit who enlivens, gives life, and that the flesh profits nothing. When He said to eat His flesh and drink His blood, He was not referring to His visible flesh, because His visible flesh cannot give life. It is the Spirit who gives life. The Lord Jesus clearly explained that we can eat Him by turning to our spirit, because He is the Spirit. In order to eat the Lord, drink Him, and enjoy Him, we must turn to the Spirit in our spirit.

The Lord said that He is the Spirit in John 6, and when speaking to the people concerning drinking Him in chapter 7, He again spoke of being the Spirit. To eat Him is to eat Him as the Spirit, and also to drink Him is to drink Him as the Spirit. Both eating and drinking are matters in the Spirit.

We need to know that God is Spirit in His essence. When the Lord Jesus spoke to the Samaritan woman, He said that the proper worship is neither in this mountain nor in Jerusalem, but that God is Spirit, and those who worship Him must worship Him in spirit. Fundamentally, God is Spirit. It is difficult to eat and drink God if we consider Him to be something visible or physical. We need to see that God is Spirit. If we understand this, it will not be difficult for us to receive God and assimilate Him.

Today our God is not merely the Holy Spirit. Much more can be said about Him. One day the God who is Spirit entered into humanity. God was born of woman and became a man. This is Jesus, the incarnated Word. At this point God the Spirit entered into humanity and was mingled with man. He put on human flesh and took the form of man. He lived a human life for thirty-three and a half years. It was a perfect human living. This was the first step.

In His second step, He died on the cross. In His death on the cross He bore our sins. He shed His blood to deal with our sins before God. While He was being judged and crucified on the cross, sin itself was being judged and crucified. On the one hand, He dealt with the problem of our sins before God. On the other hand, the sin that dwells in us was judged as well. On the cross He also crucified our flesh, the old creation, and He judged Satan and the world. He tasted death for us and destroyed the power of death. His death on the cross dealt with these six things: sins, sin, our flesh, which is the old creation, Satan, the world, and death. These six things were dealt with on the cross through the death of the Lord Jesus.

In His third step, He came out of death in resurrection, fully overcoming and transcending the realm of death to enter into God. When He entered into God, He entered into God with His humanity. When He ascended to the heavens, His humanity was also raised to the heavens.

Finally, in His last step, in His resurrection and ascension, the Lord became the Spirit. God who is Spirit was incarnated to be a man on earth. He was fully mingled with man. He passed through human living and was crucified on the cross, settling the problem of man's sins and solving the problems related to sin, the flesh, Satan, the world, and even death. In other words, He dealt with everything that stood in the way of God. Then He walked out of the realm of death and entered the realm of resurrection and ascension, bringing His humanity with Him into God. Our God has now become this Spirit. All the processes, the steps, and the elements in God are now all-inclusively in the Spirit. The Holy Spirit is no longer so simple. Within Him are many things. Within the Spirit is the Father, the Son, incarnation, union with man, human living, crucifixion, and the termination of sins and sin itself. Within this One there is the solution to the problems of the flesh, Satan, the world, and death. There is victory over death in resurrection. Within this One is also our entrance into God through the bringing of humanity into God through ascension. Today all these items are included in the Spirit.

We should remember that the God we touch today is this Spirit. The God whom we breathe in and whom we take in by eating and drinking is this Spirit. The Father is in Him, and the Son is in Him. Incarnation, union with man, human living, and crucifixion are all in Him. The termination of sins, the solution to sin and the problems of the flesh, Satan, the world, and death are also in Him. Resurrection is in Him. Man's being in God and man's being brought into the heavens are all contained in Him. All these processes and all these elements are now included in Him.

As an example, we may add grape juice and sugar to a glass of water. Then when we drink, we receive grape juice, sugar, and water. All these ingredients are contained in this drink. Now the Father is in the Son, and the Son is in the Spirit. Hence, everything of the Father is included in this Spirit, and all the experiences and attainments of the Son are also included in this Spirit. We can say that everything that the Triune God is and has done is included in this Spirit. Hence, it is convenient and expedient for us to eat and drink God, because He is now the Spirit. As long as we breathe in the Spirit, we can eat and drink God.

We need to see that God is Spirit. He has passed through incarnation, human living, death, resurrection, ascension, and glorification. All these items are now in the Spirit. The Lord said that it is the Spirit who gives life. He also said that to receive the Spirit is to drink Him. Hence, eating and drinking depend on the Spirit. The Lord also said that God is Spirit, and those who worship Him and contact Him must do so in spirit. God has given Himself to us as our food. He desires to enter into us to be our everything. He desires that we eat Him and drink Him. But how do we eat Him and drink Him? His words make it clear that eating and drinking are in the spiritual realm, not the physical realm. The physical flesh profits nothing. It is the Spirit who gives life. All we need to do is learn to exercise our spirit to contact God.

In order to receive anything, we need the proper organ. We receive sound with our ears, colors with our eyes, food with our mouth, and air with our lungs. It is clear that we need to use the proper organ to receive anything. Because God is an object, there is no way for us to receive Him with our physical senses. We cannot touch God, smell God, taste God, see God, or hear God. It is useless for us to try to contact God with our five senses. As I have said repeatedly, there is another organ within us—our spirit. Within every one of us there is a spirit. We must contact God and receive Him with this spirit.

Some people exercise their mind rather than their spirit when they pray. When a sentence comes to their mind, they utter it, and they also utter the next sentence that comes to their mind. They pray according to the thoughts in their mind. When their minds are distracted by other things, they even spontaneously pray concerning these distracting matters. Once a pastor in a denomination asked an elder to pray after his sermon. Because the elder had been preoccupied with his business while the sermon was being given, he found himself muttering something concerning his business a few sentences into his prayer. The whole congregation burst into laughter. This may sound like a joke, but we also have prayed in this way. We have prayed prayers that were not prayers. Mental prayers from the mind are frustrations. They frustrate us from eating and drinking God, and we are held back from receiving God. No matter how many mental prayers we utter, they will never touch God.

God is Spirit. Hence, receiving God and assimilating Him are altogether a matter in the spirit. We need to restrain our mind when we pray. We must exercise to pray with our spirit. Instead of spending the time to consider what to pray, we should take care of our inward feeling. As we kneel before the Lord, we may not have any words to utter. However, because of a heavy burden, a pressure within our spirit, we can still groan and sigh before the Lord. This is a very genuine prayer. Have we had this kind of experience? We generally utter groaning prayers when we are in a difficult situation, because the situation exhausts our mental capacity. When the suffering is intense, our mind is unable to control the situation, and the spirit is released through groaning before the Lord. This is the best kind of prayer. It is the most precious kind of breathing.

We must learn to stop our thoughts and contact God in spirit not only when we pray but while we are walking on the street, sitting in a bus, or working. The more we are in the spirit, the more we will touch God, and the more we will absorb Him, eat Him, and drink of Him. It is not a matter of what we pray. We will assimilate God as long as we turn to our spirit.

ASSIMILATING THE SPIRIT BEING
TO ENJOY GOD AS ONE'S ALL

If we learn to assimilate God in our spirit, we will experience Him as everything, and He will be whatever we need. As we assimilate Him this way, we will discover that God is our comfort when we need comfort. He is our power when we need power. He is the word when we need a word. He is light when we need light. He is our patience when we need patience. He is love when we need love. He is holiness when we need holiness. He is our way when we need a way. He is wisdom when we need wisdom. All parents need forbearance toward their children. Once we receive God, He becomes forbearance to us. All children need to honor and obey their parents. Once we receive God into us, there is honor and obedience. Our God is everything to us according to our need. When we assimilate Him, He is whatever we need. This is wonderful!

In a traditional wedding a pastor, based on the Scriptures, asks the husband to love his wife and the wife to submit to her husband. However, it is difficult to find a married couple who truly love one another and are obedient to one another. This is because the love that the husband needs in order to love his wife is not something that issues from teachings, nor is the obedience that the wife needs in order to obey her husband something that issues from instructions. Love is simply God Himself, and submission is also God Himself. When a husband exercises his spirit, even a little, to breathe in God, he cannot help but love his wife. Even the most unlovable wife becomes lovable. This is because God Himself is simply love. In the same way if the wife breathes in God, the Triune God, the Father who is in the Son and the Son who is the Spirit, enters into her. There is no need for teaching; she will simply obey in an absolute way. When God enters the husband, He becomes the sweet love in the husband, and when God enters the wife, He becomes the absolute submission in the wife.

Have we ever noticed the number of times the Bible speaks of what God is? God is light. God is power. God is food. God is the living water. God is healing. God is peace. The Lord says that He is the way, the truth, and the life. He is the light of the world. He is everything. Do we need boldness? God is our boldness. We are not bold because we do not have God. When we are filled with God through drinking, we will be bold. We do not have eloquence because we do not have God. In Greek the word *eloquence* is the same as the word for *speaking*. Speaking is the Word, and the Word is God; hence, eloquence is God. When we say that we do not have eloquence, we are saying that we do not have God. The brothers who give messages should no longer complain that they do not have eloquence. Saying that they do not have eloquence proves that they do not have enough God. When we are filled with God, we will surely be full of eloquence and utterance. Do we need to be persuasive? God is our persuasiveness. We do not need to worry whether our speaking is eloquent or persuasive if we are filled and satisfied with God before we speak and if we continue to breathe Him in while we speak. I do not need to speak too much regarding this. Our lack of anything is a sign of our lack of God. As long as we are filled with God, we will not lack anything. God is everything. The apostle Paul said that he could do all things through the power of the One who empowered him. God is everything. There is no thing that He is not. As long as we enjoy Him, assimilate Him, and abide in Him, we can do all things. The key lies in our receiving God with our spirit. We need to learn to receive God all day long with our spirit. We need to learn to exercise our spirit even when we are walking on the street. In our busiest moments we need to learn to fellowship with God in our spirit. Please do not misunderstand me, but we need to learn to exercise our spirit even when we lose our temper. If we learn to fellowship with God in our spirit while we are losing our temper, our temper will vanish. Whenever we are about to lose our temper, we should take a deep breath of God, and the temper will surely disappear.

Therefore, in any circumstance and at any time, we need to learn to contact God and enjoy Him in our spirit. God is the omnipresent Spirit. He is also the all-pervading Spirit; no place is too distant for Him to reach. No matter what our condition is, He is willing to draw near to us. Even when we think that we are at our worst, He is willing to be received by us. We should realize that we can receive Him and touch Him in our spirit, even at our lowest moments. Once He enters, all our problems are solved. I believe we now understand that even though we may have myriads of needs, our unique solution is the living God. He is everything. He is the solution to whatever we need. He is all in all!

CHAPTER TEN

HOW GOD BECOMES MAN'S ENJOYMENT IN THE SPIRIT

Scripture Reading: Col. 2:9; John 14:16-20; 16:7-8; 1 John 2:27; 3:24; 4:13; 5:20; Rev. 4:5; 5:6

THE NEED TO BE IN SPIRIT TO ENJOY GOD

We will continue to consider the way to contact God. In other words, we will consider how to eat God, drink God, and enjoy God. We have pointed out repeatedly that God is Spirit. Moreover, everything that He has passed through and attained is now in the Spirit. Both His incarnation, which joined God with man, and His death and resurrection, which brought man into God to be united with Him, are realized in the Spirit. He is in the Spirit, and He even is the Spirit. We must now contact this Spirit. Therefore, He clearly said that we need to contact Him with our spirit. Only when we are in spirit can we contact the Spirit. The more a man uses his mind to consider, ponder, and make judgments, the less he touches God. Our contact with man requires that we be sincere and truthful, but our contact with God requires that we turn to our spirit. Since our God is Spirit, and He is in our spirit, we can contact Him only with our spirit when we turn to our spirit.

We should pay attention to the word *spirit* and how it is used. First, God is Spirit. Second, as Spirit, God enters into our spirit. Third, we have to turn to our spirit, and fourth, we must contact God with our spirit. In summary, because God, who is Spirit, has entered into our spirit, we need to turn to our spirit and contact Him with our spirit. We need to repeatedly remind the brothers and sisters that in order to contact God, touch Him, eat Him, drink Him, and enjoy Him, we need to be clear concerning these four points. Whether or not a person can touch God depends altogether on learning the lesson of turning to our spirit and touching God with our spirit. We may have heard a thousand messages but not touched God. Learning the lesson of turning to our spirit is a secret that enables us to touch God, making it easy for us to absorb and enjoy God. All experienced believers know this reality.

GOD MAKING HIMSELF AVAILABLE
IN THE FORM OF FOOD FOR MAN TO ENJOY

God has given Himself to us to be our food. He wants us to eat Him, to take Him in as food for our life. How does God present Himself to us in order to be eaten by us? God makes it possible for us to eat Him by means of a process. For example, if we want to eat chicken, no one would expect us to eat a live chicken; rather, the chicken needs to be processed. Before it can be eaten, it needs to be killed, and its feathers need to be removed. Then it needs to be washed, cut into pieces, and cooked until it is tender. In the same way, God cannot be eaten by us without being processed. This is not so simple, because God dwells in unapproachable light. He is great and glorious. If the God who dwells in unapproachable light manifested Himself to us in His majesty, glory, and unapproachable holiness, what would we do? Would we still be comfortable sitting here, or would we all prostrate ourselves before His face?

This is not my imagination. There are many examples of this in the Bible. When Daniel saw God, his strength left him, and he fell before God. When the apostle John, who had reclined on the Lord Jesus' breast, saw the Lord's glory on the island of Patmos, he fell at His feet as if dead. It would be impossible for us to eat God if He remained in a state of unapproachable light. There would be no way for us to come near to Him. Even if He gave Himself to us as food, in this condition it would be impossible for us to eat Him because we would all be fearful and would fall down on our faces. It would be impossible for us to eat Him. Thus, it is not easy for God to make Himself available for us to eat.

We should thank the Lord that He presented Himself to man as food in the form of the tree of life with the fruit of life when He created man. Because God presented Himself to man in the form of food, Adam had no reason to be afraid when he saw the tree of life.

This is why I repeatedly say that I am afraid that God's children have never considered this matter. God has given Himself to us to be our food. He has given Himself to us in the form of food, in the way of life. In this form man is not threatened; rather, God is warm, affectionate, and easily accessible.

We should not think that God's making Himself available applies only to the tree of life in Genesis 2. One day God became flesh in the person of Jesus of Nazareth. When He came, He came as a man. But when He presented Himself to man, His way and presence suggested that He was a piece of bread. He wanted man to receive Him in the form of food. He did not come as a dignitary with outward glory. He did not convey a sense of loftiness or greatness, and it was easy for people to approach Him. It was natural and easy for people to contact Him. No matter how evil or unworthy a man might have been, there was no sense that he would be rejected. He came in the form of food, as a piece of bread.

One day the Lord Jesus went away into the borders of Tyre and Sidon. A Canaanite woman came and cried out to Him, saying, "Have mercy on me, Lord, Son of David!" The Lord said, "It is not good to take the children's bread and throw it to the little dogs" (Matt. 15:22, 26). Since the Gentile woman knew only that the Lord was a descendant of the royal house of David, she addressed Him repeatedly as the Son of David. However, the Lord's answer indicated that He was a piece of bread, because He said that the children's bread should not be given to the dogs. Although some of us may not understand the Lord's words, it was very clear to the Jews. The Jews considered the Gentiles to be dogs and that only the Jews were the children of God. The woman did not know that the Lord Jesus had come as a piece of bread. She considered Him only to be the Lord and the Son of David even though He had already declared that He was the bread that came down out of heaven when He spoke by the seashore. When the people heard that word, they did not understand. When He spoke with the Gentile woman, He repeated that He was a piece of bread given for the satisfaction of God's children, the Israelites, but He would not be given as food to Gentile dogs. The Lord said this purposely to test the woman. After hearing this, she was enlightened in her heart by the Holy Spirit. She was not provoked by the Lord calling her a dog, but she wisely responded to the Lord's word, acknowledging her lowliness and unworthiness by pointing out that even a dog could eat the crumbs which fall from the master's table.

When the Lord spoke to the woman, He was at the border of the land of Israel. The land of Israel was like a table. When God sent His Son to the land of Israel, it was like putting a piece of bread on the table. Although the Israelites were God's children, they were not proper. They despised the bread and pushed it around until it reached the edge of the table, and eventually off the table. The Lord spoke this word at a time in which He was being rejected by the Israelites and, therefore, had to retreat to the region of the Gentiles. At that time He was like crumbs that had fallen from the table. The Canaanite woman responded by recognizing that she was a dog under the table and that the Lord Himself, as bread, had fallen under the table. He was no longer in Jerusalem, because He had been chased away by those in Jerusalem and was now in the Gentile land. He had been pushed from the table by naughty children and was now in the land of the dogs. She pointed out that He was no longer the bread on the table but crumbs under the table, and that even though she was a dog, dogs eat crumbs under the table. Using His own words, the woman forced the Lord to make Himself available to her.

This shows how the Lord makes Himself available for man to eat. He is no longer One who dwells only in unapproachable light. He is no longer the One who dwells only in majesty and glory. He is no longer the One who is only in the third heaven. When He came down from heaven, He emptied Himself. When He descended from heaven to earth, He had no attractive form or beautiful appearance, much less any outward majesty. He was very simple and humble; He was a piece of bread good for food.

When the Lord came to man in the form of food, He had no outward splendor, majesty, or glory. He came in a humble way to be man's food. Anyone could touch Him and draw near to Him. If there ever has been a man who was non-threatening, that man was the Lord Jesus. When He was on earth, I do not believe there was one person who could say, "Although I would like to meet You, I am afraid of You." We cannot find such a person in the Bible. Even the weak women could come to Him and speak in a free way. They were not afraid of Him at all. Even the smallest child was not threatened by Him. No one was afraid of Him, not those who were evil, gravely ill, or leprous. Because our Lord came as food, He manifested Himself to man in a most non-threatening way. He wanted man to be fully at ease in taking Him as food and drink.

Although He appears to man as bread for food, the Bible says that all the fullness of the Godhead dwells in Him bodily (Col. 2:9). We should never underestimate the Lord. He did not have an attracting form or beautiful appearance. His outward appearance was neither significant nor threatening. However, He was not void of content. The Bible says that all the fullness of the Godhead, that is, all the fullness of God Himself, dwelt in Him. The fullness even dwelt in Him bodily. The fullness of the God of glory and of majesty, who is most holy and transcendent and who is in unapproachable light, dwelt in the man Jesus. In this Jesus, who is our food, all the fullness dwells. We should know Him to this extent.

GOD BEING ENJOYED BY MAN IN THE SPIRIT

One day Jesus told His disciples that He was going to die. When they heard this, they were surprised. He had been with them for only a short time, and they had only recently come to know Him as the Christ, the Son of God, the very embodiment of God Himself. Now He said that He was going to die. For Him to die meant that He would go away, and this meant that everything would change. The disciples were worried. But the Lord told them not to be troubled, because it was expedient for Him to go. In fact, if He did not go, He would not be able to come again. This was a strange word. If I had been Peter, I would have asked the Lord, "Why are You saying that You must come again? You are already here." We need to consider the Lord's word.

If Brother Hwang wants to serve me fresh fish, he will show me a live fish, but then he needs to take the fish away to prepare it. Although I have seen the fish, it still must go away. Brother Hwang may say to me, "Unless I take the fish away, it will be raw, and there will be no way for you to eat it. Once I take it away and cook it, I will bring it back for you to eat." When the fish came the first time, it was outside of me. When it comes the second time, it will be able to be inside of me. In order for it to come again, it must first go away. There is no need to be troubled or saddened by its going away, because we will enjoy it when it comes back.

When the Lord spoke of His going in order to come again, He seemingly said, "If I go away, the world will no longer see Me, but I will come back. And when I come back again, I will be edible and drinkable. When I come again, I will be the Spirit and enter into you and be with you always. Not only so, when I come back, you will live, just as I live, and you will know that I am in My Father and you in Me and I in you."

Before He spoke such a word, He prepared a supper in which He broke bread with the disciples, and He said to them, "Take, eat; this is My body." And He took the cup and gave thanks and gave it to them, saying, "Drink of it, all of you" (Matt. 26:26-27). Seemingly He was saying, "If I do not go, I will not be able to come back to you. I need to be crucified, not merely to accomplish redemption for your sins but in order that you can eat Me." Poor Christianity! It only sees that the death of Christ is for redemption. It does not see that Christ's death is even the more for eating. When the children of Israel killed the passover lamb, they did not merely shed the blood of the lamb for their redemption. They also ate the meat of the lamb as their food. In the same way, when the Lord Jesus went to the cross, His death was not merely for redemption through the shedding of His blood. It was so that we could eat Him, drink Him, and enjoy Him.

Thank the Lord that our Passover Lamb has been slain.

The Christ who has come to be our food has been crucified and resurrected. In His resurrection He is the Holy Spirit. The Spirit is now wonderful and mystical. All that God is and all that He has passed through are now in the Spirit. In incarnation, divinity entered into humanity, and in resurrection, humanity entered into divinity. Humanity is now in the Spirit. Now everything of the Lord is in the Spirit. Because of this the Spirit is not so simple. We should realize that all of the fullness of God is in the Spirit. The Spirit has been given, He has been poured out, and He has been breathed out. Everything is now in the Spirit. Everything has been prepared and is available. There is no further need to do anything. We should just eat.

Let me repeat. In resurrection the Lord became the Spirit. On the day of Pentecost this Spirit was poured out. The Bible says that the Spirit has even been sent forth into all the earth (Rev. 5:6). Previously God was only in unapproachable light. Then one day He came forth and appeared on the earth, but He was still limited by time and space. When He was in Samaria, those in Jerusalem could not see Him. When He was in Judea, those in Galilee could not see Him. Then He died, resurrected, and became the Spirit. Today this Spirit has been poured out and sent forth into all the earth. Our God is now in the Spirit. Today He is like the air, filling the entire earth. He is omnipresent; He permeates everything and is present everywhere. Therefore, anyone can contact Him and receive Him.

Human beings need food and drink, and they also need air. Of these three things, air is the most available. God has become so available and enjoyable to us that it is enough to just breathe Him in as air. God is Spirit, and everything related to Him is in the Spirit. In the original Greek text, *spirit* and *breath* are the same word. Today the Spirit is like the air that we breathe. He is everywhere; He permeates everything and is omnipresent. When He comes in a strong way, He can be compared to wind, and when He comes to us in a gentle way, He can be compared to breath. When we can hear or feel the movement of air, it is wind, but when we cannot hear or feel its movement, it is breath. God has been processed to the extent that He is available in every place; no one can be deprived of Him. He is just as available as air; we can breathe Him in. There is no need for us to exert any effort to breathe Him in. What a blessing this is!

A PERSON ENJOYING GOD AS THE SPIRIT

Let us now consider a person who absorbs the Spirit, that is, a person who enjoys God. We have a certain feeling when we breathe fresh air; we have a feeling of enjoyment. Similarly, whenever we touch the Spirit by breathing Him in, we have a certain feeling. We are convicted; we feel judged and condemn ourselves because the Spirit is the lamps of fire burning before the throne of God (Rev. 4:5). He is also the eyes of the Lamb (5:6). In Revelation 1:14 the eyes of the Lamb, who is the Son of Man, are like a flame of fire that shines, exposes, and judges. When the Spirit is touched by man and received into man, He becomes a shining and enlightening within man. He convicts the world of sin, righteousness, and judgment (John 16:8). When we touch the Spirit, we cannot escape being convicted. When we breathe in the Spirit, we cannot fail to be enlightened. He is the lamps of fire burning before the throne. The throne is for judgment and for ruling. Hence the lamps before the throne are the Spirit of judgment from God. This means that when the Spirit touches man, He shines the light of God's throne into man, and man sees his unrighteousness and corruption. Whenever we touch the Spirit, we feel convicted. Once God touches us, the lamps before the throne shine within us, we become bright, and our inward condition is exposed even if we were dark and confused. As the Spirit of judgment and the Spirit of conviction, the Spirit judges and convicts us. God is holy and cannot dwell with evil. Once a man touches Him, a sense of conviction comes, and his true inward condition is exposed. God's Spirit shines in man as lamps of fire, and He searches man's inward parts with His flaming eyes. Everyone who has experienced this knows that when he touches the Spirit, he is connected to God and is transparent before God. He senses that God's flaming eyes are searching through his innermost parts. Nothing can be hidden from God; nothing can hide us from Him. We sense that our entire being is brought into the light. In the light we see our sins, we are aware of our mistakes, we are convicted of our evil and corruption, and we condemn and judge ourselves. The more we condemn ourselves, the more our spirit breathes in God, and the happier we feel. This is truly wonderful. The more we condemn and judge ourselves, the happier we are inwardly, and the more we enjoy the Spirit's presence and God's infilling. Eventually, spiritual songs and praises well up within us. Condemnation and conviction are turned into praising and thanksgiving because we are filled with the Spirit as if we were drunk with new wine.

When the Spirit shines within us, exposing our condition, we should condemn ourselves and confess our sins, breathing them out. We may cry, "Lord, I was wrong in this matter, and I have sinned in that matter. I have sinned against my parents, my children, and my spouse. I am wrong at work. I am wrong in the church. There is nothing in me that is right." This is what it means to breathe out. A person who has never breathed out in this way has never breathed in God; he has never been saturated with God. When the Spirit comes, He convicts the world of sin, of righteousness, and of judgment. Therefore, when we touch the Spirit, we breathe out our sins. Not only so, whenever we breathe out, we also breathe in. How much we breathe out determines how much we can breathe in. We breathe out our sins, and we breathe in the Spirit. We breathe out the self, and we breathe in Christ. We breathe out corruption, and we breathe in the riches of God. God is in Christ, and Christ is in the Spirit. We cannot help but breathe out and breathe in when the Spirit, as the lamps and the eyes of the Lamb, judges and condemns us. We breathe out our corruption and the self, and we breathe in the Triune God. In this breathing out and breathing in, we find comfort, joy, peace, power, light, wisdom, healing, and utterance. We have everything. What we need, we find in Him because He is what we need.

The Spirit has been poured out. He has been "exhaled" and has been sent forth into all the earth. He is everywhere, and He pervades everything. He is even in us, waiting for us to breathe Him in. When we breathe Him in, we eat and drink Him. This is to absorb Him and enjoy Him. When we enjoy Him and possess Him in this way, we will spontaneously live out Christ; we will live out God. This is what it means to enjoy God.

CHAPTER ELEVEN

HOW GOD BECOMES MAN'S ENJOYMENT

Scripture Reading: Eph. 3:16-20; Phil. 2:13; Rom. 8:2; John 6:57; 15:7-8; Eph. 6:18; 1 Thes. 5:17, 19

THE CHRISTIAN LIFE BEING TO EAT AND DRINK GOD

Let us consider further the way to enjoy God by eating and drinking Him, that is, by breathing in God. I bear a heavy burden and feel that it is very difficult to speak concerning how to eat and drink God. Without a clear explanation, however, the saints may have a wrong understanding. If my speaking is taken as a method, it will result in an artificial practice. The more we imitate, the less we will eat God, and the less we will touch Him. The more we imitate, the more we are in ourselves and are artificial. It is difficult to explain how to enjoy God. There are methods we can use to touch God; we are not without a way. There is a way to touch God, receive God, and breathe in God. There is a way to do everything. However, I do not feel to give the brothers and sisters methods. Methods can become something artificial. If all we have are methods, we cannot exercise them in a normal way.

God has no desire for us to do anything for Him. He has done everything for us. However, even though He is our food, we still bear a certain amount of responsibility. Although we do not need to do anything, we still need to eat and drink Him. It is our responsibility to receive Him. We need to do only one thing: we need to receive Him, absorb Him, eat Him, and drink Him. Whether we are up to the proper standard as a Christian depends on whether we are right in the matter of eating, drinking, and enjoying God. Being a Christian depends only on our receiving God. If we have a problem with receiving God and are even a little off, we are not up to God's standard as a Christian. However, if we are proper in absorbing God, all our problems will be solved, and we will be proper Christians who match God's standard. For this reason I have stressed that only one thing matters in the Christian life—eating, drinking, and absorbing God.

THE MEANING OF EATING AND DRINKING GOD

In the preceding messages we pointed out that God requires man only to receive Him as food. He desires man only to receive Him as life by eating Him as food. God's being life to man means that He becomes every element in man. God simply desires to enter into us as food to be life and everything to us. Our responsibility is to eat and drink Him, to absorb Him. These expressions are new even in Christianity. The Christian life is simply a matter of eating and drinking God. Although this is a simple word, it is very profound.

First, eating and drinking denote a union. Brother Hwang and I are two persons. We can never be fully united. Although we can join hands, embrace each other, or even be bound together by chains, we still cannot be fully united. His breathing is his breathing, and my breathing is my breathing; there is no perfect union. The best and most thorough way for us to have a union is for me to eat him so that he can enter into me. If it were possible, I would demonstrate this. I would get a knife, cut up Brother Hwang, cook him in a pot, and eat him. Then tomorrow morning Brother Hwang and I would be fully one; we would be united and joined to such an extent that we would no longer be two persons. My breathing would be his breathing, and he would breathe within me. This shows you that the best way to be united is through eating and drinking. Many chickens, ducks, fish, and pigs have been united with us, because they have been eaten by us. In eating and drinking, two entities become one; they are joined and united together. Those who know God know that His greatest desire is to be joined to man and for man to be joined to Him. This union can take place only by eating and drinking. God comes to us as food, and we take Him in by eating. In this way God and we become absolutely one; there is a perfect union. This is the first meaning of eating and drinking.

Second, eating and drinking imply digestion and assimilation. Twelve hours after eating Brother Hwang, he will be fully digested and assimilated into me. This shows that eating and drinking include a transformation. When God is eaten by us, He becomes us.

Some may think that it is presumptuous to say this. They may consider it sufficient to say that man, who is small, low, in darkness, and evil, draws near to God. After all, God is great, high, holy, and in light, but man is small, low, evil, and in darkness. Man is privileged to be able to touch such a God. Others may think that to say that man can draw near to God through the blood of Jesus Christ is an affront to God's holiness. However, I am saying that man can eat God, and I will even go further to say that we can digest and assimilate God. Is this word too risky? No, we should not think that God will disappear by our digesting Him. To say that is heresy. However, God's intention is to become us. The only way for God, who is outside of us, to become us from within is by eating and drinking. Whatever we take into us eventually becomes us. In the same way, when we eat and drink God, He becomes us.

Third, what we eat and drink becomes our inward constituent. What I eat and drink not only is digested and transformed into me, but it also becomes part of my inward constitution.

A brother once noted that because some people eat too much beef or mutton, they have a strong smell of cow or sheep. If one eats beef three meals a day, after a while he will smell like a cow. He has not become a cow, but others will sense that he smells like a cow because the cow he has digested has become him. It has become his constitution. What we eat becomes our constitution. In the same way, when we eat and drink God, He is digested and transformed within us to become our constitution.

Finally, what we eat and drink becomes our nutrition and nourishment, and we live by it. All the things that we eat become our nourishment and inward supply; we live by them. If we do not eat, or if we do not eat enough, we will be short of an inward nourishment and supply, and we will not be able to survive. When we eat God, He becomes our nourishment and supply, and we can live by Him. Hence, the Lord Jesus says that he who eats Him will live because of Him (John 6:57). When we eat the Lord, He is mingled with us, digested by us, and He becomes our constitution, nourishment, and supply, enabling us to live because of Him. We can live, move, and work because we have eaten Him and have received Him into us as our nourishment and supply.

CHRIST BEING OUR LIFE BY BECOMING OUR FOOD

What we have said applies to physical food. The Lord Jesus, however, is the true bread which came down out of heaven; He is much higher than physical food. When He enters into us, not only is He joined to us to become part of us as our constitution, nourishment, and supply, but He also becomes our very life. Physical food can render only a certain amount of supply; it can never become our life. It can be our nourishment, but it can never be our life. However, the Lord as food to us is not only our nourishment and supply; He is also our very life. He Himself is life. In the universe only He Himself is life because only He is immortal. Only He can be considered life because everything besides Him is mortal. Only the Lord Himself is immortal and unchanging. When He is digested into us to become our constitution, nourishment, and supply, He becomes our life, and we can live because of Him.

A living organism moves and acts because it has life. If it loses its life, it is dead and ceases from all movements and activities. Every kind of life has a certain kind of living and does certain particular things. Because a fish has a fish's life, it swims. Because a bird has a bird's life, it flies. In the same way, we Christians need Christ's life because every move of a Christian depends on the life of Christ. The life we possess from birth is incapable of living the Christian life.

Once a person believes, he is regenerated; that is, God enters into him as life. He possesses God as life in addition to his human life. Our human life is totally useless in the kingdom of God. Human beings can never live the life required by the kingdom of God. Just as a fish can never fly in the air and live the life of a bird, our natural life is completely useless in the kingdom of God. Our life cannot meet God's requirements, and it is helpless in living the life that God wants us to live. For this reason we need regeneration. We need to receive Christ into us to be our life.

Christ comes into us to be our life in the form of food. He becomes our life by becoming our food. When we eat Him, drink Him, receive Him, and digest Him, He becomes our constitution, nourishment, and supply. This is how He becomes our life. When we eat and drink Christ, He becomes our life, and we can live a genuine Christian life.

LIVING THE CHRISTIAN LIFE
BY ENJOYING CHRIST

I believe that we are clearer concerning the meaning of living the Christian life. We have not been living the Christian life. Since we are saved, attend meetings, and pray and read the Bible, no one can say that we are not a Christian. However, we do not live like a Christian. We can look like a Christian and at the same time not look like a Christian, because there are two conflicting lives within us—God's life and our life. It is difficult to say who is conflicting with whom. It may be that God's life is conflicting with our life or that our life is conflicting with God's life. Whatever the case may be, these two lives are always in conflict within us.

Sometimes we may encounter a severe trial that seems beyond our power to bear. Our only recourse is to sigh before God. Wonderfully, while we are breathing out our sorrow, we touch the Lord, and the feeling of oppression in our spirit is lifted. When we touch God's presence, no burden can weigh us down, and no temptation or trial can break us. No words can describe the inward condition we experience. We are happy, shining, and buoyant as if we are already in heaven. Songs burst forth spontaneously, praises flow, and our countenance is lifted. When others see us, they sense God. This is the description of the true Christian life.

Regrettably, many believers are "five-minute" Christians. While they are singing and praising, others may exhort them with nice words and sound teachings to stand firm and trust the Lord and express concern for them, indicating that they are praying for them. However, such words of exhortation may "clip their wings," and they are no longer able to fly though they were once transcendent. Their buoyancy, praises, and Christian countenance disappear; instead, they become heavily laden and deeply troubled. They may consider what to do in such "dire" conditions and worry that since they have been encouraged, they must now trust the Lord. However, the more they "trust," the drier they become and the more they may suffer. The more they "trust," the heavier they feel and the more they want to give up. They begin to complain and murmur against God, saying, "Even though I have loved the Lord all this time, my situation has gone from bad to worse. A person who does not care for God is in a better situation than I am. God does not do anything to him, but He is harsh with me. This is not fair. God, You are not trustworthy. Why am I in this condition when I pray to You every day?" Are these believers still living like a Christian? There are many such stories.

These believers experience such a change because our exhortation interrupts their eating and drinking. If we are exercised in the matter of eating and drinking God, we will first endeavor to know whether these suffering believers have absorbed enough God. If they do not have enough God, we will not utter too many words; otherwise, we will be like Job's friends. At best, we will be like Elihu, who made God's counsel hidden through words without knowledge (Job 42:3). There is no need to say too much. We should simply fellowship a little with them and render them a supply. Then when we leave, they will have more God, and we will enjoy a filling. This is the proper way to be a Christian.

Our problem is that we have been trying to be a Christian without enjoying Christ. Even though we do not enjoy Christ, we want to be a Christian. Eventually, we lose "Christ" and are left with "ian," which is vain and meaningless. Christ is gone, and only "ian" is left. Is this not our story? Because we do not enjoy Christ, we do not live like a Christian. On the contrary, we doubt God and complain that He is not fair.

We think that God is not trustworthy or that He is not real. He becomes an abstract idea to us. Such tragic stories do happen.

Brothers and sisters, only Christ can be a true Christian. But in Himself, He can only be Christ; He cannot be a Christian. He must enter into us, be mingled with us, and come out of us in order to be a Christian. We cannot be a Christian without Him, and He cannot be a Christian without us. He has become our food; He is mingled with us and has become our life and life supply. Whenever we are enjoying Him, we are a Christian.

Without electricity, lamps cannot shine. Strictly speaking, they cannot be considered as lamps when they are not shining. They are lamps when the switch is turned on and electricity flows through them. When they are shining, they are lamps. When electricity flows through them, they are lamps. When they enjoy electricity, they are lamps. Similarly, we are Christians when we are connected to Christ, enjoy Him, and allow Him to live in us and be expressed through us. When there is no barrier between us and Him, and when He is digested by us and operates within us, we can be a Christian without trying to live like one. Because Christ is filling us and shining out through us, we will be a genuine Christian and not merely look like a Christian. This is what it means to be a Christian.

When a man is drunk with wine, he is a drunkard. A drunkard is one who drinks and fills himself with wine to the extent that his perspiration and breath smell of alcohol, his face flushes with wine, and his expressions are controlled by wine. A person is no longer a drunkard when he stops drinking, is sober, and is cut off from alcohol. We should not say that since we are saved, baptized, receive answers to prayers, and understand the Bible, we are, therefore, a Christian. We may be able to recite every verse in the Bible but still not look like a Christian. While a believer is speaking, he might not enjoy Christ or eat and drink Christ even though he is saved, baptized, and receives answers to his prayers. He has no fellowship with Christ, and Christ does not operate within Him and is not His supply. Christ is not living within him in a living and fresh way. When a believer is in this condition, he is a Christian only in name; he cannot be called a Christian in reality. He is Christless; he is a Christian who is cut off from Christ.

A Christian is a person who breathes in Christ and enjoys Him moment by moment. In everything he is joined to Christ; Christ operates within him and supplies him all the time. Christ is the embodiment of God. When He lives within us, all the fullness of God saturates us, and we are a Christian. This is what it means to enjoy Christ. This is what it means to eat and drink Him. This is what it means to enjoy God.

Every new believer has experienced this. They have eaten God and enjoyed Him. At least they have touched and contacted Him once. A person who has never touched God or contacted Him is not saved. He is merely a nominal Christian. A person becomes a Christian when he contacts God and is connected with Him. A light bulb must be connected to a power plant before electricity can flow through it. Similarly, when we are connected to God, He flows in us. This is the meaning of being saved, and this is the meaning of being regenerated. At the time of our salvation, we could not describe this in a clear way, but in retrospect, we can testify that this was truly our experience. We touched God, contacted Him, and were joined to Him. Something indescribable happened within us. We may have experienced a kind of shining, soothing, conviction of sins, or an uplifting as if we were flying, and we effortlessly overcame the world, sin, and all kinds of temptations. This is what happens when we touch God inwardly.

However, this wonderful situation in our spirit lasts only for a short period of time. Then our mind is activated, and we begin to consider the things that we can no longer do. We may say, "Since I am now a Christian, I must be proper in my behavior. Formerly I was rude to my wife, but I will now be polite to her." We make resolutions and set our mind on doing things. This is our story. We may listen to a message on living a proper Christian life by walking in a manner that is worthy of our calling. This message may strengthen our conviction, thought, and view so that we are even more determined to be a proper Christian. Since we realize that we are weak and that we cannot make it by ourselves, we may begin to pray, to trust in the Lord, and to ask others to pray for us.

Although this may work for one or two days, our true self will eventually come forth. At this point we try to control the self. However, after two days we are tired of holding back the self, and our true condition in manifested. When we pray, we complain of the hardship of being a Christian. We may ask the Lord to have mercy on us. Although it seems that we are breathing out our sins, there is actually no exercise of the spirit; we are merely exercising our mind to consider how we should control ourselves, trust in the Lord, and beseech Him for help. There is no breathing in God during the entire time of our prayer. After this "prayer," nothing changes, and we lose our temper as we have never done before. After this we feel ashamed to pray, and we have no interest to listen to a message. We see no relationship between the message and our Christian life; hence, the word that is spoken is unable to penetrate our being. We feel that being a Christian is burdensome; we cannot give up, and we have no way to proceed. We may testify that though we have done our best, the result is total failure. We are in a bind and in turmoil. Brothers and sisters, have you experienced this?

Perhaps after a long time, we are driven to our end, and we set aside a time to kneel before the Lord. This time, however, we no longer know how to pray. We can only cry out "Lord" and weep. There is no complaint of being a Christian, no pleading, and no asking God for help; we only weep. However, our weeping is actually a breathing, in which we breathe out ourselves. When there is breathing out, there is breathing in. Unconsciously, without realizing it, we are breathing in God.

After this we feel completely relieved. We are no longer cluttered, and we feel as if we are soaring in the air. When others touch us, they sense that instead of sourness and bitterness, our whole being is full of gentleness and sweetness. We have no interest to speak about this or that, but we only desire to praise and give thanks. We want to laugh and jump. It is an inexplicable experience. This is what it means to be a

Christian. Inwardly we touch Christ once again. We absorb Him, enjoy Him, eat Him, and drink Him, and He lives and operates within us once again. This is the way to live by Christ and to live Christ.

But even after this experience, we still have not learned the secret. So after two days, we pray again, "I thank and praise You, Lord. You have really helped me these past two days. But I am afraid that this wonderful situation will not last and that tomorrow I will fail again. Lord, please, please, please, protect me." Because our prayer has driven God away, our inward parts are once more in turmoil and are hardened. Before praying, we were connected to Christ, but our prayer has severed our connection with Him. Before praying, we were happy and innocent, living spontaneously in the spirit, but our prayer has driven us out of our spirit. We are now in our mind and full of thoughts; hence, we are cut off from Christ. Formerly we were blissfully ignorant; now we are clear that we are evil, unreliable, and able to lose our temper. However, those who are clear in their mind have been eating too much of the fruit of the tree of the knowledge of good and evil. Adam and Eve had their eyes "opened" once they ate of the fruit of the tree of the knowledge of good and evil. They immediately saw that they were naked and looked for clothing. Before they ate of the fruit of the tree of the knowledge of good and evil, they were blissfully ignorant. Although their eyes seemed to be closed, they lived before God. Our prayers often "open" our eyes. Even messages we hear can "open" our eyes. Before we prayed or listened to a message, we were in our spirit and were happy, free, and unconcerned. We fellowshipped with Christ in our spirit. We did not know the meaning of losing or controlling our temper, and we were not concerned or afraid of our temper. It was as if there was no such thing as temper in the universe. We simply allowed Christ to live in us. We were joined to Christ and spontaneously lived a Christian life. We were a Christian in actuality and reality. However, one message "opened" our eyes, and we were led away from our spirit to our mind. We received some exhortations and began to guard ourselves against our temper, considering how not to lose it. We began to worry about and fear our temper. Immediately we were inwardly cut off from Christ. Hence, our fear of our temper grew, and we became more likely to lose it. Once we are inwardly cut off from Christ, we lose our enjoyment of Christ and have no way to live the Christian life.

LIVING CONTINUOUSLY IN THE SPIRIT
TO ENJOY CHRIST

We need to learn not to stray away from our spirit and not to be concerned about our thoughts and so many other things. We simply need to live in the spirit. Christ dwells in our spirit, and we must learn to be connected to Him all the time. Hence, the Word says that we should abide in Him (John 15:4). When we abide in Him, we can pray unceasingly. Such unceasing prayer is not in the mind but in the spirit. When we breathe in Christ, receive Him, fellowship with Him, and are connected to Him at all times and in every place, we can pray without ceasing and without regard to a method. This does not mean that we should not have set times for prayer. We often have a need to pray at particular times. However, when we do this, we must be careful not to turn from our spirit to our mind. We do not need to be concerned about our mind or to worry about so many things. There is no need to think, worry, or consider too much. We do not even need that much teaching. We need to be a simple Christian and focus only on the fact that Christ is our life and that He is dwelling in us. We can simply enjoy Him in our spirit. When we enjoy Him and are connected to Him, we are a Christian. Whatever we ask in prayer should be out of Him; He should be the One asking from within us. Requests made in this way are surely granted, and we bear much fruit because His fullness is expressed and manifested through us. Spontaneously we glorify God and are His disciples because we are inwardly filled with Him. When we are full of Christ, we are a Christian. Christ makes His home in our heart by faith, and we are filled unto all the fullness of God. God operates in us, and the exceedingly great power accomplishes everything for us, even above all that we ask or think. We are Christians who are full of Christ and who fully enjoy God. We enjoy God Himself. Day by day and moment by moment, we are eating and drinking God. We will enjoy Him and absorb Him without a moment of interruption.

CHAPTER TWELVE

ENJOYING GOD BY PRAYING AT SET TIMES

Scripture Reading: Psa. 27:4; 84:4, 10; 55:17; 119:164; Dan. 6:10; Acts 10:2-3, 9-11, 30; Gen. 18:16-17, 22-23, 33

NEEDING A SET TIME OF PRAYER

God is Spirit, and the most appropriate way for us to absorb and enjoy Him is to turn to our spirit. Turning to our spirit is as necessary as breathing in air. We will now consider how to enjoy God from a different perspective. Although God as the Spirit is available everywhere on earth, and although we can now receive Him anywhere and at any time, those who are experienced know that we need set times to devote ourselves to absorbing God. This can be compared to breathing. There is no need to concentrate on breathing—we breathe spontaneously at any time and in any place. But everyone who is conscious of their health knows that we need to set aside time every day to breathe deeply. We should find a quiet and open space and spend some time to breathe deeply. Deep breathing is beneficial to our health. If we only breathe normally, we cannot remove more than a certain amount of carbon dioxide. In order to remove more than this amount, we must breathe deeply. It is also through breathing deeply that a fresh supply of oxygen is able to fill more of our lungs. A good exercise in deep breathing thoroughly cleanses our lungs. Similarly, our drawing near to God and breathing Him at any time is general and common. If we want to touch Him in a deep way, and if we want to breathe out our sins and absorb God so that our entire being is renewed, we need a definite time to come to God. We need spiritual deep breathing. In other words, we need a set time to come to God to pray.

We should all be clear that prayer is to breathe in God. It is to breathe out everything that belongs to us and to breathe in God and everything of Him. Prayer is a kind of breathing. Although we mention many things in prayer, our goal is to breathe. We breathe out everything that is within us through prayer. At the same time, we breathe in everything of God through prayer. This is prayer. If we grasp this meaning of prayer, we will be able to pray anywhere and any time. No matter how noisy the environment is or how busy we are, we can breathe in God. Nevertheless, there is still the need for us to set aside some time during the day for prayer. We need such a time for spiritual deep breathing so that we can absorb and enjoy God in an intensified way.

Set Times of Prayer Being Worthwhile

Regrettably, we often spend time on worthless things. We waste precious time on things of no value and neglect the most precious thing—breathing God. The psalmist says, "A day in Your courts is better than a thousand" (Psa. 84:10). This means that spending time to draw near to God and to breathe in God is most precious. Spending an hour a day to absorb God is of more value than occupying ourselves with other things for a thousand hours. Nothing in this world is more worthwhile than breathing in God.

The most precious time of our day is when we breathe in God, when we pray. Whether our time is well spent depends on what we accomplish during that time. God is the supreme blessing, the ultimate treasure of the universe. Nothing is more precious than God. Even the blessings that God gives cannot be compared with God Himself. We do not pray to receive blessings from God or even to obtain answers to our prayers. We pray to breathe in God. We receive God and enjoy Him in our prayer. Nothing can be more precious than obtaining God through prayer, but we are often foolish in our accounting; we do not know that we must do this most worthwhile thing.

In our Christian life there are two contradicting things. The first is that being filled with God through prayer gives us the most precious reward; the other is that gossip, or loose talk, gives us nothing but loss. We should consider how many hours a day we spend in loose talk. The brothers and especially the sisters often say that they are too busy to pray. But when sisters come together, they gossip a lot; they can even make time to gossip. Gossip or unnecessary talk, which are actually words that spread death, bring nothing but loss to the church. For this reason I say that we often do the most unprofitable things. We neglect the most profitable things and daily engage ourselves in the most unprofitable. If we would use a notebook to record the times that we daily spend in prayer and to record the times that we engage in loose talk, we would be surprised to see that one-tenth of the time we spend in loose talk is spent in prayer. We waste our precious time on worthless things.

Prayer is to breathe in God; it is to receive God and to absorb Him. This is priceless. Why are we not attracted to this? Our problem is that we hear many exhortations concerning breathing in God, but we spend only a few minutes breathing. We should ask ourselves of what use this is to us. We need to change our concept. Even though we are busy, we should still set aside some time to receive and absorb God. No matter how busy we are, we should daily devote some time for prayer with the sole purpose of breathing in God.

How Saints of Old Set Aside Time to Pray

There are many examples in the Old Testament and the New Testament of ones setting aside time to pray. In the Old Testament David said, "Seven times a day I praise You" (119:164). He also said, "Evening and morning and at noontime / I complain and moan" (55:17). This complaining and moaning were actually a kind of sighing before God by which David breathed out his sorrows. He did this in the evening, in the morning, and at noontime because every day begins in the evening and continues to the morning in a Jewish calendar. This verse shows that David breathed in God three times a day.

Daniel prayed before God three times a day "because he had always done so previously" (Dan. 6:10). Daniel was a man filled with God and full of His presence. The secret to his being filled with God was in his setting aside three definite times a day to absorb God and to enjoy Him.

In the New Testament there are many examples. Cornelius said that he was keeping the ninth hour of prayer in his house (Acts 10:30). This shows that every day he prayed at the ninth hour, which is about three to four o'clock in the afternoon. He kept that time of prayer in the same way that some Christians today keep the morning watch. In the same chapter Peter was praying in the sixth hour, which is at noon: "Peter went up on the housetop to pray around the sixth hour" (v. 9). The Holy Spirit recorded these instances to show that a man who enjoys God keeps specific times for prayer. Peter probably prayed every day at noon, and Cornelius probably prayed every day at about three in the afternoon.

Both the Old Testament and the New Testament show that those who truly receive God and enjoy Him have set times for prayer. We cannot be unrestricted if we expect to enjoy, receive, and breathe in God. Even though there is a side to enjoying God that is very free, there is also a side that is very restricted. In particular, new believers, who have not fully learned to exercise their spirit and are still new in the matter of enjoying and breathing in God, need a specific time for prayer.

The Time to Pray Being Determined
by One's Own Choice

The time of prayer should be determined according to a person's schedule. There is nothing legal related to this time. Peter prayed at noon, and Cornelius prayed at the ninth hour. We know that Daniel prayed three times a day, but we do not know at what times. There is no legal time. Some would rather spend time in the morning before their work to breathe in God. Others are very busy during the day and have time only in the afternoon. For them to devote twenty or thirty minutes during that period of time to absorb God is a good choice. Some sisters work at home, and it is not easy for them to find time early in the morning. They may need to wait until their children and husband leave the house and they finish their morning chores, maybe around ten o'clock in the morning. Because it is too early for them to be occupied with lunch preparation, they spend some time to quietly breathe in God. There may be some who, like Cornelius, set aside time between three and four in the afternoon. A person should determine the time that he sets aside.

However, we should never use the time before we go to bed for prayer, because when we are exhausted, we may fall asleep while praying. Hence, this is the worst time. When George Müller was asked why he devoted his mornings to the Lord, he answered that in offering a sacrifice to God, one must offer the choicest portion of fat. In contacting God we must offer the choicest part of our time. There is no set rule as to what is the choicest part of our time. With some it is the early morning. With others it is after the noon break. The decision is left to each individual.

Extra Grace That Comes with Set Times of Prayer

If we mean business and set aside a period of time to contact God every day, we will receive many unexpected blessings. God has reserved much grace for us, but we have been too busy. We have never set aside the time for God. Hence, God does not have a way to reach us. If we would set aside some time every day, not merely to pray or to breathe in God but to open ourselves before Him, we will open a door for God to do many things in us. No other time can be compared with our prayer time. The most precious things happen to us when we pray. If we would spend some time before God, not to speak to Him and not to ask Him to do things for us but to give Him the opportunity to speak to us and to do things in us, many wonderful and mysterious things will happen to us during that time. We will see visions, we will know ourselves, and God will unveil mysteries concerning His Word and grant us understanding (2:17). He will even grant us burdens and gifts that we did not possess. We will receive a special portion of grace as a special kind of enlightenment or as a rebuke, cleansing, or dealing. During this period of time God will speak and operate in us.

Therefore, this period of time is indispensable. If we take away this time, we will be deprived of opportunities to receive grace and of opportunities for God to work in us. We need to be impressed that since we know how to enjoy God, we must set aside a specific time to practice. If we fail, we will suffer great loss in our life. Whether the saints are old or young, brothers or sisters, we will all suffer a great loss if we do not spend some time before the Lord. The wisest thing for us to do is to spend some time before the Lord. We can spend one, three, seven, or even more times a day to absorb God. However, it is better not to set aside too many times a day initially. If we set aside too many times a day, we may be able to maintain it for a few days, but eventually it will become a legality to us, and we will fail. Some have practiced praising seven times a day. In my youth I also practiced this. But after a while I could not bear the burden any longer, because it became a law to me. It is best not to set too high a standard. However, we need to come before the Lord at least once every day. If we practice this, we will receive much profit.

THE WAY TO ENJOY GOD
THROUGH SET TIMES OF PRAYER

Even though there is no regulation concerning what we should do during this time of prayer, we should remember the points we considered in chapter 5. Here is a review of those points.

Seeking after God

During this time of absorbing God, we should not worry about so many things. There is no need to mention many things in our prayer. The more we pray for different things the less we touch God, the less we reach Him. Please pay attention to the word *reach*. When we pray, we must reach God. This can be compared to hitting a person. To hit a person, our hand must reach the person; otherwise, we are hitting in vain. Being concerned about many things when we pray prevents us from reaching God. In order to gain God, we must drop everything. The first point in enjoying God through prayer is to appear before Him, to seek after Him. We do not go to God to pray for things; we go to Him to seek after Him. We look for God, touch Him, and contact Him.

God is Spirit, and He lives in our spirit. When we pray, we must learn to turn inward, to return to our spirit to seek after God. We must turn to our spirit to touch Him. Once we touch Him in our spirit, we pray. This prayer reaches God.

Some brothers and sisters might not understand what it means to reach God. If I want to speak with Brother Hwang, I must go to him. Even though I may shout and yell when I find him, if his eyes are not set on mine, I have not reached him. If I want to reach him, I must either wait until he is looking at me, or I must stand in front of him and look at him. When I see his face, I can speak to him. This is what it means to reach God in our prayer. Many brothers and sisters do not do this when they pray. They are not concerned with touching God or facing Him when they pray. Instead, they pray hurriedly about many things, and when they are finished, they say, "In the name of Jesus, Amen." They do not know if the Lord is looking at them when they pray. This kind of prayer does not reach God.

When we contact God, we must exercise to turn our whole being to our spirit. We should seek Him in our spirit. We close our eyes when we pray to stop from being distracted, turn to our spirit, and touch God. For this reason we also should not be too quick to open our mouth. Rather, we should be calm and have a period of silence. Good prayer does not depend on an abundance of words. It is good to be silent at the beginning of our prayer, and it is also good to have a period of silence during our prayer. Many psalms in the Bible end with *selah*. This is the equivalent of a rest note in music notation. It tells a person to stop, to halt for a while. Because our words of prayer can distract us from the spirit, there is the need of a halt to bring our entire person back to the spirit. There are times, however, when we cannot stop; a stop may drive away the spirit. What we should do depends on the circumstance. In prayer, we need to learn to be silent. There is no need to be in a hurry. We need to be at ease and quiet.

Beholding God

Let me repeat: while we are silent, we should not try to remember many things. Rather, we should learn to praise God and behold His beauty. We are not here to tell Him many things. We are here to absorb Him and to enjoy Him. While we are in His presence, we must learn to behold Him. Some may consider that beholding God will distance us from Him. They may ask, "Since God is in us, why do we need to behold Him?" Our God is wonderful. He is the Son of Man who descended out of heaven but who is still in heaven (John 3:13). Although He has come, He remains in heaven. He lives in us, but at the same time He is in heaven. When beholding Him, there is no need for us to determine if He is in heaven or within us. Actually, when we truly touch Him and experience His countenance, we are not clear where we are. When we are truly in spirit, we have no idea whether we are in heaven or on earth.

Inquiring of God

When we learn to come to God and behold Him in a quiet spirit, we will spontaneously worship and praise Him. After worshipping and praising God, we must learn to inquire of God. We should ask if He wants us to pray about a certain matter. We should not immediately pray about different matters. Rather, we should first have a discussion with Him, asking Him if we should pray for a certain matter. All prayers should be initiated by God. He should be the one who initiates them within us.

Abraham's intercession before God in Genesis 18 is a model intercessory prayer. God wanted to destroy Sodom; however, He wanted to save Lot, and He needed a man to intercede for Lot. Everything that God wants to do to man and every grace that He intends to bestow on man can be fulfilled only after man prays. This is an unchanging principle. God intended to save Lot, but He needed a man to pray. Who could He find? He could find only Abraham, a man who lived before God.

There are two precious portions in Genesis 18. The first is "Abraham walked with them [God and the angels] to send them away" (v. 16). This is a sweet word. God came to Abraham's tent and visited him. Abraham ministered to God and fellowshipped with Him while God ate and drank in his tent.

God spoke to Abraham concerning his begetting of Isaac. After that, God finished His business with Abraham and was free to leave. But while He was leaving, Abraham walked with God to send Him away. The Bible says that Abraham was called the friend of God (James 2:23). This is vividly portrayed when Abraham sent God off. On the one hand, God visited Abraham; He ate, drank, and fellowshipped with him as a friend in his tent. On the other hand, Abraham sent God off also like a friend. It was as if God said, "Abraham, good-bye!" Then Abraham seemed to respond, "Let me walk with You a distance to send You off." They behaved like two intimate friends who were unable to part.

There are certain things that God does not reveal until we walk a distance with Him. If Abraham had not walked a distance with God that day, but had instead promptly parted with God, God would not have had a way to save Lot. When God visited Abraham, it seems as if He accomplished only that part of His business that pertained to Abraham; the part that pertained to Lot was still hidden in God's heart. God's heart was on Lot. He intended to judge and destroy Sodom, but His child Lot was still in the city of Sodom and needed to be rescued. However, God could not rescue Lot, because He needed someone who was one with Him to pray. In visiting Abraham, He settled the business He had with Abraham and was waiting for Abraham to do something for Him. But He did not say anything. When we visit friends, it is easy for us to tell them what we are doing for them. But it is not easy to ask them to do something for us. This was what happened when God visited Abraham. Although God wanted Abraham to do something for Him, it was not easy for Him to say anything, because He did not know if Abraham was willing to do it. He did not know whether Abraham was one with Him in His inward parts. It was as if God said that He was leaving, but Abraham would not let Him go; he walked with God. Then God stopped and said, "Shall I hide from Abraham what I am about to do?" (Gen. 18:17). The sending away issued in something. God said that He was going down to see the situation of Sodom, and that He was going to judge it. This word hinted at God's intention to save Lot. He did not say this in plain words.

Abraham was a man living before God, and he understood God's heart. He knew that though God did not mention Lot, He cared for Lot. Here we find the second precious word: "Abraham remained standing before Jehovah" (v. 22). In the first precious word Abraham walked with God to send Him away. In the second precious word Abraham remained standing before God. While he was standing before Him, he prayed. This prayer was intercessory prayer. Such intercessory prayer is fully initiated by God and motivated by Him. It is conceived out of fellowship with God, out of touching His heart. Abraham began to pray for Lot, but he did not mention Lot's name. It seems as if both God and Abraham were speaking in a riddle. How do we know that Abraham's prayer was for Lot? In 19:29 we are told that when God destroyed Sodom, He rescued Lot on account of Abraham. Therefore the subject of that intimate talk and riddle between God and Abraham was Lot. But God did not say that it was Lot, and Abraham did not expose it either. On the surface both were speaking about Sodom. Actually, they were speaking about Lot's deliverance. Abraham's intercession truly touched God's heart.

I hope that we would see that as we breathe in God, we should learn to touch God's heart. We should not bring many things to God, nor should we ask for many things. If we do, God will disappear, and we will not touch Him. We must learn to stop our being and touch the burden within God's heart. The most precious prayers are those that are initiated by God within us. God knows all the matters that concern us. However, we must ask ourselves if we can say, "Lord, I believe You know all the things concerning me. Although I am in a difficult situation, You have not initiated anything within me, and I will not pray for this situation." If in our prayer we can tell the Lord that we will not pray for any matter, we have learned a great lesson. At least we should pray, "God, You know that I am bearing a big burden. Do You think I should pray for any matter that concerns me?" We may then bring the matters to Him one by one. If there is an echo within when we touch a certain matter, we have touched God in that matter and can proceed to pray for that matter. But if God's presence is not there, and there is no sense of God when we touch a certain matter, we should drop that matter. Whenever we pray, we should stop immediately when we do not touch God or sense His presence. We should no longer pray for that matter. However, as soon as we touch God, we should continue praying. We should pray for the items that bring us into His presence. No matter how many burdens we have or how many difficulties we face, we should never pray according to these difficulties. Rather, we should pray according to God's initiation and presence. Prayer is fully a matter of man mingling with God. We should never utter a prayer in which we pray, but He does not pray. We cannot enjoy God in such prayers. We must have the confidence to say that He is praying as we pray. We must also have the confidence to say that our prayer follows His prayer and is directed by His prayer. In this way, He bears us in His prayer, and He joins us in His prayer. Every word of our prayer touches Him, and we enjoy Him.

Brothers and sisters, no matter what the content is of such prayer, it is initiated by God. It touches God, and it mingles the praying one with God and joins him to God. The more a person prays this way, the more he breathes in God and the more God is added into Him. The result of such prayer is not only the accomplishment of the things prayed for—this is secondary. The main result is that when one prays this way, even in the process of his prayer, he receives God and enjoys God. The primary thing is that man gains God. The secondary thing is that man's prayers are answered.

Allowing God to Finish Speaking

Lastly, one must learn the lesson of allowing God to finish speaking. This was what Abraham did. After Jehovah finished speaking, He left. We must learn the lesson of allowing God to finish speaking. We should not be afraid that this will take too much time, and we should not worry that this will delay our affairs. God cares for us more than we care for ourselves. He will not forsake us.

The importance of prayer is not in praying for things. The importance of prayer is in touching and absorbing God. Although we should have the faith that He will accomplish whatever we ask, this is secondary. We must learn to touch Him and enjoy Him. Our prayer should be directed by Him and joined to Him. The most crucial need among God's children is to learn to pray by absorbing and breathing in God. May the Lord be gracious to us and perfect us in this way.

Chapter Thirteen

ENJOYING GOD AS FOOD BY READING THE WORD

Scripture Reading: John 6:27-36, 41-43, 47-58, 60-61, 63, 66-68; 12:50; Matt. 4:4; Jer. 15:16; 2 Tim. 3:16

READING THE WORD BEING ONE WAY TO ENJOY GOD

We have considered how to enjoy God through prayer. In this chapter we will consider how to enjoy God through reading the Bible.

Those who enjoy God know that God is Spirit and that we contact Him with our spirit. There are, however, two ways or means for us to contact Him in our spirit. The first is prayer, and the second is reading the Word. A person who absorbs and enjoys God prays and reads the Word. A believer who does not pray or read the Word has stopped enjoying God. In order for us to absorb God, eat and drink Him, and enjoy Him continually, we need to pray and read the Word every day. Both praying and reading the Word are necessary. We cannot have one without the other.

Concerning breathing in God through prayer, we have pointed out that God dwells in our spirit through His Spirit. Hence, prayer is to turn to our spirit to breathe out, item by item, the things within us and to breathe in God. With the breathing out, there must be the breathing in. In this way we breathe in God Himself as well as everything related to Him. Such breathing out of ourselves and breathing in of God are genuine prayer. Genuine prayer does not depend on how many things we bring before the Lord. It depends on breathing out what is within us and breathing in what is within God. Breathing out and breathing in deliver us from everything related to us and fill us with everything related to God. Breathing in God, who is Spirit, through prayer affords us the most excellent way to enjoy God.

Prayer, however, is not the only way that God has ordained for us to enjoy Him. He has also ordained reading the Word. God created everything in this universe in pairs. In order for the human race to propagate, there is the need of both male and female. Neither male nor female alone is adequate. Transmission of electric waves requires both an antenna and a ground wire; either one alone is insufficient. In the universe there are two sides to everything. A man with only one leg can only jump and hop; he cannot walk. This is unpleasant and also awkward. Everything has a top and a bottom, an inside and an outside, a front and a back, a positive and a negative. Similarly, enjoying God has two tracks, not one. On one track our eyes are closed, but on the other track our eyes are open. One track does not require our thoughts, but the other requires our thoughts. One track begins in our spirit and is unrelated to physical things, but the other track begins with black and white letters and ends in the spirit. In order to enjoy God, we need these two parallel tracks.

When we walk, we need both left and right legs. Similarly, when we absorb God, we need to close our eyes to pray and to open our eyes to read the Word. Everyone who properly breathes in God prays and reads, and reads and prays. If we want to enjoy God, we must learn to use both feet. We must learn to take both tracks. We must learn to pray, and we must learn to read the Word.

OUR PERSON DETERMINING THE WAY WE READ

If prayer is our spiritual breathing, what is reading the word? This is a big subject. Different people receive different things when they read the same Bible. Every Bible is composed of sixty-six books, beginning with creation in Genesis and ending with an admonition that no one should add or delete from God's Word in Revelation. The Bible we have in our hands is the same, but it seems as if we read different Bibles because we receive different things. You may receive one thing, and I may receive another. We receive different things from the same Bible. A brother with a deep knowledge of God and the Scriptures once said that the kind of person we are determines the kind of Bible we have. This is absolutely true.

A young person once asked, "Why do you say that we should not lie? In the book of Joshua God blessed Rahab the prostitute who lied. She hid the spies sent from Joshua, lied, and received a blessing." I could not answer him.

An older brother who longed for his children and grandchildren to treat him well said, "The Bible is wonderful in its expounding of filial piety." He admitted that he joined Christianity because the Christian Bible provides the clearest teaching on filial piety. He even asked me to come to his home once a week to teach his descendants the teachings of the Bible. When I asked what should be the topic of the meetings, he responded, "What else is there to speak about in the Bible except filial piety?" In his understanding, the Bible was a book on filial piety.

A sister once came to me and said that she had found an important point in the Bible: husbands should love their wives. Then she asked me to visit her husband since he needed this teaching. To an old man with many children and grandchildren, the Bible is a book on filial piety, but to a wife with a cold husband, the Bible is a book on husbands loving their wives.

I am not joking. Perhaps after the sister comes, the next day her husband may come and say, "I fully agree with Christianity, because its Bible teaches wives to be submissive to their husbands. This is a very good teaching. In order to have a good family, a person must accept the Christian Bible. I hope some sisters can come to my home and teach my wife the most important subject in the Bible. This is higher than the Chinese teaching on wives nagging their husbands. The Bible says that a wife must submit to her husband, just as the church submits to Christ and as Sarah submitted to Abraham, calling him lord. No other book speaks of submission as well as the Bible does."

A thoughtful scientist once said, "When I was young, I despised the Bible, considering it to be a book of fairy tales with no scientific basis. But now I can see that the Bible contains the highest science." His word puzzled me since I am not aware of the science he was referring to. When I asked him if he was referring to John 3:16 or to 1 Timothy 1:15, he did not even know where these verses were. In his eyes the Bible was a book of science.

A lawyer once said to me, "When I was young, I was a student of law, and I opposed Christianity. I despised the Bible, thinking that it was a simple book. But after so many years, I regret not having studied the Bible. Had I read the Bible fifteen years ago, my strength of argument as a lawyer would be much better today. I have studied many books on law, but no book surpasses the book of Romans in its arguments. This book shows Paul not only as a man of eloquence but also of argument. His arguments subdue and silence men." However, he did not even know the topic of Paul's arguments.

Another man who studied literature said, "I have read many famous writings, but nothing matches the Bible in its form, structure, and literary style. The Bible contains prose, poems, historical stories, and many other things. It is like an encyclopedia." However, he did not know the content of the prose, poems, stories, and histories.

This point should now be clear. The same Bible can be a different book in the hands of different people. To a certain kind of person the Bible is a certain kind of book. Those who are full of hatred find hatred in the Bible. Those who are full of love find love in the Bible. Those who lie find lies in the Bible. Those who are honest find honesty in the Bible. The kind of person one is determines the kind of Bible he reads.

What kind of Bible do we wish to have in our hands? Do we want a book on literature, science, arguments, filial piety, love for husbands, submission for wives, honesty, or lies? The kind of Bible we have depends on the kind of person we are. Different kinds of people have different kinds of Bibles. No one can change this principle.

THE BIBLE BEING GOD'S FOOD FOR US

Since we desire to be persons who eat, drink, absorb, and breathe in God, we need a drastic change in our concept concerning the Bible. We need to see that the Bible is the food

God has given us. We read the Bible with the purpose of eating, drinking, absorbing, and breathing in God, because we know that the Bible is the Word of God. John 1 says that the Word of God is God Himself. God's Word is God's coming forth. When God is expressed and presented to us, we have the Word, the Bible. Since God wants to be our food, His expression and manifestation to man as the Word means that the Word is man's food.

Some people think that God's words are only precepts and commandments, but in John 12:50 the Lord Jesus said that God's commandment is eternal life. God's commandment is life because it is food. When we receive God's commandments, we receive them in the way of eating. When these commandments enter into us as food, we spontaneously receive life and nourishment from them. Those who have experienced this can testify that when we read the Bible with a heart to absorb God, it becomes food to us. Even a commandment such as husbands loving their wives can become food to us when we receive it in the way of absorbing God. When we do this, we are filled with God's supply and His presence as we love our wives. While we are loving our wives, God is life to us. The commandment—love your wife—becomes eternal life to us. The more we receive this commandment to love our wives, the more we sense God's presence, supply, and life.

In the same principle, if we read the portions of the Bible that command children to honor their parents, with a heart to absorb God, we will receive this commandment as our food. Then when we obey this commandment to obey our parents, we will sense the moving of the Holy Spirit; we will experience the Holy Spirit as life to us. The more we honor our parents, the more we will be filled and satisfied, and the more we will eat and drink God and be saturated with His life. This is what it means for God's commandment to be eternal life to us.

The Lord Jesus Being Food to Man through His Word

The entire Bible, from the first word to the last, is God's word. It is God's expression and His breathing out. God's word is God Himself. John 1:1 says, "In the beginning was the Word, and the Word was with God, and the Word was God." This Word is our Lord Jesus. This is wonderful. The Lord Jesus is God's Word because He is God's expression and explanation. He manifests God; hence, He is the embodiment of God. When man receives Him, he receives God Himself. With the Word is life, nourishment, and supply. God is contained in the Word; hence, when a man receives the Word, he receives everything that God is.

When the Word came to earth, He was received in the way of food. He said that He is the bread that came down out of heaven to be eaten by men. The hearers, however, were confused. The Lord sympathized with their weakness and explained to them, using the type of the offerings. When the Jews celebrate the Passover, they slaughter a lamb, shed its blood for the remission of their sins, and eat the meat of the lamb. Every Jew was familiar with this. The Lord said that His flesh is true meat and that His blood is true drink. This means that they were to eat Him in the same way that they slaughtered and ate the Passover lamb. The lamb was slaughtered to meet the need of man's sinfulness and emptiness. When the lamb was killed, its blood was shed for the remission of sins, and its flesh was eaten for the satisfaction of man. Since the Jews understood the type, they should have also understood that the Lord was the Lamb prepared by God for them. He was killed, His blood was shed, and His body was broken. His shed blood redeemed man from his sins, and His broken body released His life to enter into man for man's satisfaction. His flesh is true food, and His blood is true drink. Those who eat His flesh and drink His blood eat Him, and those who eat Him will live because of Him (vv. 55-57).

The Jews, however, were confused when they heard these words. They wondered how this man's flesh could be their food. This word was too hard for them, and they could not receive it. Brothers and sisters, the Jews were confused, and we are often confused when we read John 6. For this reason, the Lord Jesus also said, "It is the Spirit who gives life; the flesh profits nothing" (v. 63). He was not giving them His visible flesh as food. If they ate His physical flesh, they would still die; they would not have lived. It is the Spirit who gives life. This proves that the Lord did not intend for them to eat His visible flesh but to eat the invisible Spirit. His desire is to enter into man's spirit as Spirit, to be man's food and man's life, and to cause man to live by Him. Here the subject of the Spirit is introduced. Prayer is to breathe in the Spirit with our spirit. It is to touch the Spirit with our spirit.

Because the Lord was concerned that the people would still not understand, He continued, "The words which I have spoken to you are spirit and are life" (v. 63). This shows that the Lord is food to us in two ways—first as the Spirit and second as the Word. In other words, the Lord today is first the Holy Spirit, and second the Holy Bible. He is the Spirit and the Word. Today we can breathe in the Spirit by prayer, and we can touch the Word by reading. The Lord is in the Spirit, and He is also in the Word. He is Spirit, the Word is the Spirit, and the Lord is the Word. Hence, the Lord, the Spirit, and the Word are three in one. The Lord is in the Spirit, and He is also the Spirit. The Lord is in the Word, and He is also the Word. The Word is also Spirit. Let me repeat: our Lord is in the Spirit, and He is the Spirit. He is in the Word, and He is the Word. Not only so, the Word is the Spirit. The three are one. He is the Spirit for us to breathe Him in; this is to pray. He is also the Word for us to read; this is to study the Bible.

Reading the Word Being
to Receive the Lord's Word as Food

Prayer is to breathe in the Lord's Spirit, and reading is to receive the Lord as the Word. The Lord as the Word is our food. Man does not live by bread alone, because he is not composed of only a body; within man there is also a spirit. The physical body requires physical food, but man's spirit requires a different type of food. Physical food is not enough to make man live. Hence, the Lord says that man shall not live on bread alone, but on every word that proceeds out through the mouth of God (Matt. 4:4). All the words that proceed out through the mouth of God are man's spiritual food. For this reason, the prophet Jeremiah said, "Your words were found and I ate them" (Jer. 15:16).

Reading the Word with an Attitude of Eating and Drinking God

Our attitude should be that the Bible is our food. The Bible is a book of food. When we read the Bible, we should eat this food. Whenever we read the Word, we should have the attitude that we are coming to eat and drink God. If our motive is merely to study truths, analyze teachings, or understand doctrines, we are not eating and drinking God, and the Bible is a book of doctrines and teachings to us. We must have a change in concept to see that the Bible is not a book of God's teaching or truth; it is God's food for us.

I hope that we would thoughtfully receive this word. This does not mean that the Bible does not contain teachings and truths. The Bible is full of teachings and truths. However, when we receive this book merely as a book of teachings and truths, and we attempt to study it only with our mind, we are but a student of truths and a learner of teachings. The Bible will merely be teachings and truths to us; it will not be life and food to us. But if our view changes, and we consider the Bible to be God's expression and His breathing out, the Bible will be a different book to us. We will realize that since God is food to man, the Bible as His breathed-out word must also be food to man. When we come to the Bible, we must eat and drink God as our food; we must breathe in God Himself and enjoy Him. If we read the Bible this way, it will no longer be a book of teachings, commandments, truths, or doctrines. Instead, it will be God's embodiment, unveiling, expression, and exhaling. It will also be our rich food. We will receive nourishment, supply, and life from every word.

Not Studying but Eating and Drinking

Brothers and sisters, this brings us back to the matter of our person. A person who studies the Bible, seeks after teachings and commandments, investigates truths, and searches doctrines may be better than those who do not read the Bible, but he can only be second best. Second best can often be an enemy to the best. This kind of reading can either damage a person or frustrate him from touching the Lord. Many brothers and sisters often read the Bible but seldom touch God, because they are not persons who seek after God. When they read the Bible, they do not absorb God, and they do not eat and drink Him. They are students of the Bible, seekers of truths, who want to find out the logic, commandments, and precepts of God. Because they are such persons, they find the Bible to be the kind of Bible they choose to hold.

There is a heavy burden within me that God's children would realize that different kinds of Bibles and different kinds of readings of the Bible are due to the differences in our person. Strictly speaking, there are not different Bibles. The same Bible is considered different because the people reading it are different. When a person is not proper, not eating and drinking God, the Bible in his hand becomes something improper. Instead of being a person who absorbs God, he is a person who studies doctrines.

Whenever we come to the Word, we must be strict to not research doctrines. Rather, we must eat and drink God; we must absorb Him. Some brothers and sisters may still not know the difference between researching doctrines and absorbing God. There are two ways to read the Bible. The first is the common, natural way of researching or studying. Everyone comes to the Bible with a heart to study it. But we can never fully understand the Bible even if we exhaust the mind of all the scholars. The Bible can never be exhausted in this way. We should not despise this little book. I have been reading this book almost every day for the past thirty-four years. I have spent much time studying it. Eventually, I had to confess that there is no way to fully know it. The more one studies this book, the more difficult it becomes, and the more confused he becomes.

For example, Matthew 1 is a huge obstacle to every student of the Bible. This chapter on the genealogy of Jesus is a high mountain, a big puzzle. Verse 1 says, "The book of the generation of Jesus Christ, the son of David, the son of Abraham." Who is David and who is Abraham? What do the names Jesus and Christ mean? Verse 2 says that Abraham begot Isaac, and Isaac begot Jacob, and Jacob begot Judah and his brothers. Who is Isaac? Who is Jacob? Who is Judah? And who are his brothers? In verse 3 Judah begot children of Tamar. Who is Tamar? Following this there are over forty names. The first seventeen verses of this chapter are impossible to study. Even after three months of studying, we will not be clear. On the contrary, we may end up with a headache, an ulcer, or we may lose our spiritual health. Many brothers and sisters are in this condition. The more they read, the hungrier they become. The more they study, the emptier and drier they are in their spirit. This is the result of merely studying the Bible.

Let us drop all these efforts. There is no need to exert much effort. I have suffered enough already; there is no need for you to suffer more. A "chicken" has been placed before us, but we insist on picking the "bones" and studying them even though they have no nutritional value. The more we study in this way, the hungrier we become. A chicken is for us to eat; it is not for us to study. A wise man will not study the mineral content of the bones; he will simply feast on the meat. He does not try to eat the whole chicken; he simply eats until he is full.

Although this may seem peculiar, many people read their Bible in this way and therefore do not derive any benefit. They study the "bone" of the word *Abraham* or the "beak" of the word *Tamar*. We need to let go of these things. We are here to eat the flesh of the "chicken," not the "bones." When reading the first seventeen verses of Matthew 1, we should let go of the many names. But when we read verse 21, which says, "She will bear a son, and you shall call His name Jesus, for it is He who will save His people from their sins," we may understand that we are God's people, so He must save us from our sins. We may then pray, "Lord, save me from my sins." After this the Holy Spirit may speak to us and point out our sins of hitting our children and scolding our wife for many years, and that our temper is too poor. Spontaneously we should confess these sins, saying, "Lord, my temper is too poor. I cannot overcome it. I have been in sin. But You are Jesus. You will save Your people from their sins. I am Your people. Surely You will save me from my sins." When we pray this way, we are eating the "meat." Following this, we may read:

"'They shall call His name Emmanuel' (which is translated, God with us)" (v. 23). Here is a bigger piece of "meat." We may pray, "Emmanuel! God with man! Lord, You are God with man! You are God, and I am man; You are with me. You are in me, and You are in my presence." These verses alone can fill us. During the day we will be praying that Jesus is saving His people from their sins and that God is with man. This kind of reading will make the Bible our food, supply, and nourishment. This kind of reading will bring the Bible into us as our life.

We are now clear that reading the Word is not for studying, in the same way that eating chicken is not the same as studying the chicken. Zoologists and biologists study the chicken. They spend all their lives studying, but still they may not understand everything about a chicken. We are not "zoologists" or "biologists" of the Word; we are not here to study but to eat. We do not read the Word in order to study it. Let the theologians study theology. Let the students of the Bible study the Bible. We are here to eat and drink God. We are the eaters, and we want to feast on the Word until we are filled.

In conclusion, God is Spirit for us to breathe Him in through prayer, and God is the Word for us to eat Him through reading the word. The more we pray, the more we breathe in His Spirit, and the more we read, the more we eat His word. The Spirit is God, and the Word is also God. When we breathe and eat enough of God, we will be filled and satisfied with God. This is what it means to enjoy God through praying and reading.

CHAPTER FOURTEEN

HOW TO ENJOY GOD BY MATCHING READING WITH PRAYING

Scripture Reading: Psa. 119:147-148; John 15:7; Dan. 9:2-4; 2 Cor. 3:6

READING AND PRAYING NEEDING TO BE COMBINED

This is the last chapter in the series concerning how to enjoy God. God has ordained two ways for man to enjoy Him. The first is through prayer, and the second is through reading the Bible. Praying and reading the Bible are as necessary as man's two feet. In the previous messages, we combined praying and reading the Bible. Strictly speaking, we are not combining them, because they naturally go together. When we walk, we exercise our left and right feet. Every person who enjoys and absorbs God knows from experience that prayer should accompany the reading of God's Word and that reading the Bible should accompany prayer. Praying without reading is the same as walking with one foot, and reading without praying is also the same as walking with one foot. In order to walk normally on the pathway of enjoying God, we cannot have one "foot" without the other. This means that whenever we absorb God, we need to match our prayer with reading, and our reading with prayer.

It is difficult to decide whether reading or praying should come first. This is the same as considering which foot should move first when we walk. When we walk, we are unconscious of which foot moves first. Similarly, it is not only difficult but also unnecessary to decide whether we should pray or read first when we enjoy God. It is foolishness to instruct someone to always use their right foot or their left foot whenever they walk. They simply need to walk. There is no need to explain to the brothers and sisters what to do first and what to do next when they absorb God. Sometimes it may be more convenient to pray first and then read. At other times it may be more convenient to read first and then pray.

The Bible does not give us a particular sequence. In Psalm 119:147-148, when the psalmist rose in the morning, he first cried out and then mused on the Lord's word. These verses say, "I anticipated the dawn and cried out; / I hoped in Your words. / My eyes anticipated the night watches, / That I might muse upon Your word." The psalmist prayed and then read the Word. In John 15:7 the Lord said, "If you abide in Me and My words abide in you, ask whatever you will, and it shall be done for you." Here the order is first the Lord's word and then asking. In other words, the order is first reading and then praying. Which sequence is correct? Both are correct. Sometimes we pray first and then read God's Word. At other times we read the Word and then pray. This shows that reading the Word and praying go together; they are parallel to each other.

The Lord Being Enjoyed
by Us in the Spirit and in the Word

The Scriptures and our experience confirm this. We enjoy God through prayer and reading the Word. In a previous chapter we saw that the Lord is the Spirit, the Lord is the Word, and the Word is the Spirit. If the Lord did not want us to enjoy Him, He would not need to be the Word and He would not need to be the Spirit; He would not need to be our food and our drink. He is the Word, and He became the Spirit so that we can contact Him, absorb Him, eat Him, drink Him, and enjoy Him. He has only one purpose for us—that we would receive Him as the Word and as the Spirit. The Word is for us to receive. The Spirit is also for us to receive. The Word is visible and outside of us, and the Spirit is touchable and inside of us. One is visible, and the other is invisible. One is outside of us, and the other is inside of us. If we have only the Spirit and not the Word, the light we receive will not be clear. If we have only the Word and not the Spirit, the light we receive may be clear, but it will not be deep. In order to be clear, deep, accurate, and inwardly shining, we need the Word and the Spirit. The Lord must be both the Spirit and the Word.

In the book of Exodus God's presence came through the pillar of cloud and the pillar of fire. The pillar of cloud typifies the Spirit, and the pillar of fire typifies the Bible. In the daytime the pillar of cloud led God's children. At night when it was difficult to see the pillar of cloud, the pillar of fire gave them light. Actually the pillar of fire at night was the pillar of cloud in the day. Without the pillar of fire, God's children would not have had light at night. In the same way, if we only have the Spirit without the Bible, our vision of God will be unclear at "night." We thank God that He has given us both the pillar of cloud and the pillar of fire. He has given us both the Spirit and the Scriptures. When we are inwardly in the light, it seems as if the Spirit as the pillar of cloud is sufficient, but when we are inwardly in darkness, we also need the Word. However, the Bible in itself is only letters. If we do not use our spirit, the Bible will not give us life. Having the Spirit without the Word may lead to error, and having the Bible without the Spirit may lead to death. In order to be accurate and living, we need to use our spirit to contact the Spirit and the Word.

The Lord has given us the Spirit and the Bible for our enjoyment. The Spirit within us and the Bible outside of us are indispensable. It is best to mingle reading with praying and praying with reading when we eat and drink the Lord. Shortly after we close our eyes to pray, we may open them to read the Lord's word, and after reading for a few minutes, we may want to close our eyes to pray. In this way, reading and praying are mingled to the extent that our reading is praying and our praying is reading. Within our reading is praying, and within our praying is reading. The two have become one, enabling us to touch, enjoy, and obtain God.

Examples of Enjoying God
through Mingling Reading with Praying

For example, when we spend time with the Lord, whether in the morning or at any other time, we should have two kinds of Bibles. We should have the Bible that is engraved on our heart and sealed by the Holy Spirit, and we should have a visible Bible that we hold in our hand. It is preferable for the visible Bible to be a pocket-size version so that we can take it with us and read it wherever we may be. In our reading we can mingle praying with reading; we can pray-read and read-pray the Bible. This kind of reading can be done at any time. It is not legal. However, according to our experience, morning is the best time.

Meditating to Turn the Word into Prayer

When we are ready to enjoy God through prayer, we should be calm, call our entire being back to our spirit, and touch the Lord. Spontaneously we may utter a prayer, saying, "Lord, as I read Your Word, open it to me." After praying we can then read. We may read Romans 8:1-2, which says, "There is now then no condemnation to those who are in Christ Jesus. For the law of the Spirit of life has freed me in Christ Jesus from the law of sin and of death." We should not read these verses quickly. These two verses are sufficient for us to muse on. We should not muse merely on the words themselves; rather, our musing should be based on these words. In other words, we muse through and by God's Word. We can muse on the Lord, His redemption, His indwelling, our union with Him, and His being life to us. We should read the verses again, not merely with our mind but by absorbing the riches in the Word with our spirit. We may say, "There is no more condemnation in Christ. How sweet it is to be in Christ! In Adam I was condemned and destined to die, but now I am in Christ. I am a person in Christ! In Christ there is no more condemnation. Therefore, in Christ there is no death!" After musing and meditating in this way, we will spontaneously be filled with thanksgiving and praising. We may say, "Lord, I praise You that I am in Christ. I am in You. Thank You! There is no condemnation in You." It is difficult to determine whether this is reading or praying. Within the praying there is reading, and within the reading there is praying. It is our prayer, but the words are from Romans 8:1. This is to pray-read and read-pray. The two are mingled as one. The best way to absorb, eat, and drink God is to mingle our prayer and our reading in this way.

If we merely read the Bible, it will remain in our mind and be dead letters to us; we will not touch, eat, or drink God. When we turn the words that we read into prayer, the letter of the Word is brought into the realm of the Spirit and becomes a spring of water in our spirit. Hence, we are inwardly nourished and watered. After praying and reading in this way, the Spirit comes to us with the Word. We are enlightened and become clear concerning many things. By having the Spirit and the Word in this way, we enjoy God in a rich, deep, clear, practical, and strong way. We eat and drink Him and are filled with His Spirit and His word.

After some time we may proceed to verse 2: "For the law of the Spirit of life has freed me in Christ Jesus from the law of sin and of death." We may speak to the Lord in the way of praying and reading, saying, "Lord, I know that the Spirit of life is within me. This Spirit of life is the Spirit. This Spirit is within me as my life. He enlivens and invigorates me. The Spirit is the Spirit of life within me. Thank You that there is a law, a spontaneous power, within the Spirit. This law is within me, causing me to overcome the law of sin and of death. Lord, my will can never deliver me from the law of sin and of death. But I thank You that You are within me as the Spirit of life. You are the law of life, the power of life, that spontaneously delivers me from the law of sin and of death." This can be compared to reading, but it is also praying. In this way we touch God. This way of reading the Word is nourishing; it is not dull or dry. Through this way of reading we touch God, and His word is brought into His Spirit. The words of the Bible are like fine flour, and the Spirit is the oil. This kind of reading mingles the fine flour with the oil and mingles the oil with the fine flour. As a result, we are nourished and watered. This is the most profitable way to read the Word.

Supplying Ourselves and Others

Some may think that we are the only ones supplied through such praying and reading, but this is not true. As we read Romans 8:1 in this way, the Spirit may give us a feeling to pray for others. We may say, "Many brothers and sisters have not seen this grace of having no condemnation in Christ. Lord, show them as You have shown me." In this prayer we are petitioning, interceding for ourselves and for the other brothers and sisters.

After praying in this way, we may have a feeling to speak with the brothers and sisters concerning Romans 8:1. When we receive this burden, we should respond by asking the Lord if the feeling to speak with the brothers and sisters is of Him and if He wants us to speak in the meeting. The anointing may move within us, causing us to sense that it is the Lord's desire. If we have a hesitation, we may express our lack of boldness to the Lord in prayer. Our hesitation may cause us to be inwardly veiled and bound. We may sense that our hesitation has offended the Lord. We should immediately respond by saying, "Lord, if it is Your will that I speak, please strengthen and motivate me." We will then feel light within and begin to anticipate the evening meeting. Something within jumps at the thought of reading Romans 8:1.

This is not merely reading and not merely praying. After this we may intercede, receive burdens, guidance, light, and utterance. All day long we may repeat this verse, saying, "Hallelujah, there is no condemnation to those who are in Christ Jesus. When I am in Christ, who can condemn me? I am in Christ, and I can never go out. Hallelujah, I am in Christ. Hallelujah, I am not in Adam." We want to speak this to those who ride the bus with us. At work we may say to our colleagues, "Do you not know that I am now in Christ!" This verse supplies, nourishes, and waters us throughout the day. It is as if we are walking on the clouds or drunk with wine.

In the evening meeting a brother may be moved by the Spirit to select the hymn: "'No condemnation!' precious word!" (*Hymns,* #297). After the singing, another brother may offer a prayer concerning no longer being condemned. We may then stand up and ask the saints to read Romans 8:1. We may also testify concerning how the Lord has opened our eyes to see that those who are in Him are no longer condemned. As we speak, we are released and full of the presence of the Spirit. As a result, the meeting is enlivened. As soon as we sit down, a brother may ask that we again sing "'No condemnation!' precious word!" After singing, another brother may pray, "Lord, we thank and praise You. We are in You, and we are no longer under condemnation." Everyone is brought into the heavenlies. They feel that they are in the heavenly realm.

This example shows that not only are we filled and nourished, but we have afforded a way for the Spirit to supply other brothers and sisters. Many will be deeply impressed that there is no condemnation to those who are in Christ. In the next Lord's table meeting, many will offer thanksgiving and praise because there is no longer any condemnation to those who are in Christ. This is the kind of reading and praying that touches God, eats God, and drinks God. Eating and drinking in this way brings God into our being.

The Way to Enjoy God through Reading with Praying

Reading the Bible Sequentially

I believe these examples are clear. Those who are saved and love the Lord will not find it difficult to practice this. It is very simple. We can begin to practice this in the morning or before going to bed. Simply go to the Lord. There is no need to select a special portion. We should simply follow our regular reading schedule. Whether we are in Genesis, 1 Kings, Matthew, or Ephesians, every word of the Bible is God-breathed (2 Tim. 3:16). Every word is His expression and contains the Spirit of God and life. We simply need to change our way of reading from the former approach of studying with our mind to eating and absorbing with our spirit. The Bible is God's expression; it is His word. It is spirit, life, and food. We need to be clear that the Bible is not a book of teachings, commandments, or doctrines for us to study. Once we have a change of concept, half the work is done.

Emphasizing Digestion Rather Than Content

Some people propose that we should read the Bible once a year by reading three chapters in the Old Testament and one in the New Testament every day. We do not need to force ourselves to read four chapters every day. There is no need to bear the heavy burden of rushing through the Bible in this way. Today I am breaking all the chains that bind us. We simply need to find time every day to focus on eating and drinking God. We can do this once a day or two or more times a day. How do we eat? We eat by reading in the way of praying and by praying in the way of reading. There is no need to be confined to one verse or even one chapter. There is no set rule. This can be compared to eating. Sometimes we may eat one slice of bread. At other times we may eat three bowls of porridge. There is no legal requirement. There is no need to worry about how much food is in the pantry. We simply need to consider how much we can eat and digest that day. If our appetite is not good, we eat less. When our appetite is better, we eat more. We should apply this to reading the Word. The Bible is very rich. I have been reading it for thirty-four years. Sometimes when I read the Word, I can take in only five or six words. I once said that I would need a month to read through Psalm 133. Others thought that I was exaggerating. They wondered how I could spend a month to read three verses. I actually needed two months. I read it day after day. That psalm is very rich. We are not concerned with how many verses we read; we are concerned with how much we have digested. May all God's children learn this way of reading the Word—the way of eating and drinking God.

If we have the way, we can set aside other times to read through more chapters. This can be compared to quickly looking to see how much food is in the pantry. For example, we might read through all fifty chapters of Genesis in two hours. Although there is nothing wrong with this, it is different from eating a meal. This is browsing through the kitchen; it is not eating and drinking God. This is merely reading Bible stories. The most precious experience, however, is to set aside a definite time during the day to read with prayer and pray with reading, in other words, to pray-read and read-pray. Such reading does not need to take a lot of time. It is not necessarily healthy to read for a long period of time. Eating too much can lead to indigestion.

Stopping Frequently to Meditate

In this way of pray-reading one often wonders whether he is praying or reading. Our reading becomes our praying, and our praying becomes our reading. As we do this, we should also meditate; we need some "selahs." I have said that the selahs in the psalms can be compared to rest notes in musical notation. When we come to a selah, we should stop for a while; we should not hurry. It is not necessarily better to read many verses. We should stop and meditate. While we are meditating, we are turned to our inner being. Prior to this we were turned outward. But by pray-reading, read-praying, and meditating, we become an inward person. Previously we were wandering and unfocused, but through pray-reading and meditating, we become focused. Our mind no longer wanders, and our unstable soul becomes calm.

This matter has much to do with our spiritual benefit. Many of us have wandering minds. Our minds are always wandering. It is difficult for us to be calm and to pray. Hence, it is difficult for us to live in fellowship with God or to live before His presence. When we read the word by pray-reading and read-praying, we are saved from this condition. There is no need to pray too much or read too much. We simply need to read a little, pray a little, and meditate a little. However, we should not let our thoughts wander. We should meditate only on what we have read and prayed. Then our wandering mind will be rescued. We will no longer be inwardly confused, and our spirit will become strong. When we meditate in this way, there will be much prayer and intercession; we will receive burdens, guidance, and commissions from the Lord.

Interceding

This was the way Daniel read God's Word. He understood the word of Jehovah to the prophet Jeremiah concerning the seventy years of Israel's captivity. This produced a burden in him, and he turned the burden into prayer. His prayer was initiated by God's word. This corresponds to the Lord's word in John 15:7: "If you abide in Me and My words abide in you, ask whatever you will, and it shall be done for you." We do not initiate the asking; it is initiated by God's word. When the word that we read touches our inward being, it becomes a burden within us and directs us in our prayer. Such prayer is initiated by the Spirit, proceeds from God, and will be answered. In this prayer, two prayers are combined into one; God prays in our praying, and our prayer matches His prayer. Thus, we are joined to God. In this prayer our spirit and the Spirit pray together; the human and divine natures are combined. This is genuine prayer. Since this prayer is initiated by God, God will accomplish it. Since His words have entered into us, His desire becomes our desire. Since He is the motive and source of this prayer and He is flowing through us, we can ask whatever we will, and it will be done. Our asking is according to God's will because it is initiated by His Word.

Abraham was a man living in the presence of God. God visited him and fellowshipped with him, and he fellowshipped with God. When God was about to leave, Abraham walked with God for a distance to send Him off. While they were walking, God said, "Shall I hide from Abraham what I am about to do?" (Gen. 18:17). Abraham received this word. While he waited in God's presence, he received a burden and prayed. This prayer was initiated by God, not Abraham. His prayer expressed and magnified God. This was a sweet experience.

Praying with Reading
Issuing in Enjoying the Glory of God

This way of praying and reading is the mingling of God and man. This is glorious yet mysterious. The God of glory mingles Himself with us in our practical human living. He does this as the Spirit and the Word. The Spirit is in our spirit, and the Word is in our hand. The Spirit prays with our spirit and leads us to read and understand the Word. The Spirit within and the Word without correspond and mingle as one. The Word then enters into us and motivates us to pray. This prayer is the expression of the word. In this way, God works within us and is expressed through us. It seems as if man is working, but God is working. The issue of this reading, praying, and interceding is the enjoyment and digestion of God's riches. We receive God's will, His desire, and His eternal purpose, and we become a channel for His expression. Our intercession affords Him the way to accomplish His will on earth. It seems as if He is answering our prayer, but He is carrying out His will. The result is that man is blessed through the preaching of the gospel to save sinners, through the release of life to nourish the believers, and through the building up of the church. Such prayer makes us fruitful branches that glorify God. We enjoy God and are filled with Him. Hence, we express, magnify, and glorify Him. This is the issue of our eating and digesting God. God is mingled with us as one. He becomes our content, and we become His expression.

In this way God becomes everything we need. If we need patience, He is our patience. If we need light, He is our light. If we need power, He is our power. If we need humility, He is our humility. He is our magnanimity and circumspection. He is our power in the gospel and our eloquence. He is also wisdom for us to build up the church and love for us to shepherd His children.

He is our food. He is everything to us. In order to become our life, He is food to us as the Spirit and the Word. The Spirit is invisible and inside of us, and the Word is visible and outside of us. We exercise our spirit to touch God through praying and reading, reading and praying. We touch both the Word and the Spirit. The Word outside of us enters into us and is expressed through us. We pray, yet God prays. We live, yet God lives. This is what it means to eat, drink, and enjoy God. This is what it means to eat God as food and receive Him as our life. This is the mingling of God and man.

In such a living we have resurrection, the Spirit, the church, the Body of Christ, and coordination in service. The church is built, and we serve in the Body. We experience the authority of the kingdom and the throne of God. We have God's image and His glory; we have the New Jerusalem. God is mingled with man. He becomes man's content, and man becomes His expression. This is the issue of our reading and praying, praying and reading. This is the issue of our eating, drinking, absorbing, and enjoying God. May the Lord lead us into such a living through the riches of His glory.

CHAPTER FIFTEEN

RESTRICTING THE MIND AND EXERCISING THE SPIRIT IN READING THE BIBLE

Many brothers and sisters are surprised that we have held so many conferences this year. There was a conference in February, and this is our second conference in March. Some may wonder why we are speaking so much concerning enjoying God. This subject is indeed inexhaustible. In fact, the whole Bible is on this subject. In this conference, however, our emphasis will be on how to practice the enjoyment of God.

Although the saints in the church in Taipei are willing to eat, drink, and enjoy God, they feel challenged because they do not know how to eat, drink, and enjoy God. How does one read the Bible in a way that touches God? How does one pray in a way that breathes in God? Many brothers and sisters still do not know the key to these practices. For this reason, we will now concentrate on the practice of enjoying God. We will cover some crucial points related to our practice. In the following messages we will first consider the practice of enjoying God through reading the Bible and then the practice of enjoying God through prayer.

Concerning the practice of reading the Bible, we need to point out a few basic matters.

GOD BEING FOOD IN HIS RELATIONSHIP WITH MAN

When we realize that God's relationship with man is based on His being food to man, our reading of the Bible will be greatly affected. In order to enjoy God when reading the Bible, we need to understand that God's way is to satisfy man as food. In this way He can be fully mingled with man and be life and everything to man. This is a very basic matter.

We read the Bible in order to pursue God so that we can have a proper relationship with Him. Our reading of the Bible calibrates and adjusts our relationship with God. In His relationship with man, God is food to man. Hence, in our relationship with God, we should receive Him as food. We have said this many times. Strictly speaking, God does not want us to worship Him or to serve Him. He does not want us to do anything for Him. Worshipping Him, serving Him, or doing things for Him are secondary. His primary desire is to be food to us. He wants us to be filled with Him before we do anything for Him. He wants to be our food in order to fill us before we engage in any work. We must understand this point. Many people do not know how to read the Bible because they do not have a proper understanding of this basic concept.

A brother may say that he reads the Bible in order to know God's desire and walk according to His desire. Even though the brother's intention is good, and his words are worthy of praise, they reveal that according to his concept, God is looking for people who would please Him. This concept is a problem.

We must remember that God's way is to be food to man. He has no intention for man to do anything for Him. He gave us the Bible for us to enjoy Him as food. He does not want us to be under any regulations. May every child of God clearly see this matter so that he can boldly say, "I read the Bible in order to eat God. My need is to eat, eat, and eat. I am hungry, and I need to be fed. God is my food, and He is my satisfaction. He has made Himself available through His Word. When I read the Word, I am eating God." Whenever we read the Bible, we must have a simple and definite understanding that our purpose is to eat, drink, and enjoy God, because God is food.

THE BIBLE AS GOD'S EXPRESSION
BECOMING MAN'S FOOD

We also need to know that the Bible is God's very expression. The Bible is God's word, His word is His breath, and His breath is His expression. Hence, whenever we read the Bible, we need to have a clear understanding that it is God's expression. God is expressed in the Bible. When we touch this book, we should not touch merely doctrines or words; rather, we should touch God Himself. God is Spirit, and He is also the Word. When we pray, we are breathing in God, and when we read, we are eating and drinking God.

The prophet Jeremiah said that he found and ate God's words (Jer. 15:16). The Lord Jesus said that man shall not live on bread alone but on every word that proceeds out through the mouth of God (Matt. 4:4). Hence, eating God's words is not a new idea invented by us. It is a concept that can be found in the Bible.

If we read the Bible merely as doctrines and facts, we make it a book of letters. Since the Bible is the word of God, and the Lord said that His words are Spirit, if we contact the Bible with our spirit, it becomes spirit, and we eat it. The same Bible can be letter, or it can be spirit to us. Whether it is letter or spirit depends on how we read it. If we read it merely with our mind, it is letter, but if we contact it with our spirit, it is spirit.

The Bible clearly says that the letter kills, but the Spirit gives life (2 Cor. 3:6). We should never think that the Bible is always a profitable book. Many people have been harmed by the Bible. This statement seems very bold. Can the Bible truly harm someone? Strictly speaking, the Bible does not harm anyone; a person is harmed by his mind. When a person studies the Bible with his mind, the Bible immediately becomes the letter that kills. This is what harms a person. If we want to receive life, we must use our spirit because only the spirit gives life. We need to contact the Bible with our spirit. It is only in our spirit that the Bible becomes God's living word. It is only in our spirit that it is spirit and life.

I hope that the brothers and sisters clearly see this basic point. We must understand that the Bible is God's breath; it is His expression. Therefore, when we read this book, we are touching the expression of God. We should not study it as a book of doctrines. We are contacting God. May we all clearly see this point.

RESTRICTING OUR MIND AND EXERCISING OUR SPIRIT IN READING THE BIBLE

It may seem difficult to exercise our spirit and not our mind when reading the Bible. This may bother some of us. We may wonder how we can read something without exercising our mind. Nevertheless, we are saying that we should not exercise our mind in reading the Bible. Exercising our spirit and not our mind does not mean that we should absolutely forget about our mind. Rather, it means that we should touch this book with the deepest part of our being and not merely understand or ponder over it with our mind. Even though we use our eyes to read and our mind to memorize, these are not the main organs that we use. The main organ is our spirit; we read the Bible mainly with our spirit.

If we exercise only our eyes and our mind but not our spirit, the words of the Bible will not become spirit. They will not be initiated by the Spirit. The Bible then becomes a book of letters in our hand. It is something dead. This is the meaning of reading with our mind. However, if we touch the words of the Bible with our spirit, and not merely read it with our eyes, we will contact the Word with our spirit. Our reading, listening, and memorizing should merely cooperate with our spirit. The main thing is to exercise the spirit. Then the Bible will be spirit and life to us.

Here is an illustration. The Chinese sages say that if a man's heart is not in what he is doing, he can look but not see anything, listen but not hear anything, and eat but not taste anything. This is what happens when his heart is not in what he is doing. This means that we must look and listen with our whole heart. It is true that we need to exercise our eyes and our ears, but we will neither see nor hear without the exercise of our heart. In order to apprehend something, we need to exercise our heart as well as our eyes and ears. In the same way, when we read the Bible, it is possible for us to "look without seeing, listen without hearing, and eat without tasting." This, however, is not because our heart is absent; rather, it is the result of not exercising our spirit but casting it aside and studying merely with our mind. This is what it means to read the Bible without exercising the spirit. If we want to read the Bible, we must exercise our spirit. Our spirit must take the lead, and the activity of our mind must be restricted.

The mind is always a bothersome thing. It often wanders to different places and causes us to fantasize. When we are reading Genesis, our mind may wander to Revelation, and when we are reading Revelation, our mind may return to Genesis. It jumps faster than electricity. When we are not reading the Bible, our mind does not wander, but once we open the Bible, the imagination begins to operate and all kinds of thoughts come. Therefore, in reading the Bible, we must restrict our mind, that is, gird our thoughts and exercise our spirit. When reading, we must allow our spirit to take the lead and not be carried away by our thoughts. We must reject our thoughts when we read the Bible. Some may think that this is contradictory, but if we practice, we will realize that it is not contradictory. We can reject our thoughts while we are reading the Bible. We can stay away from our mind and use our spirit.

Many have the problem of reading the Bible with their mind. This is our problem when we study the Word. We think about God instead of eating and drinking Him. In a sense, we are thinking about bread instead of eating it; we even consider our imagining to be our eating. Some people think about the word instead of eating the word. They read the Bible and still feel empty in their spirit.

Some brothers and sisters may try to trap me by saying, "Brother Lee, didn't you say that we need to meditate? Why are you now saying that we should eat and not think?" If a brother exercises mainly his mind to read the Bible, his mind will wander from the New Testament to the Old Testament and from the Old Testament back to the New Testament. After reading he thinks that he has obtained something, but what he has received is in his mind, not in his spirit. He has obtained knowledge in his mind, but there is no supply or satisfaction in his spirit. This is the common problem. Either we do not read the Bible, or we fall into the trap of our mind when we read. Most of us do not remain continually in our spirit when we read the Bible.

EXAMPLES OF READING THE BIBLE

Some may understand this fellowship in theory, but they do not know how to practice it. They may not know how to restrict their mind and exercise their spirit, allowing it to take the lead when they read the Bible. A brother may be touched in his inner being and moved when he reads Romans 4:17, which says that God gives life to the dead and calls the things not being as being. Then he may immediately exercise his mind to understand this verse. He is pursuing the doctrine of this verse. Because he does not realize the weakness of the mind, he is unconsciously distracted even though he had a good beginning. Although his mind may have more ideas, his spirit is empty.

The proper way for a person to read the Bible is to guard his thoughts when touched by a verse. A person should not ask what it means to give life to the dead or to call the things not being as being. Rather, he should simply eat the Word and receive it into his spirit. He should immediately exercise his spirit to pray, saying, "Lord, You give life to the dead, and You call the things not being as being. I thank You that You are inside me and have become everything to me." When he prays in this way, he is contacting God with his spirit rather than considering doctrines with his mind. He might not understand much, but his spirit has eaten and enjoyed God because he has touched God. This is what it means to read the Bible with our spirit.

Whenever we read the Bible, we must guard ourselves against arguing over doctrines. We will not touch God if we study doctrines, because we are exercising our mind. If something touches our spirit, we must control our mind. It is true that when reading a verse we may be led to consider a second verse. However, this must be initiated by the Spirit; we should not initiate it. We must control our thoughts and not consider doctrine when we read the Word. Rather, we should exercise our spirit, and turn the word that has touched us into prayer so that we can breathe in God. While we are praying and breathing, the Spirit may point out our true condition. When reading Romans 4:17, the Spirit may point out that we are dead and that we are in a state of "not being." We should respond immediately and pray, "God, that is right! I am in a dead condition, a condition of 'not being'! But I praise and thank You because the deadness and the nothingness afford a basis for Your resurrection life to abound." In such a prayer we are not exercising our mind; rather, we are taking the Word as food and eating it with our spirit. In this way we will discover that God is the element within this food. We are contacting and enjoying God.

In another situation the Holy Spirit may point out that instead of being dead and nothing, we are alive and full of many things. We have not died and have not been brought to the point of nothingness. For this reason, God cannot work in us; He cannot manifest the power of resurrection within us. We may respond, "Lord, be merciful to me! I have not been brought to the point of death, to absolute desperation. I still have my natural strength. I am neither like Abraham nor like Sarah." We do not need to memorize these prayers. Such prayers will be given to us by the Spirit as we breathe in God.

This is different from merely studying doctrine. As a verse touches us, we should digest it with our spirit and turn it into prayer. When we pray in this way, and the Spirit speaks to us, we should again turn the words into prayer. In the end, we will be inwardly satisfied even though we may not understand much doctrine.

Brothers and sisters, this is a crucial point. If we do not practice this, we will not eat much God when we read the Bible; we will not receive much genuine supply in our spirit. We may be familiar with the Bible, knowing how one verse relates to another, but our spirit will be empty. We will not have received the supply. Hence, we must always guard against our mind when we read the Word to enjoy God. We must guard against studying doctrine. We must exercise to be limited by our spirit, and we must exercise our spirit to breathe in God by means of the Word. We should pray and digest the words of the Bible with our spirit.

If we read a portion that we do not understand, we should let it go. Even if we understand what we read, we should not consider it. Whether or not we understand a passage, we should not spend time to consider it; rather, we should restrict our mind. We should not dwell on our thoughts, nor should we try to understand too much. These are the activities of the mind. We must learn to be restricted by our spirit even when we understand what we are reading. We should exercise our spirit and turn the Word into prayer. In this way, we will enjoy God through the Word.

CHAPTER SIXTEEN

LEARNING TO BE SIMPLE TO PICK UP THE TRUE MEANING OF THE BIBLE

In this message we will consider the way to enjoy God through reading the Word. There are many ways to read the Bible. One can find hundreds of ways to study the Bible in Christianity, but I would like us to consider the best and most profitable way. We may call this the life-study way to read the Bible. This is the simplest and the most beneficial way to read the Bible.

READING THE BIBLE BEING SIMPLE

Our concept concerning reading the Bible needs to be simplified. We should not consider that it is difficult to read the Bible. Many people think that the Bible is a difficult book. They think that since the Bible is the canon of the Christian religion, they can never understand the Bible. This concept frustrates our ability to understand the Bible. However, we must consider that reading the Bible is as simple as eating. We all admit that eating is a simple matter. It is not easy to cook a meal, but it is very easy to eat the meal. This also applies to reading the Bible. God does not want us to write the Bible; He wants us to read the Bible. We do not need to invent anything or to investigate. Strictly speaking, when we come to the Bible, we come to the presence of God to be fed by God. Hence, we must first consider that reading the Bible is a simple matter.

This consideration, however, does not mean that we do not need to read the Bible. No one can say that because eating is easy, he does not need to eat. Instead, this consideration should encourage everyone to eat.

Saying that it is simple to read the Bible does not mean that it is easy to understand it. Even if I read the Bible for another six thousand years, I will not fully understand it. No one can fully comprehend the Bible. The more one reads it, the more he feels he does not understand it. Thirty years ago I thought that I understood one book of the Bible, but today I can say that I do not truly understand any book of the Bible. The Bible is very rich, and no one can fully understand it. Although it is simple to read the Bible, it is difficult to fully understand the Bible; nevertheless, it is very easy to receive food from the Bible. No matter which chapter and which verse we read, we can find rich food and be filled because the Bible is full of nutrition.

My burden is first to help us accept that reading the Bible is a simple matter. We thank God that the Bible has been written and is in our hands. It is very easy for us to obtain food from the Bible. We do not even need much education to be fed with the Bible. We can be fed even if we do not recognize one hundred percent of the words in the Bible. Reading the Bible is a simple matter.

NOT SETTING THE MIND ON STUDYING THE TRUTH

When we come to the Bible in a simple way, we should never set our mind on finding doctrines in the Bible. We should not focus on studying the Bible. When we eat, we do not set our mind to study our food. When we come to eat, it is best not to know anything. If we come with a heart to study, we will get ourselves into trouble. If we set our mind to study how the various dishes on a table were prepared and how they should taste, the food will be cold before we have finished. Others at the table will be satisfied, but our stomach will be empty. Our studying the food frustrates our eating. In the same way, when we come to the Bible, we should not come with a heart to study doctrine or to investigate some truth. If we have such a mind, we will be unable to enjoy God; we will not find food in His Word.

DROPPING OUR CONCEPTS

When we come to the Bible, we also need to drop our

concepts. We must never wear glasses that are colored by our concepts. We all have a pair of colored glasses within us that prevents us from knowing the true color and meaning of the Bible. If we wear green glasses and look at a white book, the book will appear to be green, and we will not see the true color of the book. It is difficult to find a person who does not come to the Bible with colored glasses. Those from Zheqiang wear Zheqiang glasses. Those from Shantung wear Shantung glasses. Those from England wear British glasses, and those from America wear American glasses. The type of person we are determines the kind of Bible we have, because the type of person we are determines the type of glasses we wear, and the color of our glasses determines the color of our Bible. A student of science comes to the Bible with a pair of "scientific" glasses and has a Bible of science. A student of Confucius wears "Confucian" glasses and has a Bible of Confucian teachings. A literature student wears "literary" glasses and has a Bible of literature. The type of person we are determines the type of glasses we have, and our glasses determine the type of Bible we read. Therefore, in coming to the Bible, we need to remove the glasses of our concepts before we can see the true color and meaning of the Scriptures.

After listening to the testimonies of some of the brothers concerning their reading of the Word, I realize that it is difficult to find one person who does not read the Bible with colored glasses. A person reading Matthew 11 might be touched only by the Lord's word about being meek and lowly in heart. Please do not misunderstand me. This does not mean that being meek and lowly in heart is something bad. Being meek and lowly in heart is something very good; the Lord Himself spoke this word. But all men who have some idea of ethics and morality, both from the East and from the West, focus on the words *meek* and *lowly* when they come to Matthew 11. They may actually be wearing glasses of meekness and lowliness before they read Matthew 11. There is no need for them to read Matthew 11, since they already value the concept of meekness and lowliness. Brothers and sisters, we must drop our concepts when we come to the Bible. We must take off our inner glasses; we must break them before we can see the true color and meaning of the Bible. If we bring in our concept, we will lose sight of the true meaning of the Bible.

Here is another example. Ten years ago a young brother was offended by an elder. Daily he was bothered by the thought that an elder, who should be compassionate toward others, could offend a person in such a way. This thought took root in him so that when he came to the Bible, he subconsciously looked for passages that spoke of elders being compassionate to others and of older ones being sensitive to younger ones. Although he was not looking for such passages intentionally, this concept was hidden in him. For many days his reading of the Bible was influenced by this concept. He spent much time reading the Bible but did not receive anything. Then one day he read 1 Peter 5:3, which speaks of elders not lording it over the flock but being patterns. His eyes lit up and he said, "This is so good! I have seen a great light! I did not realize that the Bible is so clear about elders not lording it over others." Dear brothers and sisters, did he really see light? If that was light, then he did not receive it from the Bible; he had this "light" before he came to the Bible. This is what it means to read the Bible with the glasses of our concepts. The result of such reading is but a projection of one's own concepts.

Here is another true story. Over ten years ago I stayed in the home of a Christian couple. One morning at breakfast we began to speak about our experience of reading the Word and praying. The husband said that he read Ephesians 5 that morning and found the good teaching of wives submitting to their husbands. The wife said that she too had read Ephesians 5 that morning and had found an even higher teaching than the one her husband had found. She found that husbands should love their wives just as Christ loves the church. The husband found that the wife should submit to the husband, and the wife found that the husband should love the wife. This shows that the way we read the Word is a reflection of our person. From our conversation it became clear that the husband felt that his wife was assuming too much headship, was not keeping her place, and needed to submit to him as her husband. At the same time, the wife felt that her husband was not sensitive enough to her and did not love her enough.

If they had not both read Ephesians 5 that morning, I would not have known them that well. Outwardly speaking, the two seemed like a very good couple, but through that conversation, I fully understood what was transpiring within them. Their reading of the Word fully exposed them.

The kind of Bible we have reflects the type of person we are. We cannot hide. If we do not want our reading to be a reflection of what we are, and if we want to have the original meaning of the Bible, we need to remove our glasses. A man from Zheqiang must remove his Zheqiang glasses, and a man from Shantung must remove his Shantung glasses. A slow person must set aside his slow concept, and a quick person must set aside his quick concept.

When I was young, I knew an old man who was a very slow person. He spoke about not being hasty in doing anything with God, because nothing hasty, quick, or hurried is from God. He said that the Bible does not give us one instance of God running, because He is a God who is never in haste, who is never quick. With God everything is slow. Since I thought this was very reasonable, I did everything slowly for a few days under the influence of this teaching. However, after a few years I heard another servant of God say that God ran at least once in the Bible. He said that in Luke 15 the father, who depicts God, ran to the prodigal son and kissed him. He showed everyone that God ran at least once. We may think that these are silly stories, but they show that the kind of person we are determines the kind of Bible we read. The Bible of a slow person confirms his slowness, and the Bible of a quick person confirms his quickness. The teachings obtained from the Bible are a reflection of the person who is reading it.

I knew a quick-tempered man whose voice was like thunder and whose face became red whenever he spoke. One day he said that in the Bible when God appears, smoke goes up from His nostrils, and His voice is like thunder (Psa. 18:8, 13). When I heard this, I knew that I was speaking to a quick-tempered man with a voice like thunder. We may think that this is funny. A mild person has a "mild" Bible, an angry person, an "angry" Bible, a rough person, a "rough" Bible, and a fine person, a "fine" Bible. There is no exception to this. Let me repeat, the kind of Bible we have reflects the kind of person we are. Consequently, it is difficult to find a person who knows the true meaning of the Bible. A person is a good reader of the Bible if he can read it according to its original taste and color.

We must consider reading the Bible to be a simple matter, and we must drop the thought of studying. Such a thought will only frustrate our reading of the Word. We also must not trust in our concepts; rather, we should drop them and throw away all our glasses.

NOT LOOKING FOR INSPIRATION

When we come to the Bible, we also should not look for inspiration. We should not try to find or create some kind of inspiration. We do not need to seek inspiration from the Holy Spirit. Inspiration from the Holy Spirit is like radio waves in the air; as long as we adjust to the right frequency in our spirit, the radio signals will come. When we purposely look for something, we oftentimes find something false. When many brothers and sisters read the Bible, they create their own inspiration. This is unnecessary. The Spirit who has been sent forth to all the earth is omnipresent and all-pervading. As long as the frequency in our spirit is right and the condition of our spirit is proper, we do not need to look for or think about inspiration when we come to the Bible; inspiration surely will come.

I hope that God's children can grasp these four points. We should realize that reading the Bible is a simple matter, we should not come with a heart to study, we should drop our concepts, and we should not look for our own inspiration. May we all practice these four points.

PRACTICAL EXAMPLES

Let us now consider our practice. When we come to read the Word, we must turn our being from outward things. This is commonly known as quieting ourselves, being calm. As soon as we are calm, our whole being can be turned to the spirit. At this point we must ignore our concepts. Instead of having the intention of investigating something in the Word, we should have a seeking heart to contact God Himself, to eat Him, drink Him, and enjoy Him through our reading. Rather than reading random portions of the Bible, we should simply follow a regular schedule and continue reading from where we stopped the day before. As we read the Bible, we should not entertain different thoughts or try to study or investigate a topic, in order for the words of the Bible to spontaneously touch our inner being.

Suppose we are reading Matthew 11. In this chapter John the Baptist, the Lord's first faithful witness, was in prison. After hearing about the miracles that the Lord performed in healing the sick, casting out demons, and even resurrecting the dead, John wondered how people who had done nothing for the Lord could receive such miracles, but he received no deliverance. Hence, he sent men to question the Lord, asking if He was indeed the coming Christ. In other words, if the Lord was the Christ, He should deliver John from prison, and if He was not, John should wait for someone else. This word was meant to provoke the Lord Jesus. The Lord replied saying, "Blessed is he who is not stumbled because of Me" (v. 6). If our inner being is touched with the Lord's response, we may say to the Lord, "Even though I have served You faithfully, and You do not seem to care for me in my sufferings and are doing many things for others who seem to have nothing to do with You, I am not stumbled by You. On the contrary, I am blessed." Such a response does not come from our concepts; it is not imagined, and it does not come from study. Rather, the Holy Spirit has touched us and inspired us as we were reading the Word in a simple way. This is the way to eat the Word.

LEARNING TO BE SIMPLE IN ENJOYING GOD THROUGH READING THE WORD

For this reason, when we read the Word, we must learn to be simple; when we eat, we are simple. We do not need to have any concepts, we do not need to have the intention of learning something, and we do not need to seek for inspiration. We simply need to read. As we read, the Holy Spirit will frequently touch our inner being with the Word. The intention to study will be a frustration to our reading. Any concepts will veil the true picture of the Bible. The thought of receiving inspiration will often produce false inspiration. We must drop these things. When we come to the word, we must be very simple, having the attitude of not wanting anything and not knowing anything. All we want is to contact God in His Word. Then according to the condition in our spirit, the Spirit will use the words of the Bible to touch our inner being in an appropriate way, and we will receive something from the Bible. When we receive, we must still restrict our mind from thinking too much. We must exercise our spirit to turn the words that touch us into prayer. Then our reading will reach a higher plane, and we will always be richly fed when we read the Word.

We may wonder how a reading that does not pay attention to spiritual inspiration can help us understand the Bible. However, those with the best understanding of the Bible read in this way. If we would daily read with the sole intention of eating the Word and being nourished by God's riches, after some time we will see that the Bible is an open book to us. While the light of the Bible will shine brightly before us, we will also feel that no one can fully understand this book. It is inexhaustible. No matter how we approach it, it always yields fresh riches and brings new nourishment.

I hope that all the brothers and sisters will take this word to be simple by considering that the reading of the Word is a simple matter. We should not try to study. We should drop our concepts, and we should not seek for any inspiration. This is what it means to be simple. If we can be this simple, our reading of the Bible will be profitable. Then when a word touches us, we must restrict our thoughts and exercise our spirit to digest the word. It is better not to have many thoughts. We must remain in the Spirit's inspiration and receive the words that touch us. Spontaneously, we will exercise our spirit to turn what touches us into prayer. In this way our reading will be an absorption of His nourishment and an enjoyment and satisfaction. As we eat God's Word and absorb God, we will enter into the experience of enjoying God through reading His Word.

CHAPTER SEVENTEEN

PRACTICING DROPPING OUR CONCEPTS TO PICK UP THE CENTRAL THOUGHT OF THE BIBLE

We need to point out more crucial points concerning our reading of the Bible.

In the previous message we saw that when a person comes to the Word, he must drop his concepts. He should not read the Lord's Word with his own ideas, nor should he seek to learn some teachings from the Bible. He does not even need to expend any effort to gain inspiration. Many times we ourselves are the problem and the obstacle in the study of the Word. Either we do not come to the Word, or we come with our own baggage. We come to the Word with our concepts or our expectations. At times we even come to the Word with our striving and effort.

OUR CONCEPTS HINDERING US FROM OBTAINING THE TRUE MEANING OF THE BIBLE

We all know what it is to have a concept. Everyone has views and a unique disposition. A person's disposition is seen in his constitution, and his constitution is expressed in his concepts. It is very difficult for a person to drop his concepts when he comes to the Word. It is difficult to find a person who comes to the Word without his own concepts. These concepts can be compared to colored glasses that frustrate us from seeing the original color and light in the Bible.

Reading the Word is wonderful. However, while those who are nonchalant, having no concepts, do not receive anything from the Word, those who are full of concepts do not receive the true meaning of the Word either. Some may think that it is not possible to come to the Word without any concepts, but this principle applies to many spiritual things. It is wrong to be full of natural concepts, and it is wrong to be indifferent and nonchalant. Those who receive something from God's Word are not indifferent. The condition of not being indifferent, however, is arrived at through a process of God's breaking. A student of the Word should not be void of all concepts, but his concepts must be dealt with and broken by the Lord. Being void of all concepts is not a condition for reading the Bible, but a person must be able to set aside his own concepts before he can read the Bible. He can be full of endeavors, thoughts, and concepts, but every time he comes to the Bible, he must set his concepts aside and drop them. May we all remember to set aside our concepts when we come to God's Word. Then we will find the true meaning of the Bible in our reading.

OUR CONCEPTS HINDERING US FROM RECEIVING THE CENTRAL THOUGHT OF THE BIBLE

Unless a person sets aside his concepts, he cannot receive the central thought revealed in the Bible. Since many of God's children are trapped by their concepts, they do not know the central and crucial things in the Bible even though they have read it for many years. They always come to the Bible with their concepts. These concepts are a veil and limitation, blocking and limiting them from seeing the central and crucial matters in the Word. Hence, they receive only superficial and irrelevant points. When they testify about reading the Bible, they speak of superficial matters. They seldom speak of crucial matters. This does not mean that the Bible does not contain crucial matters, but there is no response or reaction in them when they read the crucial matters.

This can be compared to writing on oily paper. Oily paper cannot absorb the ink. However, if one writes on tissue paper, the ink is immediately absorbed because tissue paper is ink-absorbent. The ink that is not absorbed by oily paper is easily absorbed by tissue paper. This can be compared to our reading of the Bible. We are like tissue paper in relation to some things in the Bible; we absorb them as soon as they come to our attention. We are like oily paper, however, in relation to other crucial and central matters; we repel them and turn away from them whenever we read them. We may say that we have no feeling for them. We are not touched, and the Word does not affect us.

In the previous chapter, the young man who was offended by the elders had the concept that elders should not offend young believers. This concept affected and biased his inward being so that the only portion of the Word that he responded to was 1 Peter 5. Like a piece of tissue paper that absorbs ink, he immediately absorbed the word that elders should not lord it over the flock of God but should be a pattern to the flock. However, like a piece of oily paper, there was no response within him to other crucial passages in the Bible. He would say that those portions did not touch him. However, the words did in fact touch him, but there simply was no response within him.

Whenever God's Word touches us, there should be a corresponding condition in our being that matches His touching. If our condition does not match the Word, it will not affect us, but if our inward condition matches the Word, it will affect us. If a husband expects his wife to always submit to him, he will respond to passages on wives submitting to their husbands. Likewise, if a man pursues humility, considering it to be the most necessary virtue, he will respond only to teachings on humility in his reading. As soon as he reads something about humility, there will be a response within him. He will be touched by those words. Most people who seem to dig things out of the Bible are not actually digging. The items they find were within them before they read the Bible. The Bible merely confirms what was within them. A person may be so burdened for humility that it fills his being and occupies all his thoughts. He will define a perfect man as a person who acts in humility and will define a Christian who is up to the standard as one who attains absolute humility. Since his being is focused on humility, he is impressed only with humility when he reads the Bible. Only the portions on humility are marked in his Bible, and he memorizes only the verses on humility. In his view, the Bible is a book about humility.

Strictly speaking, however, he is not responding to the word on humility that is in the Bible; rather, the word on humility in the Bible is a confirmation of his concept of humility. He finds an echo in the Bible, and he responds strongly to it.

There are many stories like this. A person may be predisposed to self-denial and constantly speak about sacrificing oneself to care for others. Since he is filled with this concept, it is not easy for him to receive any light or to be touched by any other portion in the Bible. When he reads teachings on denying the self, bearing the cross, and following the Lord, he is immediately struck with these words. Only the words *denying the self* are underlined in his Bible. His inward being is filled with the matter of denying the self, and this is the only portion he finds in his Bible. It is difficult to determine whether his self-denial originates from the Bible or from him. Nevertheless, he seems to respond to the word in the Bible.

I must repeat that the kind of person we are determines the kind of Bible we read. A humble person has a Bible on humility. A self-denying person has a Bible on self-denial. In order to read the Bible, we need to be broken. We need to receive God's breaking in order to hear what God is saying. God's ways are higher than our ways, and His thoughts higher than ours. We may think that humility is good, but there are things that are better than humility. Nevertheless, many people have never found these things in their reading.

This is a very heavy burden within me. I wish I could open my heart wide to you and speak a word from the depth of my being. I feel that my words have not penetrated into your inner being. I want to shout this point: Do you realize that the Bible you are reading does not convey the divine inspiration of God to you? The Bible you have in your hand is the same book that I have in my hand. However, when you read it, you do not receive its divine inspiration. You are reading a book that only reflects your own concepts. Even though our Bibles are exactly the same, we receive different impressions when we read them. When the Bible in our hand is framed by our concepts, it becomes a different book. We should ask ourselves how many times we have read the Bible without using the glasses of our concepts. When will we be free from our concepts?

Everyday you read your own "Bible." From the beginning of the year to the end of the year you read the divinely inspired Bible which is veiled by your concepts. You are reading the Bible according to your concepts. You are not reading a Bible that is not colored by your concepts. When you come to the Bible, you are full of concepts; you are wearing colored glasses. As a result, God's Word changes when it passes through the filter of your concepts. It is no longer in its original form. You are not reading the Bible according to God's original inspiration. You are reading a Bible that is tainted with your concepts and views. You are reading a Bible that is a reflection of yourself.

NEEDING TO GIVE UP OUR CONCEPTS
WHEN WE READ THE WORD

When I come to the Bible, I have learned to ask myself whether I am coming with my concepts or whether I am setting them aside. This is a very severe question. I pray, "Lord, I want to read Your word in an uncluttered way and receive the true meaning in Your Word. I want to receive the unadulterated Word without my concepts as a veil and a covering. I do not want to subject Your word to my views or my concepts. I want to place myself under Your Word and set aside my concepts and views."

Brothers and sisters, this is a difficult lesson to learn. It is easy to read the Word, but it is difficult to drop our concepts. Let me repeat: it is difficult to find a child of God who receives the Bible as the pure, unadulterated Word of God. Every child of God has a Bible that is somewhat altered by his concepts and views. Hence, when he comes to the Word, he is covering and limiting the Bible. He brings his feelings, concepts, opinions, and views into his reading. As a result, the Bible is changed, and its true meaning is missed. Even though he can still find superficial things, he has no way to find the basic and central items of the Bible.

THE CENTER OF THE BIBLE BEING
GOD BECOMING MAN'S LIFE IN THE SON

What is the basic and central thought in the Bible? The

basic and central thought in the Bible is God becoming life to man in the Son. This means that God has come to us as our food. God becomes life to us in the form of food. The entire Bible, from Genesis to Revelation, has only one center. There may be many other items in the Bible, but the basic, foundational, and central thought is that God desires to be life to man. God becomes life to man in the person of the Son through the indwelling of the Holy Spirit. He enters into man and is received by man through eating. In this way He is digested by man and fully mingled with man. This is the very center of the entire Bible.

Whenever we come to the Word, we must lay hold of this principle. We come to the Bible because God wants to be life to us in His Son. He wants to become our food in the Son and feed us until we are full. God wants us to receive Him through the Bible and digest Him. Therefore, whenever we read the Word, we must drop all our concepts and grasp this one unique concept, asking the Lord to control our entire being with this unique concept. If we come to the Word for any other reason, our attitude is incorrect. We should have only one consideration: we come to the Word because God is food to us through the Bible. God is life to us in His Son, and He is received and eaten by us through the words of the Bible. If we read the Bible with this unique concept, we will have the proper concept and we will find the crucial items in the Bible.

EXAMPLES OF MAN'S CONCEPTS VEILING GOD'S WORD

A brother may be touched by Psalm 51:4: "Against You and You alone have I sinned." He may realize that sin is not only before men but also before God; his sins offend men and God. Although we cannot deny that the Holy Spirit is speaking to him through that verse, he has only touched something on the surface; he has not touched a central item. We can say that he has tasted the feathers or the skin of a chicken. He has not tasted the meat. He has tasted something, but he is not satisfied. He has merely touched the skin of Psalm 51. He has not touched the spirit of the psalm, because he has not dropped his concepts. Before reading Psalm 51, he may have had a concept about living before God rather than before men and about being spiritual before God rather than before men. Since he had this preconceived concept, he was not impressed with the first three verses. Instead, he responded only to verse 4. Thinking that this word has touched and inspired him, he prays, "Yes, Lord, I have been living before men for too long. I am concerned only about others' knowing of my sins. If others do not know, I am satisfied." This response is produced in him because he has read only the words that match his concept. The crucial words in Psalm 51, however, do not affect him; he feels no response toward those words, thinking that they lack the inspiration of the Holy Spirit. Dear brothers and sisters, although reading the Word is a simple matter, our person poses a real challenge.

Another brother may read Psalm 57 and be touched by the first verse: "Be gracious to me, O God, be gracious to me; / For my soul takes refuge in You; / Indeed in the shadow of Your wings I will take refuge." Although these words are in the Bible, trusting God, taking refuge in Him, and trusting in His Word are common expressions among Christians. Every Christian uses these expressions. Even before a person becomes a Christian, he can use these expressions. These are natural concepts, and they are not part of the central and crucial things in the Bible.

According to the same principle, it is easy to pick up matters such as loving one another in the Gospel of John, because this thought is in us even before we come to the Word. Hence, when we read such passages, there is an echo and a response within us. However, we miss the other precious words in the Gospel of John, such as, "In Him was life, and the life was the light of men" (1:4); "I am the light of the world; he who follows Me shall by no means walk in darkness, but shall have the light of life" (8:12); and "in that day you will know that I am in My Father, and you in Me, and I in you" (14:20). It is difficult to find one Christian who responds to these words, but we are easily touched by the portion concerning the Lord's new commandment to love one another even as He loved us. Immediately there is an echo within us because this concept is already within us.

I hope this word will render some help. We must not only

read the Word with our spirit in a calm way, but we must also learn to set our concepts aside. We must place ourselves before the Lord like a piece of blank paper and pray: "Lord, speak to me and write on me through the words of the Scriptures. I do not want to have any concepts of my own. I do not want to have any views of my own."

Preconceived concepts within man are a strong veil, preventing him from seeing the true meaning and color of the Bible. About fifteen years ago a very intelligent sister spoke with me about head covering. To her understanding head covering was an ancient custom from the Mediterranean area; hence, the apostle wrote the passage in 1 Corinthians to tell the believers not to go against the local customs. I opened the Bible to 1 Corinthians 11:3-6 and began to read to her: "I want you to know that Christ is the head of every man, and the man is the head of the woman, and God is the head of Christ. Every man praying or prophesying with his head covered disgraces his head. But every woman praying or prophesying with her head uncovered disgraces her head...For if a woman is not covered, let her hair also be cut off." After reading, I asked her how she could think that head covering pertained to customs since the passage begins with great things like Christ being the head of every man and God being the head of Christ. She responded that even though the passage speaks of Christ being the head and God being the head, to her observation head covering was still a matter of custom. When I heard this, I closed my Bible and said to her, "You have continually used the words *to my observation*. If you continue in this way, there is no need to go to the Bible. You should wait until you finish your observations before reading the Bible." She did not understand what I meant, so she asked how long she should wait. I answered, "Perhaps fifty years. But I am afraid that you will not finish your observations before you die. Perhaps you will understand this passage only when you enter into glory. At any rate, by that time you will no longer be saying, 'To my observation,' but you will not find the true meaning of the Bible until then."

This story shows that it is difficult to find a child of God who comes to the Bible without relying on his personal observation. It is difficult to find a child of God who is free from his personal views. For this reason it is difficult to discover the great things spoken of in the Bible. About twenty years ago, as I read 1 Corinthians 11, I noted the repeated references to the word *head*. Christ is the head of every man, God is the head of Christ, and man is the head of the woman. This is the reason there is head covering. Immediately, I knelt down and worshipped God, saying, "You are the Head in this universe. Besides You, Your Son is the Head. I thank and praise You because You have also ordained man to represent You as the head. I want to cover my head before You as the Head." From that day on, I knew authority, and I began to understand submission to authority.

ASKING GOD FOR NEW THINGS

If we drop our concepts and come to the Bible for its original meaning and color, we will see the central and crucial things. But if we come full of our concepts, we will only find what is already in our concept. The Bible may be full of weighty words, but they will not touch us, because there will not be an echo or a response within us.

For this reason we must learn not to quickly accept our feelings when we come to the Word. We must test whether these feelings were already within us or whether they are revelation from the Bible. Is it something from us or something given to us by God? If it is something that is already within us, we will lose nothing by rejecting this so-called inspiration. There is no need to even pray about it. We can simply let it go and continue with our reading. If we do this, God will give us something new, deep, weighty, and great. He will give us something that belongs to the trunk, the center. These will be the eternal, precious things that are according to God's view. Only these things can feed us and fill us. May we learn the lesson of dropping what we already have when we come to the Word and ask Him for new things.

CHAPTER EIGHTEEN

IDENTIFYING THE CENTRAL AND PERIPHERAL MATTERS IN THE BIBLE

Many brothers and sisters may still not be clear concerning studying the Bible in the way of life. In this message we will consider again the matter of enjoying God through reading the Word. First, I will mention a few crucial points and then give some examples to illustrate these points.

THE BIBLE HAVING CENTRAL AS WELL AS PERIPHERAL MATTERS

In the Bible there are central matters and there are peripheral matters. In other words, some things in the Bible can be compared to the roots of a tree and others to the leaves. A tree has roots and a trunk, but it also has branches and leaves. There is a basic difference between the roots and the trunk, and the branches and the leaves. We can also use the example of a cooked chicken, which has meat as well as skin. If the feathers are not thoroughly plucked before cooking, there may even be feathers. The central matter of a cooked chicken is the meat, and the peripheral matters are the skin and feathers. Similarly, there are central matters in the Bible as well as peripheral matters. May we all bear this distinction in mind.

THE CENTRAL MATTER IN THE BIBLE— GOD IN THE SON COMING TO BE LIFE TO MAN

What is the central matter, the root and trunk, of the Bible, and what are the peripheral matters, the branches and the leaves? In the previous chapter we pointed out that the central matter, the root and foundation, of the Bible is God in the Son coming to be life to man. This simple word speaks of the very essence of the Bible. The subject of the Bible is God becoming life to man in the person of His Son. God is embodied in His Son, and He has given His Son to man. As soon as man receives God's Son, the Holy Spirit enters into man to become life to man. God becomes life to man by becoming man's food. When man receives Him as food and digests Him, He becomes every element within man. By living according to this life and by this life, man lives before God. This is the root, the foundation and central matter, of the Bible.

At the beginning of the Bible, in Genesis 1, man was placed before the tree of life. At the end of the Bible, in Revelation, the tree of life is still before man. All properly trained students of the Bible would agree that the tree of life symbolizes God revealing and presenting Himself to man as life in the form of food so that man would eat Him, thus enabling Him to become life to man. The accomplishment of this goal is recorded between Genesis 3 and Revelation 20. God has now entered into man and become life to man. God entered into man in His Son and through the Holy Spirit. He is now being digested by man to become man's satisfaction and life so that man can live by Him. Although the Bible says many things, the center of its revelation is this subject. This, however, is only a brief sketch. Many items are attached to this central subject, but we will not consider these items now.

FOUR PERIPHERAL MATTERS IN THE BIBLE

The peripheral matters, the skin and feathers, in the Bible can be grouped into four categories.

The First Category—Consolation in Sufferings

The first category is related to sufferings, consolation in trials, and deliverance from difficulties. We can find many things in this category in the Bible. Although God's central thought and goal are to work Himself into man to be man's life, from man's perspective there are many things that he must face. The first is suffering. Human life is always accompanied by sufferings. For example, I can preach the gospel to a friend and exhort him, saying, "You should believe in the

Lord Jesus. He wants to save you and enter into you to be your life." My friend, however, may respond, "My wife has had tuberculosis for three years. Can you come and pray for her? If she is healed as a result of your prayer, I will believe in Jesus." Whereas God is trying to work His Son into my friend to be his life, my friend does not understand or even care for this. Instead, he cares for his wife's deliverance from tuberculosis. God wants to enter into him to be his life, but he wants his wife to be healed. There is a conflict of interests. In such a situation God may sympathize and give in a little, causing me to respond, saying, "Has your wife had tuberculosis for three years? God is a sympathetic God. His name is also Jehovah Ropheka, Jehovah who heals (Exo. 15:26). He can heal. As long as you and your wife pray to Him, she can be healed." This word may comfort my friend, and he may return to his wife, saying, "I spoke with a preacher today. Even though I did not understand or care for what he said, he did say that there is a true and living God who can heal you. If we pray, your sickness may be healed. Why don't we try?" The two of them may pray for healing, but as they are praying, they are also providing an opening to the Lord and affording the Holy Spirit an opportunity to enter into them and work on them. The Holy Spirit may convict them of their sins and lead them to confess their sins. They may call on the Lord Jesus without much understanding and confess Him as their Savior. They might not be clear concerning who the Lord Jesus is, but by calling on Him, they can still be saved by God's mercy. On the one hand, the wife is healed, but on the other hand, God has entered into them.

Even if the wife is healed, the husband might not have a job. Hence, when we speak again, I may say, "God has cared for you. He knows your troubles and answers your prayers. Go and pray with your wife again." As long as he is only concerned about his troubles, those who try to help him can only help him solve his troubles. There is no way to help him to know God in a simple way and to experience Him as life.

The human life is full of sufferings. God knows this and, therefore, is somewhat obliged to help man before He can be life to man. I believe that the Lord allows me to say "somewhat obliged," because this is not the main work of God. But man misunderstands God and thinks that God desires only to heal people and find jobs for them. It is as if God is a free doctor and a great employment agent. People think that God is only supposed to find jobs, schools, and homes for them. Many people begin their Christian lives by asking Him to do many things for them and thank and praise Him when their prayers are answered. However, when He no longer answers their prayers, they immediately question Him, saying, "What is wrong with Jesus? Why is God partial to some people? Maybe God is not a faithful God, or maybe He is not trustworthy." They become angry and stop going to meetings or praying at home, thinking that God is not faithful and not trustworthy. There are many examples of such Christians. Many among us may even be such Christians.

Since man does not know God, he thinks that God is a goodhearted and good-natured God, who blindly dispenses love and mercy. Veiled by this misconception, he cannot understand God's desire. He does not understand God's thoughts and is completely occupied with his sufferings. Some preachers even say that man suffers because he lacks religion and that only religion can solve the problems of human suffering. They even preach that Christianity solves the problems of human life, giving examples of families whose problems were solved once they believed in Jesus. They use these words to attract people and to satisfy man's psychology, because they know that human life is full of sufferings; however, they are ignorant of God's mind.

The Bible does show that God is compassionate and cares for man. He is ready to comfort the suffering and heal the sick. Although the Bible does mention many such precious promises, these things are not the central goal in God's heart. God's central goal is not to heal our sicknesses or to remove our sufferings. His central goal is to enter into us to be our life. Because we have sufferings, sicknesses, and needs, He comforts, heals, and abides by the promises in the Bible. However, promises such as these are peripheral matters in the Bible. They are not the central matters. They are not the root and the trunk; rather, they are the branches and the leaves.

Unfortunately, we often find only these superficial and outward things in the Bible. We fail to see the central, foundational things.

The Second Category—Building Up Morality

A second category of things in the Bible is related to morality. When God enters into man to be His life, He cannot allow man to remain an evil person. As a vessel, man must be upright and proper in order to match God so that God can become his life. For this reason, the Bible speaks much concerning morality. If I want to drink from a cup, I must first clean it thoroughly and properly. Although my ultimate goal is to have a liquid inside the cup, I must first clean the cup. In the same way, when God wants to make us His vessel, to enter into us as life, He must first cleanse our vessel from sin and evil. However, this is only a peripheral preparation work.

Man is also full of concepts about morality. Hence, when he reads the Bible and finds something on morality, he heartily responds to what he reads, and he echoes it. Most people mark only the passages in their Bibles on love for one another, meekness, humility, righteousness, and justice. Everybody who comes across these passages feels that these words are great and encouraging.

This does not mean that these teachings in the Bible are bad. These teachings are good. However, we must realize that these are peripheral matters. They are not the central matters in God's will. If we can find only these matters in the Bible, then the Bible is no different from the writings of other religions or the teachings of sages. These things are absolutely not the center of the Bible

The Third Category—Guidance for Human Living

A third category of peripheral matters in the Bible is secrets on human living. How should we live as human beings on earth? How should we handle human relationships? How should we behave as parents and as children? How should we relate to our spouse? How do we make friends? What attitude should we have toward money? How should the rich live? How should the poor live? Things like these can be found in many places in the Bible. The book of Proverbs is full of such advice. These are the things that many people consider to be precious when they come to the Bible. However, these are peripheral matters, like skin and feathers.

The Fourth Category—Religious Zeal

The fourth category of peripheral matters in the Bible is related to zeal for religion. Every Christian has a zeal to serve God, to be dedicated to Him, to love Him, and to be faithful to Him. These are not bad things. They are all good, but they are religious concepts. They are peripheral matters that have nothing to do with the central point of the Bible.

Although the Bible contains these four peripheral categories of things, the central matter of the Bible concerns God becoming our life. The peripheral matters of the Bible deal with solutions to sufferings, exhortations for moral conduct, guidance for human living, and zeal for religion. When man comes to the Bible, he may be filled with concepts and needs related to these four areas, but he may also have no consciousness of God becoming our life. Therefore, he receives only peripheral things. He misses the central matter, the trunk and the root. This is a great lack in our reading of the Bible.

EXAMPLES OF READING THE BIBLE

Suppose a brother loses his job and worries continually about his employment. When he reads Philippians 4, he may not understand verses 1 through 3 but may touch something in verse 4, which says, "Rejoice in the Lord always; again I will say, rejoice." This verse is in contrast to his situation since he is not rejoicing and is unhappy about losing his job. Consequently, his attention is drawn to the word *rejoice,* but he misses the words *in the Lord.* It is as if the verse reads "Rejoice always; again I will say, rejoice." As he continues reading, he is not touched by verse 5 but is touched by the words in verse 6, which say, "In nothing be anxious." Since he has been very anxious about his job, this word is very precious to him. He feels as if the Lord has spoken to him and has touched his inner being with these words. Then he reads, "But in everything, by prayer and petition with thanksgiving, let your requests be made known to God." This word is even better, and he begins to pray, saying, "Lord, thank You and praise You that I can let my requests be made known to You by prayer and petition with thanksgiving. My request is to have a job. I need a job. You said that I should be anxious in nothing. I am not anxious anymore. I give my anxiety to You." He ultimately feels cherished after reading verse 7: "And the peace of God, which surpasses every man's understanding, will guard your hearts and your thoughts in Christ Jesus." Immediately he thanks and praises God for giving him the peace that will guard his heart and thoughts. He seems to be reading the Bible in the way of life. He has exercised his spirit, not his mind, and has digested the word through prayer, eating God through the Word. He is fed and satisfied.

Although this is good, we may ask whether the brother has eaten the meat or the feathers. Has he touched the central matters of the Bible or peripheral matters? These few verses contain central matters and also peripheral matters. The peripheral matters are attached to the central matters. Regrettably, this brother found only the peripheral matters; he did not touch the central matters. Verse 4 says, "Rejoice in the Lord always." The words *in the Lord* mean that we have a life union with the Lord, that we allow the Lord to be our life. Based on our being in the Lord and on this life union with Him, we can and will spontaneously rejoice. Verse 7 says, "The peace of God, which surpasses every man's understanding, will guard your hearts and your thoughts in Christ Jesus." The basic issue lies in the words *in Christ Jesus*. This is the central matter. Guarding is merely the result of being in Christ Jesus. But our brother only picks up the words *peace* and *guard,* not *in Christ Jesus.* He picks up only the things that are not of the Lord. He does not understand the central point. He sees only the peripheral matters. These peripheral matters belong to the first category, to consolation and deliverance from sufferings.

Then the brother reads verse 8, which says, "Finally, brothers, what things are true, what things are dignified, what things are righteous, what things are pure, what things are lovely, what things are well spoken of, if there is any virtue and if any praise, take account of these things." He is touched again. This verse is related to the category of ethics and morality. God requires that man be proper. Man should not be evil. Hence, God says that we should take account of things that are true, dignified, righteous, pure, lovely, and well spoken of. We should think of good things, not evil things, pure things, not filthy things, and lovely things, not hateful things. However, these are peripheral matters; they are not central. Because our brother's mind is full of ethical concepts, he responds immediately to these words on morality and ethics.

Our brother continues to read verse 12, which says, "I know also how to be abased, and I know how to abound; in everything and in all things I have learned the secret both to be filled and to hunger, both to abound and to lack." This word appeals to him even more because it speaks of a secret to human living, a secret related to abounding and being in lack. Then he reads, "I am able to do all things in Him who empowers me" (v. 13), and he exclaims, "I have found the secret to human living! It is to trust in the Lord." Many Christians utter these words without knowing what it means to trust in the Lord. The important words in this verse are *in Him*. We are able to do all things "in Him." The One who empowers us dwells within us. If we learn to live in Him, we find the secret to human living. It is only when we are in Him that we are able to do all things.

On another day this brother may read Galatians 1. While he is not impressed by verses 1 through 9, he is touched by verse 10, which relates to the category of zeal for religion: "Am I now trying to win the assent of men or of God? Or am I seeking to please men? If I were still trying to please men, I would not be a slave of Christ." He is touched again, and because he thinks that a Christian should be faithful to God, he turns this feeling into prayer, saying, "Lord, forgive me for being fearful of men and trying to please men. Strengthen me so that I will please You all the time and not care to please men. I want to live before You instead of before men." The prayer enables him to touch his spirit, and the more he touches his spirit, the more he is filled and satisfied.

The next morning the brother reads, "It pleased God...to reveal His Son in me" (vv. 15-16). Even though these are central verses, his inward being is like oily paper that prevents the ink from penetrating into his heart. His inward being cannot absorb these words. This brother is receiving the skin of the chicken, not the meat. God is pleased to reveal His Son in us to be our life and to become the fullness of God in us. This is the most central matter. However, when he reads, there is no response in him; it is as if these words do not exist. The only words that touch him in Galatians 1 concern being a slave of Christ and not pleasing man. This is the skin. However, he does not realize that the meat in Galatians 1 is the phrase *it pleased God to reveal His Son in me*. Although this is God's goal, he is fully occupied by religious zeal and concepts. He feels that he should be zealous for God and faithful to God, but he does not see God's central goal.

On the third day the brother reads chapter 2 of Galatians and does not see anything significant in verses 1 through 10. In verse 11 he reads Paul's rebuke of Peter, and there is an echo within him. He considers Paul to be a faithful man who did not compromise in order to preserve the purity of the gospel. He is "enlightened," and prays, "Lord, in the past some brothers have spoken erroneously in public. Please forgive me for not correcting them immediately. I am not faithful. Please give me the strength to be faithful for the defense of Your gospel so that the truth can be preserved among us." This is a religious concept. He is not touched, however, by verse 20 even though this is a precious central word, which says, "I am crucified with Christ; and it is no longer I who live, but it is Christ who lives in me."

READING THE PERIPHERALS OF THE BIBLE BUT MISSING THE CENTER

From the above examples we can see that a person who comes to the Word can find words of comfort for times of trial, words that build up human virtues, words on the secrets to human living, and words on religious zeal. However it is not easy for a person to find the central matters concerning God coming into man to become man's life. Man must be in

God before he can have true joy, before God's peace can truly guard his heart and mind, before he can have the secret to human living, and before he can do all things and experience Him as his strength in all things. The words *in Him* are central and are related to God becoming life to man in the Son. This is God's central goal.

Regrettably, man's concepts are occupied with finding solutions to sufferings, building up virtues, solving the problems of the human life, and having religious zeal. Therefore, when he comes to the Bible, he cares to receive something only from these four categories of things—comfort in trials, building up human virtues, the secrets of human living, and religious zealousness. It has not occurred to him that God wants to enter into him to be his life. God wants to be everything to him. He grasps only the superficial things in the Bible; he cannot understand the central things. Brothers and sisters, there is comfort from God in our trials according to His promises. He is able to build up our virtues and teach us the secrets to human living. He even wants us to be faithful to Him and zealous for Him, but these items are peripheral. They are skin and feathers, branches and leaves. God primarily wants to enter into us to be our life. He wants to be our food and satisfaction. When we are satisfied, He becomes our inner strength that guides us through all our trials and difficulties. When we are satisfied, He becomes our inner wisdom and our secret to human living; we will spontaneously live out His virtues. When we are satisfied, we will be on fire for the Lord, and we will be faithful to Him. The Bible is focused on the central matter. If we have the central matter, we will spontaneously have the peripheral branches and leaves.

However, when reading the Bible, we select items mainly from the four peripheral categories—comfort and deliverance in trials, building up virtues, secrets to human living, and religious zeal. Many of us were probably touched by words related to comfort and promises in trials this morning. One brother may say, "My son is far away, and I miss him very much. This morning I read a verse which says, 'In nothing be anxious,' and I prayed, 'Amen, Lord, I am now casting my anxieties on You.'" Another sister may testify, "I have been very worried about my husband's illness. While I was reading the Bible this morning, I came across the words: 'Surely He has borne our sicknesses, and carried our sorrows,' and 'by His stripes we have been healed.' I was greatly comforted." There may be many such testimonies among us. Many of us were probably touched by words related to the building up of human virtues such as humility, patience, love, submission to husbands, and love toward wives. Not all of us may have been touched by words related to secrets to human living, but I believe a few were touched this morning. Many of us may also have been touched by words on religious zeal and fervor. Some may have been encouraged by the words, "I exhort you therefore, brothers, through the compassions of God to present your bodies a living sacrifice" (Rom. 12:1). Others may have been touched by the words, "Go into all the world and proclaim the gospel to all the creation" (Mark 16:15). Still others may be led to confession by the words, "Not abandoning our own assembling together, as the custom with some is" (Heb 10:25). They may have even asked the Lord to forgive them for not attending the meetings for over half a year. Many of us may have had our religious sentiments invoked in our reading. However, it may be that only a few of us were touched by God coming to us as life in His Son.

We need to remember that promises, comfort, deliverance in trials, the building up of human virtues, the secrets to human living, and religious zeal for serving God are all superficial and peripheral matters. They are the branches and the leaves. They are the skin of the chicken. Only the meat of the chicken is central. Words such as, "It pleased God...to reveal His Son in me" (Gal. 1:15-16), "it is no longer I who live, but Christ who lives in me" (2:20), "in Christ" (3:26), and "abide in Me and I in you" (John 15:4) are central words. This is the fifth category of words in the Bible. It is regrettable that although there are many such words in the Bible, we do not realize that they are there. Instead, we see the peripheral items and miss the central words concerning God coming to us as life in the Son.

PRACTICING TO MOVE FROM PERIPHERAL MATTERS TO CENTRAL MATTERS IN OUR BIBLE READING

We should not be discouraged. Even if we do not find the central things in our reading, we should continue reading. We need to read the Bible. We can still be fed even if we only find words of comfort. Words such as, "In nothing be anxious, but in everything, by prayer and petition with thanksgiving, let your requests be made known to God" (Phil. 4:6), "casting all your anxiety on Him because it matters to Him concerning you" (1 Pet. 5:7), or "a bruised reed He will not break, and smoking flax He will not quench" (Matt. 12:20) are not bad. It is better to eat something than to have nothing to eat. Some sisters may be touched by Ephesians 5:22-23 concerning recognizing their husbands as their heads. Some brothers may be touched by verse 25 to love their wives and care for them because they are the weaker vessels. A brother who has not been meeting for half a year may repent and be recovered to the meetings after reading Hebrews 10:25. The skin is not useless, because it has helped him. A brother may be brought to repentance after reading Philippians 2:3-4. These saints may then testify concerning what they have read in the meetings, and the meetings will be living and full of the Lord's presence. When we cannot get the meat, it is not bad to get a few bites of skin. We should never stop reading. If we stop, we will go hungry.

Nevertheless, we should all gradually move from the peripheral things to the central matter. Soon we will recognize what is meat. May we never be discouraged in our reading, and may we never be satisfied with our reading. We must discern between the center and the circumference, the meat and the skin. We must realize that the Bible contains central words and peripheral words. The central words are God's goal, and the peripheral words meet our needs. If we stand only with our needs, feelings, and psychological cravings, we can receive only the superficial things from the Bible. However, if we are delivered to stand on the side of God's goal and His heart, we will find the central things. Until then we should continue with the peripheral matters so that we can maintain a proper life before the Lord to contact, absorb, and digest Him a little every day. We should not consider the central matters to be unattainable. We should never become discouraged to the point of giving up reading the Bible. We should never take this attitude. Instead, we should do our best to continue reading, even if we cannot find the central things now. We should still learn to read with our spirit, to deny our own thoughts, and to turn all the words that touch us into prayer. We should learn to receive nutrition, even from the superficial things. Then we will gain some help. If we are faithful, God will open our eyes, and we will gradually discover the central things. May the Lord be gracious to us so that we become clearer, sharper, and more skillful in our reading of the Word, and may we be able to get into the deeper things.

CHAPTER NINETEEN

EXERCISING TO PRAY IN THE HOLY SPIRIT

Scripture Reading: Jude 20

THE NECESSITY OF PRAYING IN THE HOLY SPIRIT

In this message we will practice praying with Jude 20. This verse speaks about two things. First, it speaks of being built up in the most holy faith. This is related to reading the Word. Second, it speaks of praying in the Holy Spirit. This is related to prayer. No other verse in the Bible is as concise as this verse in the matter of prayer. Prayer should be in the Holy Spirit. We should pray in the Holy Spirit. Prayer, which is a matter of man cooperating with God, must possess two natures. Prayers that come only from man, which are not mingled with God, are merely religious prayers. They do not touch God, breathe in God, or reach God. This is the reason that Jude says we should pray in the Holy Spirit. The words *in the Holy Spirit* are very good. In Ephesians 6:18 the Chinese Union Version translates this portion as *praying by the Spirit*. The meaning of praying by the Spirit is unclear. Jude, however, is translated correctly; we should pray in the Holy Spirit. Praying in the Holy Spirit means that we and the Holy Spirit must pray together.

The secret to the Christian life is to be mingled with the Holy Spirit. The spiritual life of a Christian is absolutely a matter of man being mingled with the Holy Spirit. When we are in the Holy Spirit, we have a spiritual life. When we are not in the Holy Spirit, we do not have a spiritual life. It is possible for us to have all kinds of religious activities, but if we are not in the Holy Spirit, there is no way for us to have a genuine spiritual life. This particularly applies to prayer.

Apart from the Holy Spirit we only have religious prayers that are commonly found in Christianity. These prayers have no spiritual worth before God. If we want genuine, spiritual prayers, prayers that reach God, touch God, breathe in God, and are in God, we must pray in the Holy Spirit.

BEING IN THE HOLY SPIRIT INVOLVING THE FELLOWSHIP AND MINGLING OF THE HOLY SPIRIT WITH OUR SPIRIT

Since many brothers and sisters still may not understand what it is to be in the Holy Spirit, let me explain further. God is Spirit, and we have a spirit. Our spirit is the same in nature as the Spirit of God. God's Spirit is invisible and non-material. Our spirit is also invisible and non-material. We have a spirit within us that enables us to contact God who is Spirit.

The Lord Jesus said that God is Spirit and that he who worships Him must worship in spirit (John 4:24). This means that we must turn to our spirit and exercise our spirit in order to worship and touch God who is Spirit. These two spirits, the Spirit of God and our spirit, need to fellowship with one another, live with one another, and be mingled together. For this reason Romans 8:16 says, "The Spirit Himself witnesses with our spirit that we are children of God." The word *with* reveals that the Spirit and our spirit are mingled as one.

We were created as men, and we have a spirit within us. At the time of our salvation, the blood washed us, and the Holy Spirit entered into our spirit. In the Gospel of John the Lord Jesus said that when the Spirit comes, He will be with us forever (14:16-17). He will abide within us forever. Every believer has the Spirit of God in His spirit. God's Spirit is in our spirit, and our spirit is in His Spirit. The expressions *You in Me* and *I in you* are both found in the Gospel of John (v. 20). This transpires in our spirit. *You in Me* means that our spirit is in His Spirit, and *I in you* means that His Spirit is in our spirit. The phrase *abide in Me and I in you* means that our spirit abides in His Spirit, and His Spirit abides in our spirit (15:4). These portions of the Scriptures describe a condition in our spirit.

Some may ask how we know that such a condition exists in our spirit. How do we know that the Spirit of God abides in our spirit and that our spirit abides in His Spirit? In other words, how do we know that there is a fellowship and mingling between the two spirits within us? This is something every believer can easily know. For example, even though our outward circumstances may be painful and difficult to bear, we have a sweet sense of consolation and unspeakable joy deep within us. This sense of comfort and joy comes from experiencing God. It is a sense of being before God, of being together with Him. At other times we may be bewildered, not knowing what to do. If we would look to the Lord, the condition within us would be bright and transparent. We would spontaneously be clear concerning how to proceed. This condition deep within us is the story of God's Spirit being mingled with our spirit.

Sometimes we may feel dry, empty, and unsure of ourselves even though we are lacking in nothing outwardly. We may feel ill at ease whether we are sitting, walking, or lying down. This reveals that our spirit is short of God's presence; our spirit is lacking the nourishment of the Holy Spirit. There is a lack between our spirit and the Spirit.

These examples help us to understand what it means for God's Spirit to be in our spirit and for our spirit to be in His Spirit. Once we understand the story of mutual fellowship between these two spirits, we can understand what it means to be in the Holy Spirit. To be in the Holy Spirit is absolutely a matter in our spirit.

There is a story about a brother whose countenance was glowing with an indescribable joy as he was working. He was so happy that he was even laughing. This caused his colleagues to ask what was happening to him. They thought that it was something psychological. He responded that since they did not have Jesus within them, they could not understand what was happening. He said that his joy was the issue of his spirit fellowshipping with the Spirit of God within him. Hence, he could not help but be happy. He said that if his happiness was merely something psychological, it would be unnatural and forced. When his spirit fellowshipped with the

Spirit of God, all of his burdens disappeared. He could not help but have a happiness that came from the depth of his being.

This is a story about being in the spirit. As long as we touch God's Spirit with our spirit, such an experience will follow. Although we cannot see the Spirit of God with our eyes or feel Him with our hands, we can clearly sense Him when He touches us within. On the evening of His resurrection the Lord Jesus breathed into the disciples and said to them, "Receive the Holy Spirit" (John 20:22). The Lord Jesus used breath to represent the Holy Spirit. This is very meaningful. Although we can neither see nor touch air, we know that it has entered us because we feel inwardly relieved, refreshed, and comforted. In contrast, when there is insufficient air in a room, we feel stuffy and uncomfortable. This is a good illustration. This also applies to the Holy Spirit within us. When we are short of the Holy Spirit, we feel oppressed, bound, and constricted within, but when we fellowship with the Holy Spirit, we are immediately relieved and refreshed. This condition indicates that the Holy Spirit is within us and that He is mingled with our spirit. This proves that our spirit abides in God's Spirit and that His Spirit abides in our spirit. In other words, we are abiding in God, and God is abiding in us. This is absolutely a matter in the spirit.

PRAYING IN THE HOLY SPIRIT
BEING TO PRAY IN THE MUTUAL FELLOWSHIP
OF THE TWO SPIRITS

To pray in the Holy Spirit is to pray in the mutual fellowship of the two spirits. Our spirit must touch the Spirit, and the Spirit must touch our spirit. It must involve the two spirits mingled together. When we follow the Spirit to pray in this way, we are praying in our spirit, and we are praying in the Holy Spirit.

We often say that prayer brings us God's presence. But what does this mean? Our prayers bring us God's presence when we pray in the Spirit. Then every sentence of our prayer is solid and touches God. When we pray in this way, our prayer has touched God's presence.

Perhaps some brothers and sisters do not understand what it means for our prayer to be solid and to touch God. Here is an illustration. If I attempt to hit Brother Hwang but miss him, my blow is not solid. But if I hit him blow after blow, my blows are solid. The more I hit, the more excited and satisfied I will be, because my hitting is not in vain. We have probably had the same experience when praying. When we pray, we may sometimes feel that the words are lost in the air. They do not hit the mark. None of the words seem to touch God, and it seems as if God is not present. This means that our prayer is not solid. This is an indication that we are not praying in the Spirit. It also shows that we are not abiding in the Spirit. Because we are praying apart from the Spirit, our prayer seems to hit only the air; it is not solid, and it does not touch God. However, when we pray in the Spirit, we feel that the more we pray, the more we touch God and our words touch God. We feel as if we are filled with God. Our God is not only in heaven; He has also entered into us. This is wonderful. The more we pray in this way, the more we are inwardly enlightened, comforted, satisfied, nourished, joyful, and anointed. These feelings indicate that we have received God in our prayer; we have breathed in God. Only this type of prayer is genuine, spiritual, and of value. Only this kind of prayer should be offered up in the universe. All other prayers are religious, formal, and outward, having no value.

The brothers and sisters should now understand what it is to pray in the Holy Spirit. If someone still does not understand, he may not be saved; he may not have the Spirit of God within him. Any person who is saved has the Spirit of God within him and should have had such experiences. There should be an Amen within him, witnessing that the more he prays, the more he touches God and is filled with God. The more we pray, the more satisfied and comfortable we feel.

There are, however, times when our prayers seem to chase God away. At such times we may be forcing ourselves to pray. We, therefore, feel empty and dry within and have a desire to finish our prayers. If we have all had this experience, we know the difference between these two conditions and consequences of prayer.

LEARNING TO RESTRICT OURSELVES AND TO TURN TO OUR SPIRIT IN PRAYER

Some brothers and sisters may be clear concerning praying in the Holy Spirit, but they might not know how to enter the Spirit. Every person who learns to pray encounters this problem. We often have distracting thoughts when we kneel down to pray. When we try to reject one thought, another comes. While we are dealing with the second thought, another one invades our mind. The thoughts come like a swarm of bees. They buzz around in our mind and prevent us from praying. If we are unable to control our thoughts, we may become angry and declare that we will not pray any more. In this situation we have failed. Many times our distracting thoughts are a frustration to our prayers. They cause us to turn away from our spirit so that we cannot pray.

Our thoughts distract us because we are loose persons before the Lord. An undisciplined and loose person has distracting thoughts. If we are undisciplined and loose before God, we will be unable to be calm. We will have wandering and distracting thoughts if we are loose before the Lord. The looser we are before the Lord, the more distracting our thoughts will be. By the Lord's grace, if we learn to control ourselves, our thoughts will come under control. When we stop to pray, we will immediately be calm, and it will be easy for us to turn to our spirit.

Please allow me to say that I have seen many brothers and sisters—sisters more so than brothers—who are very loose in their speaking. This does not mean that they use unclean words, but they are undisciplined in their speech. When they converse with others, they do not seem to be able to stop speaking. Since they are undisciplined and loose in their speaking, their thoughts fly all over the world. After speaking in this way, they may need to wait until the next day before they are able to pray since they are unable to be calm and turn to their spirit. Even if they wake up early in the morning, they may still have all kinds of thoughts racing through their mind, and therefore, they still cannot pray. Everyone who is plentiful in words cannot pray. When a person speaks continuously, his entire being is led astray. His entire being is captured by thoughts that wander all over the world. He has no way to stop his being, and he cannot pray. Therefore, a person who learns to pray must learn to control his speaking. He must learn to restrict his being, not only in one thing but in everything.

Many saints have learned some lessons in the matter of restricting themselves. Some are able to stop themselves in the midst of their temper and turn to God to confess and pray. Such prayer and confession are altogether a matter in their spirit. Such a person can easily pray in his spirit. This does not mean that a person who readily loses his temper can easily pray in his spirit. Rather, a person who can control himself even while he is losing his temper tends to find it easy to turn to his spirit to pray.

There are, of course, many brothers and sisters who cannot control themselves once they lose their temper. Even when others try to stop them, they are unable to control themselves once they lose their temper. They do not know what it means to be under control. They can be compared to a car that has no brakes; they are unable to stop themselves. It is not easy for such a person to turn to his spirit and pray. He may need to wait for a week before he can pray again. His entire being has been expended through his temper.

This illustration should help us to see that if we want to learn to pray, we must learn to control ourselves before God. If we control ourselves in ordinary things, it will be easy for us to control our thoughts when we pray. Our thoughts will be submissive, and it will be easy for us to stop, be calm, and turn to our spirit. We will easily be disentangled from our thoughts in order to turn to our spirit. A person who wants to learn to pray in spirit must learn to control himself at all times.

We often classify people as either extroverts or introverts. It is difficult for those who are extroverted to learn to pray. They seem to be able to do everything, but it is difficult for them to be calm in order to pray. It is, therefore, difficult for them to absorb and enjoy God, not to mention the fact that they have many unanswered prayers. This is a great loss. It is profitable for a person to devote some time every day to calm his thoughts and turn his entire being to God in order to contact Him. However, such a person must be one who restricts himself. If we want to learn to pray in the Holy Spirit, we must learn the lesson of restricting ourselves in our daily life, controlling ourselves in everything. If we can control ourselves in this way, it will be easy for us to stop our activities and pray.

LEARNING TO BEHOLD GOD BEFORE WE PRAY

If we are able to restrict ourselves and turn to the Spirit in this way, we should not immediately open our mouths to pray. In chapter 5 we considered ten points we should pay attention to when we pray. After being calm we should behold God. This means that in order to pray, we must first touch God. We must first touch God before we can pray. This means that our spirit must touch the Spirit of God. When we are busy with many outward things, there is no way for us to touch God. When we want to pray, we must free ourselves from all affairs, stop our mental activities, and turn our entire being from outward things to our spirit. We must learn to exercise our spirit to touch God's Spirit. Then we will learn to behold God. Because God is Spirit and dwells in our spirit, it is not difficult to touch Him. When our entire being is occupied, and we live in our mind, God seems to disappear. However, He has not disappeared; rather, we have turned our backs on Him. We are not beholding Him. But as soon as we are free from our thoughts and turn from the outward things to our spirit, we touch God immediately. This is to behold God, and this is to touch His presence in our spirit. As soon as we touch God in our spirit, we feel solid within; we feel that we have the anointing and the moving of the Holy Spirit. At this point we can open our mouths to pray.

BEING AIDED TO TURN TO OUR SPIRIT
BY READING THE WORD

Some may say that it is difficult to turn to their spirit and behold God in this way. New believers may find it difficult to practice praying in this way. If a person cannot turn to his spirit or be calm, he can start by reading the Word. He can then use the words of the Bible to calm his thoughts in order to turn to his spirit. He can turn any words that touch him into prayer. This is an easy way to turn to our spirit.

Some saints are able to turn directly to their spirit without any help. Whenever they want to pray, they only need to close their eyes, and they can stop their entire being. Sometimes they do not even need to close their eyes; they can turn to their spirit even while others are talking beside them. They are not bothered by distractions. One brother said that he had learned to pray even while others were fighting in front of him. He could calmly pray to touch the Lord, sense His presence, and be brought into the Holy Spirit, no matter how loudly they shouted. Such a person is very experienced in his spirit; his spirit is very strong. He is able to control himself and is not bothered by anything. When he wants to pray, he can turn his entire being to his spirit.

However, many brothers and sisters have not learned to pray in this way. They cannot even be calm when they are alone, not to mention being calm when others argue and fight in their presence. This shows that they are not restricted before God and that they are immature in the Lord. We should never think that a person is mature simply because they have been a Christian for many years. Maturity does not depend on the number of years one has been a Christian, and it does not depend on the amount of teaching a person knows. Rather, maturity is related to our ability to be calm and turn to our spirit when we pray. If we can do this, we are somewhat mature. If we cannot, we are still quite young and cannot restrict ourselves. For this reason, we must continue to exercise until we can stop ourselves and turn to our spirit when we are ready to pray.

We may not find it easy when we begin to practice, and we may need to use the Bible. If so, we can read through the Bible slowly, allowing God's Word to touch our inward being. We can then turn the words of the Bible into prayer. In this way, it will be easy for us to be calm and turn to our spirit. Then we will behold God, we will see God; our spirit will contact God, and we will be able to offer genuine prayers.

As we utter such prayers, we still need to pay attention to

the matter of touching God. Once we stop touching God, we should not force ourselves to pray. We should, rather, continue reading the Word. We should use the Bible as a support to help us enjoy God through prayer. When we are calm and can touch our spirit through reading the Word, we can start praying again. In short, we do not need to force ourselves to pray whenever our spirit is dry and we cannot touch God. If we force ourselves, our spirit will receive no benefit but may actually be harmed. We should rather stop our prayer and continue reading the Word.

PRACTICING TO PRAY BY TOUCHING GOD IN THE SPIRIT AT ALL TIMES

The only prayers that touch God are those offered in the Spirit. Only through such prayers can we receive God. We should pray in this way, not only in the morning when we contact God but also in our time of prayer during the day. We should always feel the watering, anointing, and divine presence while we pray. But if we feel dry and void of God while we pray for a particular matter, we should stop praying and change the direction or subject of our prayer until we touch God. Then we can continue praying. In this way we can remain in the spirit while we pray.

We need to practice praying in the Holy Spirit. May the Lord be gracious to us so that we learn to pray in the Holy Spirit. May we have prayers that touch and absorb God.

CHAPTER TWENTY

PRACTICING TO PRAY ACCORDING TO THE SENSE OF THE SPIRIT

Scripture Reading: Rom. 8:26

We need to say something more concerning the matter of prayer.

TRUE PRAYER BEING A MINGLING OF GOD AND MAN IN THE SPIRIT

True prayer involves two parties—God and man. Such prayers are the issue of the Spirit of God being mingled with man's spirit and of man's spirit being mingled with the Spirit of God. When a man exercises his spirit to pray, he is praying with his spirit in God's Spirit, or we can say that God's Spirit is praying in his spirit. In such prayers it is difficult to differentiate whether man's spirit is praying or God's Spirit is praying, because man's spirit and God's Spirit are fully joined together. The human spirit and the divine Spirit are intimately joined during prayer. As we pray, God and man are joined together in the most thorough and perfect way. However, there are many prayers in which God and man are not joined together. These are prayers in which man is not praying in his spirit but rather praying by himself with his mind. These prayers are outside of God; they are merely human prayers in which God is not mingled with man. I hope we all understand that prayer is absolutely a matter of God being mingled with man. Our prayers must be in the Spirit.

TRUE PRAYER BEING MAN'S RESPONSE TO GOD'S INITIATION

Since prayer is an expression of the union of God and man,

no true prayer can be uttered without God's initiation. If a prayer is not initiated by God, it is not genuine prayer. All those who truly know the meaning of prayer know that prayer is not merely a matter of God being mingled with man but a matter of God initiating something within man. Hence, when we pray, we must learn to be calm and not follow our thoughts. Instead, we should turn from our mind to our spirit and follow the sense within our spirit. In genuine prayer a person has a certain sense in his spirit even before he prays. This sense in the spirit is initiated by God's Spirit within our spirit. When the Spirit of God mingles with our spirit, He initiates or suggests something in our spirit, which is not necessarily in the form of intelligible words. Many times it is merely a sense or a feeling in our spirit.

Therefore, when we pray, we must not only turn to our spirit, but we must also wait on God's initiation. We should be calm and turn to our spirit. At the same time we should not be too quick to utter something. Rather, we should wait for God's initiation and the sense in our spirit. Please remember that everyone who opens his mouth quickly speaks invariably from himself and from his own initiation. Whenever we pray, we must learn to turn to our spirit. Then we must learn to wait for God's initiation. We should be calm and touch the sense in our spirit in order to pray according to that sense.

THROUGHOUT THE PROCESS FOLLOWING THE SENSE THAT GOD HAS INITIATED IN THE SPIRIT

In genuine prayer the initiation and the entire process must be from God's urging. An electrical sound system is driven by electricity to transmit sounds. Not only are microphones and loud speakers driven by electricity, but the entire process, including the amplification and transmission, is driven by electricity. In the same principle, God should be the initiator of our prayer, and the entire process of our prayer should be an experience in which God prays with us and mingles Himself in our prayers.

Since the presence of God and our mingling with Him are absolutely related to the sense in our spirit, we should learn to allow our inner sense to be the initiating and motivating element within us when we pray.

It is wonderful that we are often able to comprehend the feeling in our spirit when we pray. At times a feeling may lead us to confess our failures and shortcomings or to pray for the church. Another feeling may lead us to pray for a brother in difficulty or to pray for the message meeting on the Lord's Day. We may even have a feeling to praise Him, thank Him, or exult Him. Sometimes we may have a feeling not to pray for anything, or even to praise or thank Him, but simply to bow down before Him and worship Him. There is no need for words or sounds. We simply prostrate before God in silence and worship Him. The more we worship, the fresher our spirit becomes, and the more we are satisfied. As we worship, we feel that we are touching God in our spirit. This is a prayer of worship that is generated by the feeling of the Holy Spirit within us.

As soon as we understand the meaning of these feelings from God, we should follow them in prayer. We should never restrict ourselves to the topic that we decided on prior to our prayer. If we restrict ourselves in this way, we will be in our mind, and we will be the initiator and motivator of our prayer. Our spirit is not the only requirement for proper and genuine prayer. Prayer must be a joint prayer in which God is mingled with our spirit. In this prayer God and man mingle together, and God is the Initiator and Motivator. Spiritual prayer is never directed by our mind, memory, or thoughts. It is directed by the sense in our spirit, and this sense comes from God's initiation.

Hence, in genuine prayer we pray together with God; we pray by accompanying Him. We pray according to the feeling that God gives us. This enables God to pray with us in our prayer. We are praying, and He is also praying. He and we pray together. He is within us; He is praying one with us. This is indeed an amazing matter.

Whether or not such prayers are answered is secondary. The primary matter is that we pray by following the sense in our spirit; we allow God to pass through us and to mingle Himself with us. In this way we enjoy God and absorb Him. Even though we may offer supplication for the church, for a brother in dire need, or even for ourselves, our main sensation will be that we have absorbed God and have been filled with Him.

Of course, there are times when we misunderstand the feelings from God. For example, when the inward feeling urges us to pray, we may think that we should pray for our children. But as we begin to pray for our children, the inner sense wanes, and we feel that something is not right within. When a brother likes what he is hearing, his countenance is bright, and he is happy, but if something is said that he does not like, the expression on his face will change. If there is a change in our conversation, his countenance may become bright once again. We have all experienced this. This also happens in our fellowship with the Lord. Sometimes we may sense God's presence, as if He is smiling within us. If our prayer is against the inward sense, we feel cold and withdrawn within. When this happens, we should change the direction of our prayer. We should never think that we must finish our own prayers before responding to the sense from God. If God is not praying with us, and our prayer is not touching God, we should stop praying as soon as the sense within begins to wane, in order to check the inner sense. If the sense is leading us to pray for the church, we should immediately pray for the church. If we do so, the inner sense will become bright, and we will touch God's presence again. This is the way to continue in prayer. If we follow the inner sense, God's Spirit will follow our prayer, and we will receive more feelings. Our responsibility is simply to pray according to these feelings. Verbalize the feelings one by one. This is genuine prayer that breathes in God. Through such prayer, we are in God, we breathe Him in, and God is in us. In such prayers we obtain God even before our prayers are answered. This is what it means to enjoy God and absorb Him through prayer.

THE PRINCIPLE OF ENJOYING GOD THROUGH PRAYER BEING TO FOLLOW THE SENSE OF THE SPIRIT

Regrettably, many brothers and sisters are ignorant of these inward experiences. Although they long for prayer that enjoys God and occasionally have enjoyable experiences, they do not know the key to prayer and are ignorant of the principle that governs prayer. Therefore, they are never sure when they touch God. Sometimes they touch God accidentally, but they do not realize that they have enjoyed God. Moreover, they cannot describe such an experience as enjoying and breathing in God. They only know that they prayed for twenty minutes in the morning, and that they had the savor of heaven while they prayed. The next morning they try to enjoy God by praying in the same way, but it may not work. They try to repeat the experiences of the previous day, but it does not work. They muster their will, exercise their mind, act according to their memory, and try to repeat their prayer from the previous day. The more they try, the drier they become. After praying for a while, they are depressed and empty within, and they do not understand what has happened. This experience is the issue of not praying according to the sense in their spirit. The prayer they offered the previous morning was according to the sense of their spirit, even though they might not have known what they were doing. However, when they tried to consciously repeat the experience, they fall into a formality and are no longer in their spirit.

After this, the brothers and sisters lack assurance in their prayers. They no longer know how to pray to obtain peace in their spirit. Whenever they try to repeat an experience, it is usually a failure. Such failures usually lead to discouragement and a lack of desire to pray. Eventually, their prayers become somewhat routine and unnatural. After a few weeks they may accidentally touch God again. They may sense His presence and inwardly feel satisfied. However, they are unable to repeat this the following day and are thus confused. These experiences are the issue of not touching the key to prayer. They do not know the principle that governs prayer.

There are principles that govern the matter of touching God in our prayer. This is like tuning a radio. If we want to listen to a particular broadcast, we must turn to the right frequency. Those who do not know the right frequency can only search blindly. When they stumble upon it, they listen to the broadcast. When they do not stumble upon it, they are not able to listen to the broadcast. They have no certainty.

However, those who know the frequency simply turn the dial and immediately listen to the broadcast. The same is true with prayer. In order for us to touch God in our prayer, we must follow the principle that governs prayer. Those who do not know the principle may only experience it accidentally, but those who know the key to prayer find it very easy to touch God in their prayers.

Some often say that they pray in the Lord's presence. This, however, is the speaking of a novice. Our prayer is not a matter of the Lord being present with us but a matter of inwardly touching the Lord. For example, radio waves are always in the air. As long as we adjust a radio to the correct frequency, the radio waves will be received. Similarly, the Holy Spirit is present in every place at every time. He is with us at all times and in all places. Regrettably, the "radio" in our spirit is not always adjusted to the right frequency. In one instant we may be in our mind and not touch anything. The next instant we may be in our spirit and immediately touch the Spirit.

We should now understand that the governing principle to touching God is to follow the sense in our spirit when we pray. If we do this, it will be easy for us to absorb God and enjoy Him in our prayer. We should pay attention to understand and exercise according to this principle.

THINGS TO CONSIDER CONCERNING THE SENSE OF THE SPIRIT

Those who are experienced in prayer know that there are many things to consider related to the sense of the spirit. If the sense in our spirit is for us to pray rapidly, we should pray accordingly; otherwise, we may lose the Spirit. Sometimes the sense in our spirit may be to pray slowly, requiring us to utter the words one by one; otherwise, we may lose the Lord's presence. At other times the sense in our spirit may be to stop praying. If we do not stop, we will be cut off from the sense in our spirit. There are also times when the inner feeling does not allow us to stop, even if we have other matters to take care of. We should always follow the inner feeling when we pray, not praying according to ourselves.

There are times when the inner feeling may lead us to

weep, even if we are not accustomed to crying. If we try to hold back the tears, we will lose the Spirit, but if we weep or cry, the Spirit will be released. We should follow the leading in our spirit regardless of our environment.

At other times we may not be led to cry, and if we do, we will lose the leading of the Spirit. Sisters, however, seem to be more prone to cry. Some sisters cry whenever they pray. These tears may actually frustrate the Spirit and cause them to lose the sense of the Spirit.

These are not exaggerations. One basic lesson in prayer is that we must always follow the initiation of the Spirit. If we follow Him, He will follow us. This experience is altogether in the realm of our spirit. May we all practice this kind of prayer. Whenever we pray, we must stop and turn to our spirit. Next, we must not initiate prayer from ourselves. Rather, we must allow God to deposit His feelings within us and pray according to these feelings. Whether the feeling is to pray rapidly or slowly, to cry or to laugh, we should follow the feeling absolutely. All experienced believers know that we absorb God in such prayers, and we are brought into God; God fills our being, and we are saturated with Him. This is genuine prayer to which the Lord hearkens.

Regrettably, we are not always able to follow the leading in our spirit. Our memory, will, thoughts, and opinions form the biggest inward barriers. For example, we may decide to pray for certain matters or persons regardless of the feeling in our spirit. When we set ourselves to pray, we do not care for the feeling in our spirit. We care instead about what we have decided and what we can remember. There is a problem if we are unwilling to surrender our mind, memory, and decisions to the Lord. In our prayer we must surrender ourselves to the Lord and cooperate with Him. We must let Him lead us in our prayers; we should not take the initiative. We must be active only in following the Lord, in being submissive to Him, and in not taking the initiative. Even if the greatest enterprise in the world is about to fall upon us, we should not pray for it without the leading of the inward feeling. We should only follow the feeling in our spirit.

When we enjoy God through reading the Word, we need to

drop our views and concepts in order to receive the central matters in God's Word. This principle also applies to prayer. When we pray, we need to drop our decisions and thoughts in order to pray according the sense in our spirit. Regrettably, since most of our prayers are initiated by us, they are apart from the Spirit. If the Lord is not one with us in our prayers, we will not touch and absorb God in our prayers.

When we pray, we must learn to turn to our spirit. We must learn to set aside our feelings, opinions, ideas, memory, and decisions and pray solely according to the feeling in our spirit. Only then will God follow us in our prayer. As we follow the sense in our spirit, God will follow our prayer. We may utter a sentence, and the Lord will give us more feelings, which will lead us to utter another sentence. This sentence will lead to more feelings. This kind of prayer is breathing prayer, prayer that reaches God. The more we pray, the more we touch God's presence and the more we absorb God Himself. The more we pray, the more we are filled with God. This is to enjoy God. The matters in our petitions are secondary. The important thing is that we have reached God, gained God, and absorbed God. This should be our experience every time we pray.

In order to have prayers that enjoy God, we must reject everything that disrupts the feeling in our spirit. In particular we should not be occupied with many thoughts. Sometimes we should even avoid considering many Bible passages. Instead, we should use the Word to calm our thoughts. However, under normal circumstances, we should exercise to be calm without relying on the Bible. Even praying with the words of the Bible can be a frustration if it is not according to the sense in our spirit. We may lose God's presence.

ALL PRAYERS NEEDING TO BE
ACCORDING TO THE FEELING OF THE SPIRIT

I hope that we would all see that when we turn to our spirit, are calm, and pray according to the feeling in our spirit, God will entrust many important matters to us for supplication. All we need to do is to follow the feeling in our spirit and pray the prayers that He initiates one by one. We will fulfill a great ministry of supplication in this way. Not only do we need to touch God in the morning when we eat, drink, and enjoy Him through reading and prayer; we need to touch God, pass through God, and allow Him to pass through us in our ministry-fulfilling prayers, our supplicating prayers. In our prayers, God and us, we and God, should be mingled together. Whenever we pray, our prayers should be inward prayers that come from touching God. All normal prayers are prayers according to the sense of the spirit. Such prayers come from our enjoyment of God and are actually an enjoyment of God. The more we pray this way, the more we will absorb God and enjoy Him.

CHAPTER TWENTY-ONE

THE PRACTICE OF INTERCESSION, BEHOLDING, WAITING, AND MUSING

Scripture Reading: John 15:7; Eph. 6:18-20; Ezek. 22:30; Psa. 27:4, 14; 104:34

We will now consider intercession, beholding, waiting, and musing in relation to prayer.

We are familiar with the terms *intercession, beholding, waiting,* and *musing*. However, with spiritual matters, the most common things are often the most crucial and difficult to achieve. It is often difficult to thoroughly and genuinely fulfill an apparently simple spiritual task. Many Christians know what intercession means, but not many are able to intercede. Many know what it means to wait on God and muse upon Him, but few have truly learned to wait on God and muse on Him. These are very common matters among Christians, but they are also things that are seldom done well. May we all practice not only to enjoy God through reading the Word and prayer but also to intercede, behold, wait, and muse in our prayers.

INTERCESSION

Let us first consider intercession. Genuine prayers are prayers in which man is mingled with God in spirit. Hence, all genuine prayers are initiated by God. All prayers that are mingled with God are surely initiated by Him. In such prayers, God prays in man, and man prays in God. These prayers involve two levels.

In order to pray in this way, a person must be calm and turn to his spirit. He must learn to drop his own concepts and enter into God. When a person drops his concepts and enters into God, it is easy for him to sympathize with God's heart, to be concerned for God's interest, and to live in complete conformity to God's desires. When this is a person's condition, the Lord will surely be pleased to open His heart to him, and it will be easy for him to know the Lord's will. He does not need to exert much effort to touch the Lord's desire. He merely needs to contact the Lord, and he will know what is of concern to the Lord today.

This is the source of all genuine prayers. When the Lord's mind becomes ours, we know what He wants, and we begin to care for His desires. Once we care for the Lord's desires, we will intercede for them. Knowing God's desire forces us to bear the work of intercession before Him.

Let us consider Abraham's intercession for Lot. Abraham learned to live before God. He was one who knew God's desire. When God visited Abraham, He said, "Shall I hide from Abraham what I am about to do?" (Gen. 18:17). Since God and Abraham were intimate friends, God opened His heart to him, and He told Abraham that He had come down to look at the condition of Sodom and to judge it. When Abraham heard this, he knew that God's heart was focused on Lot, who was in Sodom. Although God did not mention Lot by name, the fact that He spoke of the place where Lot was gave Abraham a hint of God's heart. Abraham knew that God cared for Lot, who was living in the city of Sodom.

As soon as Abraham understood God's heart, he knew that God needed someone to be one with Him to pray for Lot. Abraham knew that if there was no one on earth to communicate with the God in heaven, God would have no way to communicate His heavenly will to earth. God needed a man on earth who was in touch with Him and in harmony with Him. There was a need for harmony between heaven and earth. In order for God to work on earth, He had to find someone who would echo His heart, who would be concerned for what was on His heart. Abraham was God's friend; he not only sympathized with God but also was one with Him. Hence, God could confide in Abraham what He was about to do on earth.

As soon as Abraham knew God's heart, he tarried before

God and began his work of intercession. When we read Genesis 18:22-33, we see that every word of Abraham touched God. Abraham reminded God that He is the Judge of all the earth, who needed to act justly, and asked if He could destroy the righteous with the wicked. Abraham did not mention Lot by name, but Lot was one of the righteous ones. Strictly speaking, his prayer was not for Sodom but for Lot who lived in Sodom, in the same way that God's heart was not on Sodom but on saving Lot who dwelled in Sodom.

When we enjoy God in prayer, we also enter into intercession. When we drop our thoughts and care for God's inward parts, it is easy for us to know His heart. Once we know His heart, we must call on Him and intercede. In Ephesians 6:18-19 Paul says that we should petition concerning all the saints and, in particular, to petition for him the apostle. Few people can petition concerning all the saints. A person who can petition for God's church and His servants is one who drops his concepts and ideas, turns to his spirit, and cares for God's heart. Such a person knows God's will and can pray for God's desire. God cares for His church, His saints, and His servants. It is easy for believers who live in their spirit, who have dropped their concepts, and who have God's mind to touch God's heart concerning the church, to understand His care for His children and His expectation of His servants. Such persons can intercede and will intercede because God's Spirit is moving in their spirit and stirring them up to pray for God's concerns. God is concerned about the church, and they pray for the church. God is concerned about the saints, and they pray for the saints. God cares for His servants, and they pray for God's servants.

Those who intercede for the church, the saints, and God's workers can do so because they live in their spirit and touch God. It is difficult for a person who does not live in his spirit and who only hears reports and exhortations to approach God or intercede for others. If he tries to intercede, it will be apart from God. He will become drier and emptier as he prays, and he will not have the assurance that his prayers will be answered. Such intercession is a labor apart from God. It can be compared to Peter's labor when he went fishing in John 21. His nets were empty even though he labored all night. His labor was in vain.

This is not proper intercession. If we learn to enter into God by dropping our concepts, turning to our spirit, and caring for His desire, we will touch His heart and know His interests. Spontaneously we will be motivated by God to intercede. Such intercession is solid and touches God. Moreover, we are inwardly fed and established in our faith, and we have the assurance that God has heard our prayer. We have the faith that God will bless the church, the saints, and the workers according to our prayers. These prayers are initiated by God. This is what the Lord meant when He said that if we abide in Him and His word abides in us, whatever we ask will be done for us. Such asking does not originate from us. When we enter the Lord's presence, live in Him, abide in Him, and touch His heart, we have His desire. Then our asking is fulfilled because it comes out of His desire.

A brother once said that he had been praying for a long time according to the Lord's promise in John 15:7 of giving us whatever we ask. However, his prayer to graduate from the university, marry a college graduate, and have a wonderful family had not been answered. He could not understand what was wrong and wondered whether the Lord's word had failed. I asked him to read the verse again. He read, "If you abide in Me and My words abide in you, ask whatever you will, and it shall be done for you." I responded, "We cannot delete the first two clauses from the sentence. First we abide in Him and His words abide in us. Then we ask, and it is done for us. You would not have such desires if you learned to abide in Him, and His words were in you. Rather, you would know God's heart. His will would be your will, and His desire would be your desire. Then whatever you asked would be done for you."

Many of our prayers are not the issue of abiding in Him. We pray according to our concepts and desires. These prayers do not touch God and are not answered. In order for our prayers to touch God and receive answers, they cannot be initiated by us. We must first be mingled with God and allow

Him to initiate and motivate our prayers. Only these kinds of prayers are worthwhile and receive answers.

In the Old Testament God wanted to bless the Israelites and to perform wonderful works among them. Yet He could not find one person to pray for this. Then He spoke using an illustration of the need for someone to stand in the breach of the wall. However, He could not find anyone (Ezek. 22:30). To stand in the breach is to be one who touches God's heart, lives in God, cares for God's desire, and prays accordingly.

In this verse God could not find anyone on the earth who would stand on the earth for this. There was no one who would be joined to Him and echo His heart by praying for what concerned Him. Consequently, He had no choice but to give up on the nation of Israel. He could not find anyone who would echo His heart, anyone who would learn to live in Him, to care for His desire, or to respond to His desire and call on Him to do something on earth. As such, He could only sigh in resignation in heaven.

There were probably many people praying at that time, but their prayers did not touch God. They lived outside of God and did not touch His heart. In the same way many believers pray outside of God, and their prayers do not count in the eyes of God. They have not learned to turn to their spirit or to enter into God. They have not learned to drop their concepts and care for God's desire. They have not touched God's heart or allowed God to initiate their prayers. As a result, their prayers, whether they are for themselves, for others, for the church, or for the work, are all outside of God. Since their prayers are initiated by themselves, God does not pray in their prayers, He is not mingled with them, and He does not respond to their prayers. These prayers do not touch God or reach God, and they do not receive many answers or see much result.

If we want to learn the work of intercession, we must learn to turn to our spirit, enter into God, drop our concepts, and care for God's heart. When we do this, spontaneously He will show us His desire, and He will motivate us to pray. The more we pray this way, the more we will touch God's heart. We will touch God and be filled, and something solid will remain in us. After we pray this way, we will have the faith and the deep assurance that our prayers have been answered. Intercession is fully a matter of being in the spirit.

We will now consider beholding God, waiting on God, and musing on God. Some brothers and sisters consider these to be difficult exercises. The key is being in our spirit. As long as we are in our spirit, these are easy. If we are not in the spirit, they are difficult.

BEHOLDING

Most people understand beholding the Lord to mean looking up at a God who sits far above in the heavens and who sends His light down to men. They consider beholding God to be looking up to such a light. According to our spiritual experience, however, this is not the meaning of beholding God. Beholding God is to gaze and look at God.

When I meet with a friend, we typically look each other in the eye and measure each other before we say anything. Sometimes after speaking, we look at each other again before we depart. Our looking at each other conveys a kind of warmth and intimacy. It is impossible for two persons to speak to each other without looking at each other. In the same way, beholding God means to gaze on Him when we pray. After we pray a few sentences, we should turn to gaze on Him again. If we do not turn to God or do not fix our gaze on Him but instead hastily utter a few words, it will be difficult for us to enjoy God. When we pray, we must be calm, turn to our spirit, and gaze on Him. Then according to the feeling within, we can speak to Him under His gaze. We should continually behold Him. Such beholding is very precious.

Of course, beholding transpires only in our spirit. We do not behold with our physical eyes. Our eyes are closed when we pray; we do not see anything. In our spirit, however, we are before God and look at Him face to face. We gaze on God by exercising our spirit.

WAITING

Many people think that they need to wait on God when He does not answer their prayers. Generally speaking, this can be considered as waiting on the Lord. This is an outward waiting. However, we are speaking of the waiting that transpires in our spirit. Suppose we are calm and turn to our spirit, but we do not sense that we have the presence of God. As a spiritual fact God never leaves us, but in our experience we may sense that He is far away or that He is near us. At times we may feel that He is near, but He has not initiated anything. When this happens, we should not say anything quickly. Rather, we should spend some time to wait in His presence.

God should always take the full initiative in our prayer, and we should simply follow. We should pray according to the feelings He gives us. In the same principle, sometimes He purposely delays His coming so that we learn to wait on Him. We cannot care merely for our convenience. We must care for His convenience and wait. We should never be rash or impatient. For this reason the psalms say that we should wait on the Lord.

This kind of waiting is not an easy matter. We would not consider two hours to be too long to converse with a close friend, but we would consider two hours to be a long time to wait. Waiting requires patience. When we pray, there is also the need to wait on God. Sometimes God likes to test us in our prayer. If He does not seem to be near us after we turn to our spirit, and there are no feelings within, we should not initiate anything. If there is no feeling within, there can be no prayer. We should learn to wait. When He moves, we should follow, and when He does not move, we should wait on Him.

Can we spend half an hour to quietly wait on Him without uttering any words? Can we happily tell others that we spent our morning waiting on the Lord in this way? Can we wait for a long time without praying to Him? Perhaps after waiting for some time, we may need to say, "Lord, I must go to work. I am unable to wait on You any longer." Can we do this?

If we desire to enjoy God in prayer, we must learn these lessons. It is difficult for rough and rash people to pray. In the Old Testament the priest's garment had bells at the hem. The sound of the bells was to warn the high priest not to be careless (Exo. 28:34-35). Those who come before God must not be careless. The Lord prefers us to listen to Him. Hence, He rebuked Martha for being so anxious and troubled about many things (Luke 10:41). I do not believe Martha could wear the priestly garment without there being the sounds of bells everywhere. Many people are like Martha. Those with quick and rash temperaments cannot pray. We have to learn to wait patiently on the Lord.

MUSING

Good prayer often does not need many words. At times we do not need to say anything when we pray. We can simply muse on God. He cares for our musing. Psalm 104:34 says, "May my musing be sweet to Him." Prayers in which we continually speak to God may not be good prayers. In good prayer we behold God and muse upon Him.

We may think that musing is something of our mind, but it is actually connected to our spirit. We actively muse upon the attributes of our God in our spirit. He is fine, tender, careful, dignified, glorious, and great. We muse upon His dealings with us and His promises to us. As we muse, our inner being is filled with much feeling. Our musings are prayers, and at the same time they are not prayers. They are like words, yet they are not like words. They are thoughts that arise from our inner being and are a delight to God.

In summary, we should turn to our spirit to touch God in prayer. These prayers do not require many words. Sometimes it is best to spend some time to look at God or remain silent in His presence. We should learn to pray in this way. We should never pray with our own burdens; rather, we should set aside our burdens. We should say, "Lord, I give all my burdens to You and come to You with an unloaded spirit." We should be calm, turn to our spirit, and behold Him. We should then pray according to the inward sense. As we pray, we should continue to behold Him. We should also wait and muse on Him. If we do this, we will touch and absorb God richly through prayer.